Indie Cinema Online

Indie Cinema Online

SARAH E. S. SINWELL

Rutgers University Press
New Brunswick, Camden, and Newark, New Jersey, and London

Library of Congress Cataloging-in-Publication Data

Names: Sinwell, Sarah E. S., 1976– author.
Title: Indie cinema online / Sarah E. S. Sinwell.
Description: New Brunswick: Rutgers University Press, 2020. |
Includes bibliographical references and index.
Identifiers: LCCN 2019040027 | ISBN 9781978814691 (paperback) |
ISBN 9781978814707 (hardback) | ISBN 9781978814714 (epub) |
ISBN 9781978814721 (mobi) | ISBN 9781978814738 (pdf)
Subjects: LCSH: Motion pictures—Distribution. | Motion pictures—Production and direction. | Motion pictures—Technological innovations. |
Digital media—Influence.
Classification: LCC PN1995.9.D57 S56 2020 | DDC 384/.83—dc23
LC record available at https://lccn.loc.gov/2019040027

A British Cataloging-in-Publication record for this book is available from the British Library.

♾ The paper used in this publication meets the requirements of the American National Standard for Information Sciences—Permanence of Paper for Printed Library Materials, ANSI Z39.48-1992.

www.rutgersuniversitypress.org

Manufactured in the United States of America

This book is dedicated to my parents

Contents

Introduction: (Re)Defining Independent Cinema in an Era of Convergence 1

1. Indie via Instant Viewing: Now Streaming on Netflix and Hulu 25

2. Simultaneous Release Strategies: Soderbergh and the Screening Room 45

3. DIY Distribution: YouTube, *Four Eyed Monsters*, and *Girl Walks into a Bar* 65

4. The Fourth Screen: Sundance, Shorts, and Cell Phones 87

Conclusion: The Future of Indie Cinema Online 105

Acknowledgments 113

Notes 117

Bibliography 149

Mediagraphy 169

Index 175

Indie Cinema Online

Introduction

(Re)Defining Independent Cinema in an Era of Convergence

I became interested in the growth of indie cinema online during the cultural moment in which I realized that I was more likely to watch the most current indie films on streaming services such as Netflix, rather than rent them from my local video store in Providence, Rhode Island, Acme Video (which closed in January 2014). My love of cinema stemmed from childhood visits to the Cable Car Cinema (also closed as of 2018) and the Avon Cinema in Providence, as well as the multiple independent video stores I frequented in Alexandria, Virginia (Video Vault, which closed in 2010); Atlanta, Georgia (Videodrome, which is one of the few video stores across the United States still in business); and Bloomington, Indiana (Cinemat, which closed in 2009). As of this writing, I am lucky enough to live in a city that still hosts a local video store. The Tower Theatre Archive in Salt Lake City, Utah, includes more than 12,000 film titles that are often available only on VHS or DVD. But this video archive is in constant flux as its owner, the Salt Lake Film Society, struggles with how to maintain the collection while also trying to appeal to a viewership and audience that has now transitioned to streaming these titles online on sites such as YouTube and the Criterion Channel.

As I came closer to the completion of this book, the narrative of independent filmmaking online became more and more intertwined with television, web series, and other alternative forms of programming. As audiences move from the theaters, to their living rooms, to their tablets and cell phones, how filmmakers produce, distribute, and exhibit their films impacts the audience's ability to access indie content. Whereas it seems like there is an infinite array of indie content online, it is also limited by the means of distribution and exhibition. Thus, this book examines the ways in which online distribution and exhibition patterns are changing how audiences access indie cinema.

Though the terms "indie" and "independent" are often used to describe films and media outside a specifically American context, this book will examine the production, distribution, and exhibition of contemporary American independent cinema online as a set of texts, practices, and institutions that is constantly evolving in relation to Hollywood, art cinemas, and other forms of media in the contemporary era. For instance, following the 2013 Sundance Film Festival, the Sundance Institute announced that it would be partnering with an online video platform called Reelhouse, enabling filmmakers from the event to self-distribute their work online.[1] Including everything from feature films to documentaries to shorts, Sundance's partnership with Reelhouse reflects the shifting distribution practices of the film industry in an era of media convergence.[2] As more and more films are being distributed digitally and eliding theatrical release altogether, the future of independent cinema lies in its convergence with other digital platforms.

With the advent of online streaming (on sites such as Netflix, Amazon, and Hulu), video-on-demand services (available on iTunes, YouTube, Hulu, and Amazon), and simultaneous release strategies or day-and-date releases (on DVD, on demand, and in theaters), more and more audiences are consuming independent movies online. In January 2011, the *Wall Street Journal* announced that video on demand (VOD) was filling the revenue gap for indie films. Independent studios saw their share of box office revenue decline to 19 percent in 2010, from 33 percent in 2001, whereas in 2010 VOD made $1.8 million (up 21 percent from 2009) and digital downloads accounted for $695 million (up 16 percent from 2009).[3] Audiences and markets for independent cinema are in transition, from movie theaters to our televisions, computers, tablets, and cell phones. In an era of convergence, watching indie films online is certainly a much cheaper option than going to the theater. Whereas a movie ticket might cost between $8 and $20, online films may be available for free (on YouTube and other sites), on demand (for as little as $.99), or for a low subscription fee (as low as $7.99 a month). In this context, the audience demographics for indie films online are also changing. For example, according to Pew Research, online audiences tend to be younger than theatrical audiences for indie films. In fact, most internet video users are age eighteen to twenty-nine.[4] This impacts the ways in which online video streaming services such as Netflix and Hulu are appealing to younger viewers with original series such as *Stranger Things* (Netflix, 2016–present) and *East Los High* (Hulu, 2013–2017).

As Patricia Zimmerman argues, in the twenty-first century, "The difference between a studio production and an independent production resides no longer in production values, narrative structure, or casting, but in distribution, exhibition, marketing, and product tie-ins."[5] Though Zimmerman overstates the historical break between past and present incarnations of independent cinema here, it is worth noting that distribution *continues* to be one of the ways in which independent cinema is defined.[6] As both Michael Newman in *Indie: An American Film Culture* (2011) and Yannis Tzioumakis in *American Independent Cinema* (2006) have noted, independent cinema had consistently been defined in relation to both distribution and exhibition. In particular, independent cinema in the "Sundance-Miramax" era was constructed in relation to art house cinema and other alternative distribution and exhibition venues. Tzioumakis argues that the definition of independent cinema has continually expanded and contracted in relation to historical, economic, industrial, and cultural discourses.[7] Independent cinema is not defined *only* in relation to its production but rather via its distribution and exhibition. To this end, *Indie*

Cinema Online maps out these various discourses as a means of investigating what happens when indie films are not found in the cinema itself, but online.

The title of this book refers to the key theoretical terms that I will be (re)defining, namely, "indie" and "cinema." Within the context of convergence cultures, these terms have become particularly vexed and deserve further investigation. In the next section, I will discuss the term "indie," in terms of how it is defined both within the film industry itself and within film and media culture more generally. But I would also like to speak to the use of the term "cinema," which refers to the film, movie, or motion picture itself as well as to the theatrical venue in which films are shown. I have chosen to use the term "cinema" (rather than "film," "movie," or "motion picture") because of its explicit relationship to the film object itself *and* its modes of exhibition. Indeed, even the changes in the name of the Society for Cinema and Media Studies (formerly the Society for Cinema Studies) comment on the constantly shifting meanings of these terms within the discipline itself.[8] Thus, in *Indie Cinema Online*, I use the term "cinema" to refer to film objects (and their place within media history), as well as film's malleability.

It is important to note that the "always controversial" nature of the term "cinema" is not at all a new phenomenon. As Anne Friedberg points out in her essay "The End of Cinema" (2000), the invention of the television, cable, remote control, and VCR also marked anxieties not only about the end of cinema but also about the relationship between film studies, media studies, and convergence.[9] Scholars within the fields of film, media, and screen studies have all endeavored to investigate the utility of these various terms and debates in an attempt to mine their respective theoretical possibilities and revolutionary potential.[10] I use the term "cinema" both to create a space for indie cinema *online* within film and media studies and to acknowledge the social, technological, and cultural changes that are involved in making that distinction. Indeed, the term "cinema" also acknowledges that many of the films screened online are not actually made on film, but via digital technologies.

At the same time, the changing meaning of cinema in a digital age refers to the idea that films are no longer screened primarily in movie theaters, but in the home, at the doctor's office, and on airplanes, as well as on television screens, computers, iPods, and cell phones.[11] As many critics have argued, film, television, and other media have their own historicities that must be studied in context.[12] Participating in the continually burgeoning academic work on the history of nontheatrical cinematic exhibition within media studies, *Indie Cinema Online* studies how American independent cinema and convergence culture(s) interact technologically, industrially, and culturally in a nontheatrical and online context.[13]

To this end, *Indie Cinema Online* redefines American independent cinema in the age of convergence by taking into account the multiple discourses through which it has been understood within the current media industry. Examining the ways in which independent film production, distribution, and exhibition are changing in a digital age, *Indie Cinema Online* focuses on the advent of online streaming (on Netflix and Hulu), the continuing utilization of simultaneous release strategies (in theaters, on television, on DVD, and streaming), the screening of indie films on YouTube, and the creation of independent film channels and their online web series (on SundanceTV), as a means of investigating indie cinema's historical evolution in online spaces. In this way, I argue that independent cinema must not be limited to films that are theatrically released, but also includes films that are released simultaneously or even solely online. Documentaries, in particular, are one genre of independent films that are succeeding far more in an online context than through theatrical release.[14] The ability to access independent cinema online not only creates new audiences for independent cinema but also redefines independence itself. Interrogating "independent cinema" and "convergence culture" as terms that are both difficult to define and more and more intertwined in the digital era, I argue that as independent cinema moves from the movie theater to online venues, its meaning is more and more intertwined with mainstream interests such as Amazon and Google.

This introduction is divided into six sections. First, I discuss the ways in which independent cinema has been defined and redefined in relation to Hollywood. Then, I examine how ideas of indie cinema intertwine with concepts of art cinema and international cinema. I then provide a brief history of independent cinema in the United States from 1989 to 1999, when "indie" became its own market within the film industry. Next, I provide a brief overview of independent nontheatrical exhibition and distribution practices. Then, I define the term "convergence culture" as a means of analyzing the transformation of indie cinema from 1999 to the present as it became available online. Finally, I provide an overview of the chapters included in this book.

(Re)Defining Indie Cinema

The title of Chris Holmlund and Justin Wyatt's edited anthology *Contemporary American Independent Film: From the Margins to the Mainstream* (2005) draws attention to the evolving nature of independent American cinema and its relationship to Hollywood.[15] Focusing on the intertwining of corporate interests with independent filmmaking, the popularity of indie films such as the Miramax-produced *Gangs of New York* (Martin Scorsese, 2002), the "indie success story" *My Big Fat Greek Wedding* (Joel Zwick, 2002),[16] and the star-studded *Little Miss Sunshine* (Jonathan Dayton and Valerie Faris, 2006) attest to indie cinema's continuing symbiotic relationship with the Hollywood machine. In fact, as Chris Holmlund, Justin Wyatt, Geoff King, Alisa Perren, and Michael Newman have noted, the term "indie" has become a brand used to market more "alternative" or "marginal" films to mainstream audiences.[17]

In this context, independent cinema emphasizes the fluidity of boundaries (economic, narrative, and stylistic), as well as the nebulousness of current definitions of Hollywood and countercinematic practices. Jim Hillier also defines independent cinema as work that is different from the dominant or the mainstream.[18] But, above all, indie cinema has been defined in relation to

Hollywood itself.[19] As Chuck Kleinhans argues, "'Independent,' then, has to be understood as a relational term—independent in relation to the dominant system—rather than taken as indicating a practice that is totally freestanding and autonomous."[20] Geoffrey Gilmore, director of the Tribeca Film Festival, includes the film's low budget and whether creative control over the film lies in the hands of the filmmaker (rather than the studios) as factors contributing to whether or not a film is independent.[21] And Roger Ebert, film critic for the *Chicago Sun-Times*, points out that an independent film is often made because "it expresses the director's personal vision rather than someone's notion of box-office success."[22] These multiple definitions of indie cinema draw attention to its shifting meanings, within the film industry itself, as well as among scholars, critics, filmmakers, and so on. In this section, I will briefly discuss how indie cinema has been defined and (re)defined as a cultural category, in terms of its industrial and economic constraints, as well as its audiences and its alternative distribution and exhibition practices.

Independent cinema has historically been constructed in relation to the film industry itself, filmic texts, production values, and even cultural mores. As Jennifer Holt and Alisa Perren have argued, the study of media industries requires a focus on "texts, markets, economies, artistic traditions, business models, cultural policies, technologies, regulations and creative expression" as "sites of struggle, contestation and negotiation."[23] Continuing in this vein, in her book about Miramax in the 1990s, *Indie, Inc.*, Alisa Perren argues that indie cinema can be defined by (1) its source of financing, (2) the industrial affiliations of its distributor, (3) the sites in which it is exhibited, (4) the status of its talent in relation to Hollywood, and (5) the "spirit" of the film (usually interpreted to mean its aesthetic or generic ties to commercial or alternative media traditions).[24] *Indie Cinema Online* focuses on these changing industrial practices and cultural meanings as a means of mapping out a new online space for the production, distribution, and exhibition of American independent cinema. In this context, this book also focuses on the ways in which American independent cinema in an era of convergence continues to be intertwined with both mainstream and corporate interests.

Calling a film "indie" tends to conjure up images of a quirky, low-budget, character-driven, formally experimental film screening in the local art house cinema.[25] In his book *Indie*, Newman refers to such quintessential indie films as *Pulp Fiction* (Quentin Tarantino, 1994), *Happiness* (Todd Solondz, 1998), and *Juno* (Jason Reitman, 2007) as exemplifying what he calls indie film culture. He argues that "viewers are encouraged to see independent films as more socially engaged and more formally experimental than Hollywood; more generally, they are encouraged to read independent films as alternatives to or critiques of mainstream movies."[26] Constructing indie cinema as a film culture, Newman proposes that indie cinema as a cultural category can only be understood within its historical, institutional, economic, narrative, generic, and formal contexts. Geoff King's *American Independent Cinema* also maps out the relationship between Hollywood and independent cinema, pointing out the ways in which indie cinema has been shaped by industrial constraints, narrative strategies, formal innovations, and generic transformations.[27]

In her book *Independent Film in the United States, 1980–2001*, E. Deidre Pribram argues that independent film is a "distinct system of cinematic representation" shaped by both Hollywood and avant-garde film practices.[28] Describing indie cinema as a "discursive formation," Pribram constructs an idea of independent cinema as a set of cultural practices that includes representational, institutional, reception, and historical discourses.[29] To this end, Pribram analyzes the ways in which indie cinema can be understood in relation to distribution but also as a "part of the 'taste-setting' business of defining and demarcating that also functions as the dissemination process for independent productions."[30] In this vein, Yannis Tzioumakis also constructs American independent cinema as a "discourse that expands and contracts when socially authorized institutions (filmmakers, industry practitioners, trade publications, academics, film critics, and so on) contribute towards its definition at different points in the history of American cinema."[31] Taking into account these multiple discourses within their own historical, cultural, social, and industrial contexts, *Indie Cinema Online* focuses on shifting online distribution and exhibition practices as a means of redefining American indie cinema in an era of media convergence.

Indie Cinema, Art Cinema, and International Cinema

The relationships between art cinema, international cinema, and indie cinema have been discussed by numerous authors, including Rosalind Galt and Kyle Schoonover (*Global Art Cinema*, 2010), David Andrews (*Theorizing Art Cinemas*, 2013), James Tweedie (*The Age of New Waves*, 2013), John White (*European Art Cinema*, 2017), and Geoff King (*Positioning Art Cinema*, 2019).[32] Theorizing the distinctions between these categories presents many of the same challenges as theorizing the relationships between Hollywood and indie cinema as "relational concepts." In perhaps the two most famous early essays that define art cinema, David Bordwell's "The Art Cinema as a Mode of Film Practice" (1979) and Steve Neale's "Art Cinema as Institution" (1981), the authors argue that art cinema can be defined as (1) a mode of film practice, (2) a history (post–World War II), (3) a set of formal conventions that includes a stress on visual style, (4) a set of viewing procedures, and (5) as being in opposition to classical narrative cinema.[33] Art cinema is primarily defined by Bordwell and Neale in relation to the distinctions between Hollywood cinema and European art cinemas such as Italian Neorealism, German Expressionism, and the French New Wave. Pointing out how art cinemas avoid cause-and-effect linkages, incorporate realism, lack a goal-oriented protagonist, violate time and space, and utilize open-ended narratives, Bordwell and Neale primarily examine art cinema as both a cinematic style and an institution. More recently, however, other film theorists have extended these ideas of art cinema as a means of comparing it not only with Hollywood but also with indie cinema, global cinema, and the avant-garde.

As David Andrews argues in *Theorizing Art Cinemas*, art cinema can be understood as a "subcultural aggregate" that is a more flexible category that is not dependent on ideas of high and low art and cultures, but rather encompasses multiple forms of art cinemas, from European art cinemas, to Asian art cinemas, to indie cinema, to New Hollywood, to the avant-garde and cult cinemas.[34] In this mode of understanding, Andrews defines art cinema as "cinematic high art" that is "value-oriented," including a multiplicity of forms and contexts.[35] Early definitions of indie cinema fit into this mode of thinking, since indie cinema is also associated with art and value, exhibiting in art cinemas, museums, and film festivals, and playing with traditional modes of form and content. Thus, Andrews notes that indie cinema may be understood as "Hollywood art films" that capitalize on their association with art and with industry.[36] The analysis of indie cinema in this book continues in this vein by drawing on the tensions between art and industry as indie cinema continues to be impacted by the transition to the digital age.

In *Positioning Art Cinema*, Geoff King notes the following about art cinema: "Like 'indie' or 'independent,' the term usually serves as a marker of distinction from dominant industrial-commercial institutions, particularly but far from only Hollywood."[37] Defining art cinema as "a field of circulation and consumption, mediated by various institutions and critical discourses," King argues that art cinemas imply differences in production, consumption, and institution (including finances, circulation, and distribution), as well as differences associated with narrative and form.[38] In this way, art cinema is also associated with cultural value and social status. King contends that "American indie cinema has also tended to be downplayed in accounts of art cinema . . . because of a general tendency to position it less highly in prevailing film-cultural value hierarchies."[39] Thus, King points out that there is an overlap in art cinema and indie cinema that includes festivals, critics, art house exhibition, auteurs, and tone.

In fact, numerous critics, including Chris Holmlund and Justin Wyatt, Michael Newman, Alisa Perren, Yannis Tzioumakis, and others, have pointed to the necessity of understanding indie cinema as a distinctly *American* film culture.[40] From its association with the Sundance, Slamdance, and Tribeca film festivals, to specialty film divisions such as New Line and Miramax, to its nominations at the Independent Spirit Awards, indie cinema has often been understood in relation to *American* national cinema cultures and institutions. As these authors have pointed out, however, the lines between American and international cinemas continue to blur as distribution and financing networks transform to include more and more funding support from abroad. In fact, as will be discussed in later chapters, the distribution of independent films on global streaming sites such as Netflix and YouTube is further evidence of the difficulties of navigating the term "indie" in the age of media convergence.[41]

A Brief History of Indie Cinema (1989–1999)

Beginning in 1989, with the success of *sex, lies, and videotape* (Steven Soderbergh, 1989) at the Sundance Film Festival and continuing through to the early years of the 2000s with the rise and fall of Miramax, an increase in the number of theaters and home video sales enabled many independent films to be released in more venues than ever before. The 1990s in particular saw increased opportunities and capital in producing and financing indies, with the rise of ancillary markets, cable channels, and film festivals. The proliferation of film schools across the country made it possible for more and more aspiring filmmakers to get involved in the industry, as did the creation of the Sundance Film Festival as well as more and more regional film festivals. At the same time, organizational support for indie films from organizations like the Independent Feature Project and the Association of Independent Video and Filmmakers provided additional funding for indie filmmakers.[42]

As Yannis Tzioumakis has noted in his discussion of American independent cinema in the age of convergence, "Starting from this wider context, the year of *sex, lies, and videotape*, and more generally 1989–1990, was also the period when Hollywood cinema became deeply integrated within the structures of entertainment conglomerates, signaling the arrival of a new phase in the history of the US (and international) media industries, and not just American independent cinema."[43] Thus, American independent cinema at this time was particularly entwined with the interests of Hollywood. As Tzioumakis notes, "This 'reconglomeration' came into full force in 1989–1990 with Sony's takeover of Columbia (1989), the Time Warner merger (1989), the takeover of MCA Universal by Matsushita (1990) and Disney's aggressive expansion to other media segments following the announcement (in 1990) of the 'Disney Decade,' a corporate plan to reinvent and expand Disney on a global scale in the 1990s."[44]

In fact, the term "independent" has most often been explained through its relation to economics or financing—as a film produced outside of Hollywood and outside the mainstream studio system. Since the mid-1990s, negotiating the relationship between independent and commercial cinema has become even more challenging as the major studios purchased distributors of art house fare.[45] The 1990s, in particular, saw industrial transformations in terms of how independent films were being produced, distributed, and exhibited. Noting the ways in which the creation of "major independents" like New Line and Miramax remapped the symbiotic relationship between indie cinema and Hollywood in the 1990s, Justin Wyatt points out that the crossover popularity of films like *The Crying Game* (Neil Jordan, 1992) and *Pulp Fiction* (Quentin Tarantino, 1994) created new markets for independent films by "targeting audiences beyond a narrow art house niche."[46] When, in May 1993, Disney acquired Miramax, and the Turner Broadcasting Company merged with New Line, these major independents refigured the relationship between Hollywood and independent cinema as one of interdependence. As Alisa Perren has noted in *Indie, Inc.*, acknowledging the "potential economic *and* cultural value of niche films," Miramax became a model for creating specialty divisions for indie films.[47] In fact, these specialty divisions jump-started the indie boom of the 1990s and redefined indie cinema as a commercial enterprise.

Since the 1990s, American independent cinema has become more and more mainstream with the continuing influx of semi-indies and mini-majors within the industry due to the rise of mergers and leveraged buyouts by studios like Disney, Universal, and Time-Warner.[48] The use of the term "Indiewood" is a continual reminder of the industry's inability to separate independent films from their Hollywood counterparts, in terms of both their economic and studio backing and their content.[49] Following the Independent Spirit Awards in 1999, James Schamus remarked that the independent film movement had been successfully integrated into mainstream, corporate interests. Citing the rise of specialty film divisions and independent cinema's continued relationship to a small group of global conglomerates, he expressed concern over the possibilities for creating a space for indie films in a market increasingly driven by star-studded casts and blockbuster franchises.[50] As Tzioumakis notes in his discussion of the classics divisions and specialty labels of the Hollywood studios, more independent stand-alone distributors "suddenly found themselves in a position where they had to compete with companies that had the financial backing of entertainment corporations and access to their resources."[51] In this way, the studio divisions also became what Tzioumakis calls "an industry phenomenon," which functioned in direct competition to independent distributors such as New Line and Miramax.[52] In fact, *Variety* critic Charles Lyons points out that in an economy in which independent films must consistently engage with corporate industries in order to distribute their films, indies can now be described as "dependies."[53]

However, prior to its breakthrough moment in 1989, when Steven Soderbergh's *sex, lies, and videotape* turned the concept of independence into a marketing tool,[54] American independent cinema was arguably more marginal, more experimental, and more "independent." Films like John Cassavetes's *Faces* (1968) and Jim Jarmusch's *Stranger Than Paradise* (1984) certainly seem to have little in common with more recent independent fare like *Little Miss Sunshine* (Jonathan Dayton and Valerie Faris, 2007), *Juno* (Jason Reitman, 2008), *Black Swan* (Darren Aronofsky, 2010), *Spotlight*

(Tom McCarthy, 2015), and *Get Out* (Jordan Peele, 2017).[55] In fact, Geoffrey Gilmore of the *Nation* discusses many critics' unwillingness to include these more popular, mainstream, star-studded, and bigger-budget films within the category of independent cinema. Instead, he argues that "the definition of independent filmmaking is both elusive and evolving."[56]

Today, in an era in which independent films have bigger budgets, greater star power, and higher production values, negotiating the relationship between commercial and independent cinema has become even more of a challenge. Now, with the advent of online and digital media technologies, films continue to be produced, distributed, *and* exhibited independently of the studios. With the advent of digital video and digital distribution, it is even easier to get an independent film both produced and distributed. But the ease of creating a film outside Hollywood does not necessarily mean that it will reach audiences. Since there are now so many independent films being made, it is less and less likely that the film will actually be distributed theatrically. Rather, indie films are now being viewed on televisions, computers, tablets, and cell phones. Thus, *Indie Cinema Online* focuses on these shifting digital distribution and exhibition practices as a means of (re)defining American independent cinema in an era of media convergence.

Indie Cinema, Online Distribution, and Nontheatrical Exhibition

From the creation of United Artists by D. W. Griffith, Charlie Chaplin, Mary Pickford, and Douglas Fairbanks in 1919, to Francis Ford Coppola and George Lucas's founding of American Zoetrope in 1969, to Mel Gibson's release of *The Passion of the Christ* in 2004, filmmakers both within and outside of Hollywood have been struggling to release their work despite the constraints of the studio system. In fact, as many critics have noted, the position of independent films as independent has often hinged on their inability to conform to studio and big-business models of production, distribution, and exhibition.[57] Endeavoring to break away from these studio models, independent filmmakers from John Cassavetes (*Shadows*, 1959; *A Woman under the Influence*, 1974) to Kevin Smith (*Clerks*, 1994; *Red State*, 2011) have produced, distributed, and exhibited their films using a do-it-yourself (DIY) model.[58] But, as indie films become increasingly available online, distributing and exhibiting them outside the confines of corporations like YouTube and Google is becoming more difficult.

Within the film industry, theatrical release is still the primary standard by which films' successes and failures are judged. The "Indie Oscars" or Independent Spirit Awards still define indie films only as features that receive a theatrical release (or that screen at one of the more prestigious film festivals).[59] On the Independent Spirit Award FAQ page, it is noted that to be eligible for an Independent Spirit Award, (1) all submitted films must be at least seventy minutes long; (2) eligible films must have either played one week in a commercial theater or have been shown at one of the following six film festivals: the Los Angeles Film Festival, New Directors/New Films, New York, Sundance, Telluride, or Toronto; and (3) eligible films must be made for no more than $20 million, including postproduction. The films are also defined by their "uniqueness of vision" and "original, provocative subject matter." As noted on the Independent Spirit Awards FAQ page, "Film Independent does not—as of 1994—define 'independent' strictly on the basis of financing."[60] In 2019, The Directors Guild of America also announced that day-and-date releases would no longer be eligible for its top award, which would now be titled "Outstanding Directorial Achievement in Theatrical Feature Film."[61]

Thus, while the industry itself continues to define indie films according to the older theatrical model of the "Sundance-Miramax era,"[62] indie film culture in the era of convergence is continuing to transform these definitions, ushering in what Barbara Klinger calls "the golden age of the short"[63] and creating online film festivals (like Tribeca). In fact, many scholars have discussed how the transition to home video has also impacted the ways in which cinema viewing practices have shifted in an era of convergence. In *Beyond the Multiplex*, Klinger discusses the ways in which cinema has evolved as a result of the home viewing experience. Addressing the nontheatrical exhibition contexts of film viewing on VHS, DVD, cable TV, and the internet, Klinger notes that there have been transformations in film viewing as a result of its immersion within the home. Investigating these shifting viewing practices, she contends that film viewing in the home incorporated both new film formats (including the short) and repeat viewings (on VHS and DVD). Joshua Greenberg also discusses the transition from film to home video in his book *From Betamax to Blockbuster*, arguing that one of the reasons VHS formats flourished in the 1980s was because video distributors and retailers came to be understood as mediators between film producers and consumers.[64] These modes of distribution on video, from the home, to the electronics store, to the video store, map out the shifting audiences for films outside of their theatrical context. In the era of digital convergence, indie cinema's meaning is continuing to transform as it becomes more immediately available (via streaming), more accessible (via simultaneous release strategies), more DIY (via digital distribution), and more portable (via iPods, laptops, and tablets).

Beginning in the early years of the 2000s, there have been numerous changes in the indie market, including the decline of DVDs, the rise of Redbox and online streaming, the growth of multiplexes and the decline of art cinemas, the emphasis on original television series over motion pictures, the global growth of locally based film operations, and the overabundance of media options.[65] These factors have contributed to the need to consider indie distribution and exhibition strategies within an online context. In her essay "Digital Deployment(s)," Patricia Zimmerman proposes the idea of rethinking independent cinema as "a form of cinema that moves across different platforms and through different audiences and economies."[66]

In his book *Indie 2.0*, Geoff King argues, "The advent of inexpensive digital video as a production medium and of broadband internet as a channel for distribution, sales and other activities combined to create the possibility of unprecedented freedom from external controls and restraint."[67] In fact, as Tzioumakis states, "Indeed, one could argue that, since the late 2000s, filmmaking activity at the margins of the independent sector has done nothing short of 'de-institutionalising' and destabilizing American independent cinema."[68] Thus, in an era of media convergence, and with increasing access to broadband internet (both for filmmakers and for audiences), it is necessary to consider the multiple ways in which cinema circulates in culture, not only within the cinema itself but also on our computers, tablets, and cell phones.[69] To this end, *Indie Cinema Online* analyzes the ways in which nontheatrical distribution and exhibition practices on computers, tablets, and cell phones impact indie cinema audience's online viewing practices. In the next section, I argue for the continual rethinking of convergence culture with these transformations within indie cinema in mind.

Rethinking Convergence Culture(s)

This book revisits the much-discussed term "convergence culture" as a means of mapping how independent cinema is changing in relation to a variety of terms, including but not limited to "new media," "transmedia," "emergent media," "digital media," "digital culture," and "cybercultures."[70] These terms reflect the moment of transition from which convergence culture emerges. In fact, the increasing number and variety of terms used to describe this cultural shift draw attention both to its popularity as a field of study and to the difficulties involved in defining these categories.

One of the most established theorists within this field, Lev Manovich, uses the term "new media" to describe "the cultural objects which use digital computer technology for distribution and exhibition."[71] This definition explicitly accounts for the idea of media as digital, technological, cultural, and influencing distribution and exhibition practices. In this sense, *Indie Cinema Online* is a book about new media, but unlike many other texts within this (inter)disciplinary field, it does not analyze the ways in which these media forms are *new*; instead, it investigates *how* these new digital technologies impact film culture.[72] As Barbara Klinger observes in *Beyond the Multiplex*, film culture incorporates what Tom Ryall calls an "ensemble of practices."[73] These practices take into account multiple modes of film circulation, distribution, and exhibition in context, including the histories, institutions, and ideologies surrounding them. *Indie Cinema Online* intervenes in this discussion by arguing that concepts of independent cinema are being redefined as a result of these technological, industrial, and cultural changes. As cinema within the digital era continues to evolve, its place within the media industry and within media culture is also changing. Though terms such as "new media," "emergent media," and "digital media" describe the cultural and technological moment that this book addresses (referencing the continual transformation of media in the digital age), I choose to use the term "convergence culture" because of its explicit investment in the integration of studies of the media industry and its audiences with both technology and aesthetics.[74]

In his book *Media Convergence*, Tim Dwyer notes that media convergence must be seen as a rhetorical construct.[75] Thus, convergence must take into account the industrial, cultural, social, ideological, textual, and economic shifts that occur with the advent of new media and communication technologies. Like Tzioumakis, Dwyer posits the need to consider how *discourses* of convergence frame changes in media policy, media usage, and industrial transformations.[76] Framing indie cinema via these multiple discourses, *Indie Cinema Online* investigates the role of corporate ownership in shifting indie distribution and exhibition practices as a means of mapping out how indie cinema's meaning is changing with the advent of convergence culture.

Henry Jenkins's *Convergence Culture: Where Old and New Media Collide* is certainly one of the most significant texts in the field of convergence culture studies.[77] This book includes Jenkins's seminal definition of media convergence as "the flow of content across multiple media platforms, the cooperation between multiple media industries, and the migratory behavior of media audiences who will go almost anywhere in search of the kinds of entertainment experiences they want."[78] In *Convergence Culture*, Jenkins defines the terms of convergence and provides a theory of the intersections between old and new forms of media. Analyzing such media texts as *Survivor* (CBS, 2000–present), *American Idol* (Fox, 2002–present), the *Harry Potter* and *Star Wars* franchises, and *The Matrix* (Lana and Lilly Wachowski, 1999), Jenkins argues that old media forms are not being replaced, but their meaning is shifting as a result of the introduction of new media technologies. In his studies of popular television shows and Hollywood films, Jenkins discusses the central concepts of participatory culture (in which "fans and other consumers are invited to actively participate in the creation and circulation of new content"), the divide between producers and consumers, and the relationships between amateurs and professionals in a Web 2.0 world.[79]

Rather than analyzing the ways in which new media displaces old media, *Convergence Culture* examines how old and new media converge, interact, and intertwine in an ever-changing media economy. Jenkins describes convergence as representing "a paradigm shift" toward interdependence of different media delivery channels and more complex relationships between corporate media and what he calls "bottom-up participatory culture."[80] In this context, Jenkins is particularly interested in how audiences "talk back" to corporate media via online participatory practices. However, his media study is limited to popular (Hollywood) texts. I argue that independent cinema should also be studied in relation to convergence because of its particularly vexed relationship to corporate media that is embodied by the Hollywood machine.

In this way, *Indie Cinema Online* both builds upon and rethinks the ways in which Jenkins defines convergence in terms of how it functions in relation to American independent cinema. I argue that the relationship between grassroots and corporate media has significance not only because of its impact on the producers and consumers of independent cinema but also because of how those texts circulate within society. Whereas Jenkins focuses his discussion of convergence on the fans and audiences of these texts and how they interact with them, *Indie Cinema Online* analyzes the ways in which the online presence of independent films redefines independent cinema via new modes of online distribution and exhibition.

Thus, I also use Manuel Castells's idea that within convergence culture, the coexistence, interconnections, and interdependence between mainstream media, corporately owned media, and autonomous, independent media create new spaces for communication, power, and counterpower within contemporary culture.[81] As Castells notes, convergence refers to the confluence of "specific technologies into highly integrated systems within which old, separate technological trajectories become literally indistinguishable."[82] These shifting interrelationships among technologies, industries, texts, and economies are mapped onto the interrelationships between mainstream media culture and indie cinema. Within the context of *Indie Cinema Online*, in a market that is increasingly tied to Hollywood and studio interests, indie cinema is attempting to create a space for itself within this continually contested media terrain. The presence of indie cinema on multiple platforms and multiple devices also questions the ways in which indie cinema engages with other forms of media, such as the television, computer, tablet, and cell phone. In this context, as many critics have noted, these platforms are now intertwined in ways that traditionally have been understood as separate.[83] Yet, as I will describe in later chapters, the interrelationships between these media forms are continually up for debate as the lines between them are blurring more and more with the advent of digital and online distribution and practices.

In the introduction to their special issue of *Cultural Studies* published in 2011, "Rethinking Convergence/Culture," James Hay and Nick Couldry also stress that it is necessary to rethink Henry Jenkins's understanding of convergence as a culture.[84] Investigating the links between media, film, and cultural studies, Hay and Couldry question the ways in which convergence has been constructed as both a "culture" and a "new culture." As Hay and Couldry note, many convergence culture theorists, including Henry Jenkins and Burgess and Green (the authors of *YouTube*), tend to read convergence through the lenses of interactivity, DIY, and grassroots media.[85] As Sarah Kember and Joanna Zylinska point out in *Life after New Media*, one of the problems within new media studies is the focus on "false divisions" such as analog versus digital, private versus public, and mass versus participatory.[86] Ignoring the politics of labor, history, and culture involved in these technological and industrial transitions, many theorists also often ignore the ways in which these ideologically loaded terms are given cultural value, especially within the political economy of contemporary media. Thus, Hay, Couldry, and other contributors to this special issue argue that it is necessary to rethink the binaries between corporate interests and grassroots media proposed by Jenkins, Burgess, and Green. Instead, they propose a rethinking of convergence in relation to hybridity and multiplicity that encompasses a variety of convergence *cultures*.[87]

A study of convergence cultures that acknowledges the particular modes and practices of the American independent film industry necessitates a new understanding of convergence in all of its cultural, societal, economic, and industrial contexts. *Indie Cinema Online* argues that the industrial and cultural meaning of the terms "DIY" and "grassroots" changes in relation to independent cinema, since it is a media environment that is *already* defined in terms of both resistance and opposition to corporate and mainstream interests.[88] Without the well-defined and guaranteed audiences of these larger media franchises, independent films must engage with the advent of these digital technologies in their own unique ways. In this way, the study of independent cinema in an era of convergence also has larger implications for how cinema itself is seen in increasingly "uncinematic" online spaces. *Indie Cinema Online* argues that it is necessary to take into account these shifting modes of distribution and exhibition if we are to define both cinema and indie cinema in the age of digital convergence.

Accessing Indie Cinema Online (1999–Present)

Each chapter of this book focuses on one of four ways in which independent cinema has been transforming in relation to convergence cultures over the past two decades: immediacy, accessibility, grassroots/DIY participation, and portability.[89]

As Jay David Bolter and Richard Grusin argue in their classic book *Remediation*, one of the defining characteristics of new media is immediacy. For Bolter and Grusin, immediacy within new media refers to the realism of virtual reality, 3D, CGI, and so forth; at the same time, it also refers to the transparency of the interface.[90] In other words, within new media contexts, there is a desire for audiences/viewers/users to have an immediate relationship with the medium. In relation to indie cinema online, this immediacy takes the form of instant streaming via sites such as Netflix and Hulu. Analyzing the ways in which the availability of independent films online through Netflix and Hulu streaming has impacted the visibility and popularity of independent filmmaking, chapter 1 argues that the immediacy of screening indie films through online streaming has created a new (nontheatrical) audience for indie film. Immediate access to these sites online not only redraws the relationships between film, television, and new media as these sites screen both television and cinematic content but also creates the fantasy of immediate access at the click of a mouse.

Continuing in this vein, the idea of accessibility within indie cinema online focuses on the ways in which simultaneous release strategies create new opportunities for audiences to access independent films outside of a theatrical context. When independent films are released simultaneously in theaters, on demand, and on DVD, audiences that may not be geographically close to an art cinema gain access to films that they may not be able to view otherwise. In chapter 2, I argue that independent cinema's use of simultaneous release strategies is different from that of Hollywood precisely because it is increasingly less available via theatrical release. For instance, whereas independent films may be simultaneously released in theaters, on demand, and on DVD, bigger-budget Hollywood films can afford to stagger these releases and still capitalize on their sales. Released simultaneously in theaters, on cable and satellite television, and on DVD, films such as Steven Soderbergh's *Bubble* (2005), Kevin Smith's *Red State* (2011), and Bong Joon-ho's *Snowpiercer* (2013) push the boundaries of how independent films are produced, distributed, and exhibited within the context of contemporary digital media platforms. This chapter argues that with the production of these films on digital video, as well as their day-and-date releases in theaters, on DVD, and on television, simultaneous release strategies are transforming current film viewing practices and encouraging audiences to watch indie films on multiple devices in a variety of nontheatrical venues.

Chapter 3 explores the ways in which the availability and accessibility of digital film distribution on YouTube create a space for nontheatrical exhibition and DIY distribution for independent filmmakers. Grassroots and DIY forms of distribution are especially important for independent filmmakers who may release entire films online in the hopes of getting their work seen by a larger audience. DIY distribution also provides the possibility of earning enough money to recoup the costs of making the film and finance its theatrical release. However, despite the growth of opportunities for self-distribution within contemporary convergence culture, companies like YouTube, Google, and Lexus often capitalize on the work of independent filmmakers who are unable to release their films through more traditional means of theatrical distribution. Online streaming sites like the YouTube Screening Room promote a DIY idea of independent filmmaking, yet they also mask the ways in which the exhibition and distribution of these films are funded through corporate sponsorship. Focusing on *Four Eyed Monsters* (Buice and Crumley, 2007) and the YouTube Screening Room, this chapter argues that YouTube capitalizes on independent filmmakers and DIY distribution as a means of selling its own aesthetics of quality cinema.

In chapter 4, I analyze the SundanceTV website and its web series of short films as a means of exploring the interrelationships among independent cinema, marketing, and new digital media technologies. Independent film organizations like SundanceTV have created programming specifically for portability and cell phone viewing, ushering in a new era of the digital short. In terms of aesthetics, cinematic form, and style, these digital shorts investigate indie cinema via new modes of visuality, textuality, aurality, and haptics. At the same time, they also promote convergence with other media industries, institutions, and technologies, investigating the interrelationships between film, television, and music via the cell phone. Analyzing Sundance web series such as *Green Porno*, *Seduce Me,* and *The Art of Seduction*, this chapter redefines the spaces for production, distribution, and exhibition for independent cinema online via portability and the digital short.

Finally, in the conclusion I explore the future of independent cinema within the context of convergence culture. Through an analysis of the changing meaning of independent cinema online, I posit that the future success of independent cinema online necessitates a reimagining of the relationship between independent film online and its audiences. Across these chapters, independent cinema and convergence cultures emerge as discourses that enable not only new online audiences but also new possibilities for indie mediamakers to reclaim alternative spaces for distribution and exhibition.

1

Indie via Instant Viewing

Now Streaming on Netflix and Hulu

As the 2018 Academy Awards approached, the question as to whether such Netflix films as *Mudbound* (Dee Rees, 2017) and *Okja* (Bong Joon-ho, 2017) would receive Oscar consideration came to the fore. In order to be eligible for the Oscars, films must be publicly exhibited "for paid admission in a commercial motion picture theater in Los Angeles County." This is significant for films on streaming services such as Netflix and Hulu, since they may not be exhibited publicly (or they may only receive an extremely limited theatrical release).[1] Purchased for $12.5 million at the 2017 Sundance Film Festival and the first Netflix feature film to compete in the Academy Awards, *Mudbound* won no Oscars, but it did receive four nominations, including Best Adapted Screenplay, Best Cinematography, Best Supporting Actress, and Best Original Song. Whereas it received an extremely limited theatrical release in only eleven U.S. cities on the same day it became available for online streaming in November 2017, six months later more than 20 million hours of *Mudbound* had been streamed on Netflix.[2] Though *Okja* did not receive any Oscar nominations, during its screening at the Cannes Film Festival, the Netflix title card was reportedly booed, and Cannes later announced that films that do not receive theatrical exhibition in France would no longer receive consideration at the festival.[3] With these limited theatrical releases, Netflix films such as *Mudbound* and *Okja* are pushing the limits of traditional modes of theatrical exhibition by dramatically shortening (and even eradicating) the strategy of windowing (the time between theatrical release and distribution on home video or streaming sites). Usually averaging about four weeks, the theatrical windows on streaming sites such as Netflix and Hulu are shrinking to zero or just a few days.

John Fithian, president of the National Association of Theatre Owners, stated, "We see Netflix as basically trying to use theaters as a marketing platform for awards and to get their subscribers juiced about their movies. But we don't see them seriously interested in the business of theatrical exhibition."[4] Offering up new possibilities for accessing the means of production, distribution, and exhibition, streaming sites such as Netflix and Hulu create new online spaces (and nontheatrical audiences) for independent films. In this chapter, I focus on the ways in which instant access to independent films online redraws the relationships between independent film producers and the corporate entities that distribute and exhibit these films on new media and online platforms. Analyzing the ways in which the availability of independent films online through streaming has impacted the visibility and popularity of independent filmmaking, this chapter argues that the immediacy of screening indie films via Netflix and Hulu has created new (nontheatrical) access to distribution and exhibition while also limiting the possibilities of this access, since these companies' film catalogs frequently vary according to their ill-defined distribution deals with larger companies such as Fox and Disney.

As Barbara Klinger has noted in *Beyond the Multiplex*, cinema exists as a "schizophrenic identity"; "it exists as both a theatrical medium projected on celluloid and as a nontheatrical medium."[5] As she writes, cinema has always existed outside the confines of the theater itself: in "street carnivals, amusement parks, opera houses, tents, ocean liners, airplanes, schools, prisons, churches, museums."[6] Thus, it is not only in an era of media convergence that cinema has existed outside the multiplex. Since its inception, cinema's distribution and exhibition patterns have been constantly in flux. In the current era of media convergence, cinema's meaning is being rewritten as viewers experience cinema on their computers, tablets, and cell phones. However, this proliferation of screens impacts not only the content that is available but also the audience's viewing patterns, particularly in terms of access and control.

Chris Anderson points out in his book *The Long Tail: Why the Future of Business Is Selling Less of More* that companies like Netflix and Hulu seem to offer unlimited access to programming.[7] However, this chapter will argue that this seemingly unlimited access is in fact limited by the ever-changing film catalogs of these sites. As Chuck Tryon notes in *On-Demand Culture*, "Despite the promises of digital utopias, on-demand culture is characterized not by universal access but by the process of limiting and restricting when and where content is available."[8] This chapter addresses the ways in which these restrictions and limitations impact the availability of independent films on Netflix and Hulu.

These new modes of independent film viewing have led indie viewing audiences to move from outside the cinema into the home, car, subway, train, and bus stop. This mobility of video access across platforms such as phones, tablets, and laptops has also enabled indie audiences to grow. Whereas prior to these streaming practices, indie films were primarily available at art house theaters (often only in urban centers) or video stores,[9] online streaming brings both more availability and more variety to audiences that otherwise may not have had access to these independent films.

Thus, this chapter investigates not only the ways in which streaming video technologies have cemented viewers' desires for on-demand culture but also how this has impacted the popularity and growth of independent cinema online. As Wheeler Winston Dixon notes in *Streaming: Movies, Media, and Instant Access*, the streaming landscape is in a state of "constant permutation."[10] Though, at the time of this writing, other streaming sites such as Amazon, Criterion, Kanopy, SnagFilms, Rivit, NoBudge, IndieFlix, and Tugg also host a variety of independent films, this chapter addresses both Netflix and Hulu as two of the streaming sites in which independent films are most prolific.

Taking a three-pronged approach to this study, I will first focus on the ways in which media convergence structures streaming sites such as Netflix and Hulu by mapping out how indie film production, distribution, and exhibition are shifting in this context. Next, I will focus on independent programming itself as a means of defining the relationship between Netflix, immediacy, and indie branding. Finally, I will examine the ways in which Hulu's corporate interests intertwine with those of independent and documentary filmmakers. To this end, this chapter aims to uncover the ways in which online streaming on Netflix and Hulu both enables and limits modes of access to independent films.

Infinite Access to Indie Cinema? Netflix, Hulu, and Media Convergence

This section examines the ways in which media convergence impacts access to independent films on Netflix and Hulu. I use the term "convergence" because of its explicit investment in integrating studies of the media industry and its audiences with changing media distribution and exhibition practices.[11] As Henry Jenkins has famously argued, media convergence is "the flow of content across multiple media platforms, the cooperation between multiple media industries, and the migratory behavior of media audiences who will go almost anywhere in search of the kinds of entertainment experiences they want."[12] In this context, convergence "represents a paradigm shift" toward the interdependence of different media delivery channels and more complex relationships between corporate and independent media. At the same time, as Bolter and Grusin indicate, the convergence of the telephone, television, and the computer leads to a seemingly endless supply of entertainment.[13] As streaming services such as Netflix and Hulu continue to grow, so, too, does access to independent programming.

In his discussion of the histories of the videotape and the VCR, *Inherent Vice: Bootleg Histories of Videotape and Copyright*, Lucas Hilderbrand points out that issues of access, aesthetics, and affect are also intertwined with video technologies.[14] He argues that the VCR suggested "a shift toward a sense of access entitlement" and "a critical starting point in what might be called on-demand culture, wherein audiences want access to entertainment on their own terms: what they want, when they want it."[15] In *Videoland: Movie Culture at the American Video Store*, Daniel Herbert has noted that "video stores increased Americans' *degree* of access to movie culture . . . [and] fostered a conception of media abundance and catered to people's sense of entitlement to this abundance"; video store culture enabled viewers to access video content physically, as "tangible, portable objects."[16] The invention of the remote control and the VCR afforded viewers more control over video content, enabling them to replay, slow down, and fast-forward at their leisure. The invention of online streaming not only allows this kind of control over content but also provides a fantasy of immediate access to a seemingly unlimited library of video content.

This concept of unlimited access and unlimited mobility can also be linked to Chris Anderson's concept of the long tail,[17] which points to the idea that companies such as Netflix and Hulu would "thrive on selling niche content rather than focusing solely on blockbuster hits."[18] This is particularly significant in relation to the digital distribution of independent films, since they are included among this niche content. As Chuck Tryon notes in his book *On-Demand Culture: Digital Delivery and the Future of Movies*, this concept of "platform mobility" encompasses "the ongoing shift toward ubiquitous, mobile access to a wide range of entertainment choices."[19] At the same time, "the introduction of platform mobility complicates traditional concepts of medium specificity, creating a situation in which many of the technological and physical properties associated with film and television as media may no longer be relevant, forcing us to rethink our understanding of the media."[20]

As Michael Newman points out in *Indie: An American Film Culture*, "Independent cinema has come to signify a parallel American cinema of feature films for exhibition venues that are alternatives to mainstream first-run exhibition."[21] In his discussion of film festivals, he notes that they "adopt art world categories rather than mass culture categories to classify films and identify their significant traits."[22] In the cases of Netflix and Hulu, it is the algorithms that create this taste culture as they encourage viewing of their own original programming as well as alternative categories such as "Independent Films with Strong Female Leads" or "Quirky Romantic Independent Comedies." This also points to the ways in which the audience for independent film is changing as a result of these streaming options.

Expanding on Newman's ideas, this chapter also points to the ways in which indie is constructed as a taste culture. According to Newman, indie cinema offers "an elite, culturally legitimate alternative to the mass-market Hollywood offerings of the multiplex."[23] To this end, streaming sites such as Netflix and Hulu incorporate ideas of indie cinema as high culture as a means of reinforcing streaming as a viable option for quality media viewing. This construction of indie cinema as "quality" and "high culture" also combats anxiety about the large quantity of banal programming on such sites.[24] Yet, the ephemerality of these online locations for the streaming of independent films also points to the ways in which streaming is full of both endless possibilities (seemingly unlimited titles) and limitations (films may only be streamed for limited periods due to licensing restrictions).

At the same time, this chapter also addresses the growing integration of television and film as these online streaming services create not only feature-length independent films but also independently produced documentaries and television series intended for indie viewing audiences. Much of the media climate associated with the rise of streaming platforms such as Netflix and Hulu reveals the convergence of film and television formats. In his essay "Indie TV: Innovation in Series Development," Aymar Christian discusses the ways in which the industrial and distribution strategies for independent film change in the online video market.[25] As Adam Sternbergh has noted in his blog for *Slate*, "The same swashbuckling energy that gave rise to the indie-film movement has migrated to TV programming online. By this analogy, Netflix is

Miramax, Amazon is Fox Searchlight, and your laptop is the Sundance Festival—a clearinghouse for potential breakouts waiting to be discovered. . . . Companies like Netflix and Amazon have one crucial advantage: They have a well-built technical infrastructure but little programming experience, while companies like HBO have excellent programming expertise but are playing catch-up on the technical end."[26] This reference to the independent film distributors and studio specialty divisions is also a reminder of how streaming and online distribution function similarly to the "Miramax-Sundance era" as indie distribution patterns continue to function relationally with those of Hollywood studios and large media conglomerates like Netflix, Amazon, and Hulu. This merging of film and television markets also points to the ways in which media convergence is dependent not only on technology but also on finances and content.

Netflix Unlimited: Producing and Distributing Indie Content on Demand

Netflix was created in 1997 by Reed Hastings and fellow software executive Marc Randolph. First designed as an at-home DVD delivery subscription service, its primary appeal was unlimited DVD deliveries for a low monthly rate without the late fees incurred at brick-and-mortar video stores such as Blockbuster or Movie Gallery. In 2000, Netflix launched the personalized movie recommendation algorithm that used Netflix members' ratings to predict choices for all its members. As David Herbert has noted in *Videoland*, this algorithm depersonalized and desocialized the mechanism for movie recommendations, focusing on big data rather than the idiosyncratic suggestions of the video store clerk.[27]

From 2006 to 2008, Netflix partnered with subsidiary Red Envelope Entertainment to finance and distribute independent and documentary films such as *No End in Sight* (Charles Ferguson, 2007) and *Two Days in Paris* (Julie Delpy, 2007). Then, finally, in 2007, Netflix added a streaming service to its programming. And, in 2010 the company's CEO, Reed Hastings, announced, "We are now primarily a streaming video company delivering a wide selection of TV shows and films over the Internet."[28] In fact, Netflix is now responsible for the largest portion of internet traffic in North America; in 2018, it accounted for more than 15 percent of the world's internet traffic.[29]

As of 2018, Netflix had 125 million members globally (including 55 million subscribers in the United States and over 200 countries in Latin America, Asia, and Europe); in 2018 alone, Netflix invested more than $12 billion in new content.[30] With this continuing growth and its 112 nominations for the prime-time Emmys in 2018, Netflix is now calling itself the "world's leading Internet television network."[31] This transition to creating original television programming such as *Lilyhammer* (2012–2014), *House of Cards* (2013–2018), *Hemlock Grove* (2013–2015), *Arrested Development* season 4 (2013), *Orange Is the New Black* (2013–2019), and *Sense8* (2015–2018) points to a shift in Netflix's branding as it imagines itself as a television network such as HBO or AMC rather than simply a DVD or streaming delivery service. However, as Netflix continues to invest in the financing, production, and distribution of independent and documentary films, its focus on these converging media formats also continues to grow.

Netflix adds hundreds of on-demand streaming independent films to its library every year. Even schools such as the New York Film Academy suggest to their students that they attempt to get their films distributed on Netflix.[32] However, a film must already have demonstrated audience appeal and critical buzz before Netflix will even consider adding it to its site. Steve Swasey, vice president of Netflix corporate communications, has noted that

> For independents to get picked up by his company for distribution, they need a mixture of some or all of the following: queue demand, critical appeal, sizeable audience appeal, buzz, and film festival premieres. He says these are in no specific order and declines to give a specific number of requests needed for the Netflix queue. "If your film was profitable and gained plenty of exposure, the film's audience should be there to help support

> your film on Netflix," Swasey says. "If your film got folks in their seats at film festivals and you spent time on marketing and building an audience then your chances are slightly higher."[33]

This draws attention to the ways in which Netflix is already building on other elements of the independent film world (including film festivals, cinephilia, art house audiences, etc.) as a means of further investing in growing its content. In fact, in 2009, Netflix partnered with the nonprofit arts organization Film Independent to fund the "Netflix FIND Your Voice" filmmaking competition. Philip G. Flores, who won the competition, directed *Almost Kings* (2010), a coming-of-age film starring Alex Frost and Billy Campbell. This prize, worth more than $350,000, included a premiere screening of the film at the Los Angeles Film Festival and distribution on Netflix. Thus, Netflix is investing in new filmmakers not only via distribution but also via production. At the same time, the contest's focus on theatrical release as well as digital distribution points to the ways in which the two are still intertwined in the independent filmmaking industry.[34]

From 2006 to 2008, Netflix utilized its content acquisition firm Red Envelope Entertainment to finance, executively produce, and distribute films in exchange for either exclusive DVD rights or revenue sharing.[35] To this end, Netflix executively produced features such as John Waters's *This Filthy World* (Jeff Garlin, 2006) and the documentary *This Film Is Not Yet Rated* (Kirby Dick, 2006), as well as distributing films such as Ross Kauffman and Zana Briski's Oscar-winning *Born into Brothels* (2004) and the Duplass Brothers' *The Puffy Chair* (2005). In search of a variety of international, independent, and documentary films that were either looking for or had lost their distribution deals, representatives of Red Envelope also attended the Sundance and Toronto film festivals and eventually picked up distribution deals for David Lynch's classic film *Eraserhead* (1977) and Tim Robbins's *Embedded Live* (2005).[36]

Significantly, this move into production, distribution, and financing focused primarily on independent films and documentaries. Notably, most of Netflix's distribution deals were made with suppliers smaller than Lionsgate.[37] In 2008, however, Netflix shut down Red Envelope Entertainment. As writers for the *Los Angeles Times* noted, Netflix closed Red Envelope because the company was concerned about competing with the studios and did not want to jeopardize its relationships with them, since it still wanted to maintain access to more mainstream studio fare.[38] Over its short life span, Red Envelope acquired 126 films, including the Golden Globe–nominated *Sherrybaby* (Laurie Colyer, 2006) and Cannes Palme d'Or winner *4 Months, 3 Weeks and 2 Days* (Cristian Mungiu, 2007).[39]

As CEO Reed Hastings noted in 2004, Netflix customers rented *Whale Rider* (a 2002 New Zealand and German coproduction directed by Niki Caro) as often as more mainstream blockbusters such as *The Hulk* (Ang Lee, 2003) or *Charlie's Angels: Full Throttle* (Joseph McGinty Nichol, 2003).[40] This, in turn, also allowed Netflix to enhance its cultural cachet.[41] Via its recommendation algorithm, it could steer customers toward these independent, international, and documentary titles in its own collection as a means of encouraging the viewing of films that otherwise might not be seen by the Hollywood blockbuster viewing audience. On Netflix's home page, customers are encouraged to view "Netflix Originals" such as *Arrested Development* (Netflix, 2013, 2018), *Brahman Naman* (Qaushiq Mukherjee, 2016), and *The Fundamentals of Caring* (Rob Burnett, 2016). In this way, Netflix promotes both its brand of quality programming and its original titles.

With the advent of its original programming such as *Lilyhammer*, *House of Cards*, *Hemlock Grove*, *Arrested Development*, and *Orange Is the New Black*, Netflix is now rebranding itself as "the world's leading internet television network." Formerly known primarily as a DVD-by-mail distributor, Netflix is now marketing itself as a brand-new television viewing experience. Investing more than $10 billion per year in content licensing and creation, Netflix is rebranding itself in relation to industrial concepts of "quality television" as a means of competing with other television content producers. In competition with television networks such as HBO, BBC, and AMC and sites such as Hulu and Amazon, Netflix has more recently made the transition to producing online original content. In particular, Netflix is comparing itself to AMC (focusing on high-quality television shows such as *Mad Men* [2007–2015], *Breaking Bad* [2008–2013], and *The Walking Dead* [2010–present]). In fact, in 2018, Netflix tied with HBO for total wins at the Emmy Awards for its limited original series *Godless* (2017) and its period drama series *The Crown* (2016–present).

Selling itself as "commercial-free unlimited-viewing subscription TV," Netflix is also fulfilling the media user's fantasy of immediate and unlimited access. Netflix enables viewer control over the viewing experience by charging no cancellation fees; allowing the pausing, playing, and stopping of content at any time on multiple devices; and personalizing its membership screens and recommendation algorithms. In his essay "TV Got Better," Chuck Tryon notes that "Netflix's self-promotion places emphasis on its ability to deliver the promise of prestige, plenitude, and participation to its subscribers, through a mix of technological and aesthetic appeals that are meant to position Netflix as the future of television. Through these discourses, Netflix has situated itself as the future of television."[42] By releasing entire seasons of television programs like *Arrested Development* and *House of Cards* at one time, Netflix encourages (and rewards) binge watching. Thus, the experience of watching Netflix not only includes viewing quality original programming that is unavailable in other places, but there is no pesky delay between episodes as all episodes are released simultaneously. However, though Netflix may offer unlimited viewing, the programming it offers is not as unlimited as it seems. In the comments sections of its website, numerous Netflix members lament the loss of particular networks (Starz), shows (*Sports Night*), or recent seasons of specific programs (*Dexter* seasons 5–8). And, since HBO GO is now one of its main competitors, HBO programming probably will not arrive on Netflix Streaming anytime soon.[43]

As Blake Hallinan and Ted Striphas have noted in their study of the Netflix Prize, Netflix's audience has gradually moved away "from an undifferentiated mass toward an aggregation of highly differentiated micro-audiences."[44] In fact, "Netflix chief content officer Ted Sarandos has said that all that data means that Netflix has a very 'addressable audience.' Unlike the traditional broadcast networks or cable companies, Netflix doesn't have to rely on shoveling content out into the wild and finding out after the fact what audiences want or don't want. They believe they already know."[45] Andrew Karpen, CEO of the New York–based film distribution company Bleecker Street Media (distributor of *Beasts of No Nation* [Cary Fukunaga, 2015] and *Captain Fantastic* [Matt Ross, 2016]), notes that "'the audience has gotten more fragmented' as individualized communication on social media has supplanted mass-market sources of information like newspapers and broadcast television."[46] Karpen adds that an understanding of the core audience is necessary in order for him to get involved with a project, stating, "If we can't determine that core audience, then chances are we are not going to get involved in a film because it's that important in the marketplace."[47]

In recent years, Netflix has cemented its relationship with the independent film viewing community by becoming a key contributor to the Independent Spirit Awards voting process, making the Spirit Award–nominated films available to voters via the Netflix website. "It bothered me that it was always the most widely distributed films that were winning Spirit Awards," says Sarandos. "It bothered me even more that every year there were a half-dozen films without distribution, films that maybe 100 out of the 9,000 (voters) actually saw. . . . We're using our sponsorship to not just grow our brand, but to try and grow the whole eco-system of independent film."[48] *IndieWire*, the daily news site focusing on the independent film community, now incorporates weekly articles with titles such as "What's Streaming on Netflix This Week" or "11 Great Indie Films from the '90s Streaming on Netflix Now." This association of Netflix with other independent film organizations such as the Independent Film Channel (IFC), Sundance, the Independent Spirit Awards, and Film Independent also continues to give the company the cultural cachet associated with high culture and art house cinema.

Discussing the future of independent and Sundance films on Netflix, Ted Sarandos said, "There is a long tail, but it needs a big head. . . . Making arthouse films and Sundance movies on its own can never be a sustainable big business. But the economics of it are the same. We can draft off a bigger business, so people come in for something else and you have their attention and, 'Oh, I want to see this new thing.' You don't know the star or the director, you just know the premise, and you have this algorithm that they are putting in front of you that you trust, so you try it."[49]

However, despite this fantasy of unlimited viewing, many critics have pointed out that Netflix's catalog of independent and international films has been dwindling as of late. For instance, *Sweet Sweetback's Baadasssss Song* (Melvin Van Peebles, 1971) is no longer available on Netflix in the United States, and neither are many of Woody Allen's films, including *Take the Money and Run* (1969) and *Sweet and Lowdown* (1999). In fact, now that Netflix makes twice its profits from streaming rather than DVDs, it seems that the company is no longer investing in purchasing rarer or out-of-print DVDs.[50] In its 2013 PR video, Netflix proclaimed, "With every title we add, we remain focused on our goal of being an expert programmer offering a mix that delights our members rather than trying to be a broad distributor. We're selective about what titles we add to Netflix. . . . we can't license everything and also maintain our low prices. So we look for those titles that deliver the biggest viewership relative to the licensing costs. This also means that we'll forego or choose not to renew some titles that aren't watched enough relative to their costs."[51] This statement functions as a response to many members' concerns that Netflix does not include every film title in its library and that many of the titles that stream on the site are there only temporarily. As Netflix acknowledges its move toward becoming the "Internet's largest television network," it is moving further and further away from its role as curator of a vast DVD library. In fact, since 2014, Netflix's U.S. catalog has shrunk by 31.7 percent.[52] However, in 2016, Morgan Stanley released a new survey of the video streaming industry pointing out that the quality of Netflix's original programming (which includes series such as *House of Cards* and films such as *Beasts of No Nation*) has now surpassed that of HBO.[53]

In 2012, Netflix signed an exclusive deal with Disney through which it gained streaming rights to all theatrically released Disney films starting in 2016.[54] According to its website, from September 2016, Netflix became "the exclusive US pay TV home of the latest films from Disney, Marvel, Lucasfilm and Pixar."[55] This means that other sites such as Hulu, Amazon Prime, and Starz could no longer carry Disney new releases such as *Zootopia* (Byron Howard, Rich Moore, and Jared Bush, 2015), *The Jungle Book* (Jon Favreau, 2016), and *Finding Dory* (Andrew Stanton, 2016).[56] This collaboration with Disney enabled Netflix to compete with other sites such as Hulu and Amazon as these streaming services continued to grow, but Netflix's deal with Disney ended in 2019, at which time Disney created its own streaming service.[57]

In 2015, Netflix released the viewership numbers for its first foray into original film distribution, *Beasts of No Nation*.[58] After noting that the film had been streamed more than 3 million times in North America in its first two weeks, Netflix's head of content acquisition, Ted Sarandos, told *Deadline*, "I think [it's] a bigger audience than any specialty film could ever hope for, in its first two weeks of release, and maybe for its entire run. And we're just starting. . . . We are just thrilled with the total audience reach of this film, not just in North America, but the world."[59] At the same time, however, the release of *Beasts of No Nation* also points to the continuing issue of day-and-date releasing. Though the film was very successful streaming on Netflix, it was controversial because it was released theatrically at the same time. Major theater chains such as AMC, Regal, and Cinemark chose not to show *Beasts of No Nation*, since it broke the traditional ninety-day home entertainment debut window.[60] Thus, Netflix is also pushing the boundaries of cinema by utilizing simultaneous release strategies (which will be discussed in the next chapter).

Branding Hulu, Branding Indie: Independent Documentaries and Corporate Interests

Founded in 2007 as a means of creating ad-supported on-demand streaming video for NBC, Fox, ABC, and more than 400 other content companies, Hulu is a free and legal online video service most often associated with television programming. In 2017, Hulu made more than $1 billion in revenue and reached over 17 million subscribers to its paid subscription service.[61] Though Hulu is primarily seen as an online viewing space for popular television shows like *The Daily Show* (Comedy Central, 1996–present), *Family Guy* (Fox, 1998–present), and *The Handmaid's Tale* (Hulu, 2017–present), as well as television clips, upcoming trailers, and webisodes, Hulu has also recently become an online screening space for independently produced feature films and documentaries. Since a small percentage of these films screen theatrically, Hulu is creating a space for them to screen online.

With the advent of online streaming on Hulu, more and more audiences are consuming independent films online (on their televisions, computers, tablets, and cell phones), thus reversing a tradition in which television was the primary exhibition space for documentary films. As scholars such as Patricia Zimmerman and Betsy McLane have noted, since the 1980s, television has opened up new horizons for documentary film in particular, providing money, audiences, and distribution for films that could not be released theatrically.[62]

Today, television continues to be a space for documentary viewing, with the advent of cable and satellite television stations such as HBO, the History Channel, and the Discovery Channel. By devoting one section of its site entirely to documentary, Hulu has continued in this vein by providing a screening space that is separate from the television, Latino, kids, and other sections of the site. Now that users and subscribers are explicitly searching for documentary content on Hulu, this focus on documentary films legitimates their popularity in a space in which more than 70 percent of Hulu's users still view primarily television content. Thus, by diversifying its programming to include not only documentary films but also half-hour original documentary series, Hulu is creating new audiences for independent documentaries online.

Hundreds of independent documentaries such as Martin Scorsese's biography of Bob Dylan, *No Direction Home* (2005), Steve James's Oscar-nominated *Hoop Dreams* (1994), and Morgan Spurlock's *Supersize Me* (2004) and *Comic-Con Episode IV: A Fan's Hope* (2011) have been available for viewing on Hulu. Hulu has also signed deals with Kino Lorber and SnagFilms, an online ad-supported documentary film website. Additionally, Hulu has hosted a number of curated series of documentaries, including a series entitled IndieWire Picks: Inspired by the 2013 Oscar Doc Nominees. These films included David Singleton's film *The Flaw* (2011), chronicling the aftermath of the 2008 financial crash, and Judith Ehrlich and Rick Goldsmith's documentary about Pentagon insider Daniel Ellsberg, *The Most Dangerous Man in America* (2009). In this context, the use of indie branding combines with the cultural cachet of the Oscars to promote films that otherwise may not have achieved wider recognition, large-scale popularity, or even theatrical release.

In fact, the Hulu website continually utilizes discourses of independence and quality to underscore its focus on "premium content." Up until 2015, Hulu's paid subscription service, Hulu Plus, stressed the use of indie branding by companies like Miramax and Criterion as a means of encouraging viewers to subscribe for a monthly fee of $7.99.[63] In addition to creating a space for classical Hollywood, foreign, and art cinema online, Hulu's paid service made available canonical documentaries such as Orson Welles's *F for Fake* (1973) and Albert and David Maysles's *Grey Gardens* (1975) and independent films such as John Cassavetes's *A Woman under the Influence* (1974), David Lynch's *Eraserhead* (1977), and Steven Soderbergh's *Schizopolis* (1996). Thus, the quality content associated with indie cinema as a taste culture is associated with the Hulu name. In 2016, however, Criterion left Hulu to join FilmStruck, a new streaming service launched by Turner Classic Movies; in 2018, FilmStruck announced it would shutter its services and Criterion would find a new home on the Criterion Channel.[64] In fact, more and more streaming services are continually entering the streaming market, especially services that include niche content such as Crunchyroll for anime fans and Shudder for horror fans.

Hulu has also invested in original programming in the documentary format, creating three half-hour original documentary series that capitalize on the branding of indie auteurs: Morgan Spurlock's *A Day in the Life*, Richard Linklater's historical travel show *Up to Speed*, and Kevin Smith's "movie revue" series, *Spoilers with Kevin Smith*. These shows mimic the television programming on such networks as the Travel Channel, the Biography Channel, AMC, and Bravo. Aired exclusively on Hulu, these original programs are attempting to draw in both television-viewing and independent cinema–viewing audiences. At the same time, the creation of these original programs is an attempt to move away from the TV programs provided by ABC, Fox, and NBC and "sets Hulu on a course of semi-independence, where it can produce shows outside of its parent companies' content."[65] By appealing to indie and documentary audiences, Hulu is also creating a space for reimagining itself outside of its corporately owned sponsorship.

In fact, Hulu executives have seen the viewership statistics for documentaries climb as the company has added more intriguing titles. Documentaries like David Modigliani's 2008 film, *Crawford* (about George W. Bush's move to Crawford, Texas, shortly after announcing his candidacy for president), and Rob Epstein's *The Times of Harvey Milk* (1984) have generated a huge amount of chatter in Hulu's comments section. A Q&A with Modigliani also generated heavy traffic for Hulu, indicating that there is a clear opportunity for Hulu to serve as a forum for documentary fans to interact with filmmakers.[66] At the same time, this use of online streaming also capitalizes on the ways in which social networking is part of the Hulu experience. Unlike DVD culture or theatrical releases, Hulu builds upon the shared culture of social media as a means of promoting its online content.

Conclusion

In an era in which video streaming is now outperforming DVD sales, the use of online distribution and exhibition spaces such as Netflix and Hulu has become even more necessary as indie filmmakers attempt to navigate a variety of online media spaces. Without the well-defined and guaranteed audiences of larger media franchises, independent films online must engage with the advent of these digital technologies in their own unique ways. These alternative distribution and exhibition venues and cross-media platforms are especially significant given the high costs of both theatrical exhibition and DVD distribution. Because independent films are increasingly less available via theatrical release, filmmakers may choose to release their films on Netflix or Hulu not only in the hopes of getting them seen by a larger audience but also with the possibility of earning enough money to recoup the costs of making these films and financing their DVD releases.

As of the end of 2015, streaming services such as Netflix, YouTube, Hulu, and Amazon accounted for more than 70 percent of peak internet traffic in North America.[67] Broadband internet service tracking firm Sandvine CEO Dave Caputo stated that, "Streaming Video has grown at such a rapid pace in North America that the leading service in 2015, Netflix, now has a greater share of traffic than all of streaming audio and video did five years ago. . . . With Netflix, YouTube, Amazon Video, and Hulu increasing their share since our last report, it further underscores both the growing role these streaming services play in the lives of subscribers, and the need for service providers to have solutions to help deliver a quality experience when using them."[68]

According to chief content officer for Netflix, Ted Sarandos, "Netflix routinely provides some 75% of DVD and electronic revenue for specialty films, and for foreign and documentary, even more than that."[69] Thus, independent filmmakers who are having trouble distributing their films theatrically are turning to Netflix and Hulu (and other sites such as iTunes and Amazon) as a means of getting their films seen by larger audiences. In fact, as Liesl

Copland, head of Red Envelope Entertainment, has noted, filmmakers and the industry need to move away from focusing so much on theatrical exhibition. According to Copland, "It's incumbent upon them to release movies more cost effectively and more creatively and accelerate the downstream windows for independent film. I would hope the indie sector at large realizes how much it benefits from getting to Netflix or iTunes or whatever cost-effective ancillary platforms as quickly as possible, and not chase theatrical revenue."[70] Nevertheless, getting independent films released on online streaming sites and finding independent film fare available for streaming online also pose their own challenges.

Members of the International Documentary Association recognize that video on demand is the future of documentary distribution.[71] At a panel at the South by Southwest film festival (SXSW), founder of the Film Collaborative Orly Ravid, president of Magnolia Pictures Eamonn Bowles, and a variety of other independent filmmakers and professionals gave a presentation entitled "How I Learned to Stop Worrying and Love VOD."[72] Using their release of *American: The Bill Hicks Story* (Matt Harlock and Paul Thomas, 2009) as a model, they argue that the future of independent and documentary film distribution is video on demand. Advocating ad-supported VOD strategies for documentary films such as those used by Hulu, these industry professionals noted that VOD distribution strategies often provide significant revenue generators and may lead to additional viewing on cable and satellite services.

On Hulu, 50 percent of the ad revenue goes back to the filmmaker. After a $750 fee, this means a film that generates $1,500 in ad revenue on Hulu will break even at a 50 percent revenue share. In contrast, iTunes splits revenue sales 70/30 (70 percent to the filmmaker), whereas Netflix licensing fees vary on a film-by-film basis. Jon Reiss, a filmmaker and media strategist and the author of *Think Outside the Box Office: The Ultimate Guide to Film Distribution and Marketing for the Digital Era*, warns that these models are constantly changing; he encourages filmmakers to read the fine print and exhaust multiple options, including not only ad-supported streaming but also direct distribution models, and urges filmmakers to consider digital rights in relation to foreign sales.[73] But for many unknown independent and documentary filmmakers, Netflix and Hulu may be the best option among these, especially if the film has not received much critical acclaim or its content is not immediately marketable to wider audiences. In fact, the anecdotal evidence from *Crawford*'s run on Hulu shows that the film's online exposure gave a nice lift to its DVD sales. As a result, Hulu has pursued relationships with additional independent documentary distributors such as Cinetic, Cinelan, B-Side, and SnagFilms (the parent company of *IndieWire*).

Though Netflix's and Hulu's audiences still watch mostly television content, rather than movies or documentaries, the numbers are growing. Of course, the futures of Netflix and Hulu are unknown, and the market for online streaming is in constant transformation due to these streaming sites' continual investment in their own corporate interests. However, it is clear that in the contemporary market, online streaming and on-demand video services are continuing to grow. Accessing this programming instantly and on demand is also creating wider audiences for independent and documentary films online. Thus, the role of streaming in the independent and documentary filmmaking marketplace is still up for negotiation, but at least for the moment, its investment in indie programming continues to grow.

2

Simultaneous Release Strategies

Soderbergh and the Screening Room

After having just received an Oscar for *Still Alice* (Richard Glatzer and Wash Westmoreland, 2014) at the 2015 Academy Awards, Julianne Moore critiqued day-and-date releases, arguing that "a movie never looks the same on television."[1] Noting the significance of both the aesthetics and the experiential components of theatrical exhibition, Moore is among numerous actors and filmmakers such as James Cameron and Christopher Nolan who oppose the idea of releasing films in theaters, on demand, and on DVD on the same day. This cultural moment in 2015 was particularly noteworthy for simultaneous release strategies, also called day-and-date release strategies, since it followed the release of Evan Goldberg and Seth Rogen's film *The Interview*, the largest ever day-and-date release by Sony Pictures Classics. Though *The Interview* earned only $2.8 million in four days at the box office, it received $15 million in online sales (and was rented and purchased more than 2 million times) in the five days after it first became available on December 24, 2014.[2]

Pushing the boundaries of how films are distributed and exhibited, simultaneous release strategies challenge the traditionally revered space of the theatrical window as the first and ultimate form of film exhibition. As Sony Picture Classics copresident Tom Bernard stated, exhibitors are the gatekeepers who "choose the movies that are worthy of playing in theatres."[3] Whereas many exhibitors within the industry have critiqued day-and-date strategies and how they might impact the bottom line (profit and ticket sales), these strategies also question who the arbiters of taste are in the cinematic world. Whether a film is worthy of playing in theaters also calls into question the value of low budget, nonstudio productions that do not have the same financial backing, merchandising, and advertising budgets as Hollywood films. Simultaneous release strategies also problematize whether the exhibitors should be the ones deciding which movies get a theatrical release. This also has implications for independent filmmakers who may not be able to release their films theatrically and are therefore trying to get them released via more DIY strategies such as video-on-demand (VOD) and day-and-date releases.

Speaking to the problem of windowing, National Association of Theatre Owners (NATO) chief John Fithian argues, "Though one-off and radical simultaneous release experiments garner some media attention, the reality is that major distributors believe that theatrical exclusivity drives the entire business."[4] As noted in the introduction to this book, the problem of theatrical releases continues to be an issue for independent filmmakers who must release their films theatrically or at major film festivals such as Sundance, Telluride, or Toronto in order to garner critical acclaim and future distribution. Simultaneous release strategies create new opportunities for audiences to access independent films outside of a theatrical context by making it possible for them to access indie films online. When independent films are released simultaneously in theaters, on demand, and on DVD, audiences that may not be geographically close to an art house theater gain access to films that they may not be able to view otherwise.[5]

Released simultaneously in theaters, on cable and satellite television, and on DVD, films such as Steven Soderbergh's *Bubble* (2005), Kevin Smith's *Red State* (2011), Edward Burns's *Newlyweds* (2011), Lars von Trier's *Melancholia* (2011), and Bong Joon-ho's *Snowpiercer* (2013) draw attention to the constantly transforming hierarchies and interconnections between production, distribution, and exhibition within the context of contemporary digital media platforms, especially within the independent film industry. In this chapter, I argue that independent cinema's use of simultaneous release strategies is different from that of Hollywood precisely because independent films are increasingly less available via theatrical release. For instance, whereas independent films may be released simultaneously in theaters, on demand, and on DVD, bigger-budget Hollywood films can afford to stagger these releases and still capitalize on their sales. This chapter argues that the simultaneous release strategies of films such as Soderbergh's *Bubble* and Smith's *Red State* are transforming current film viewing practices and encouraging audiences to watch indie films on multiple devices in a variety of nontheatrical venues.

To this end, this chapter is divided into three sections. First, I will provide a short industrial history of simultaneous release strategies and day-and-date releasing. Second, I will focus on Soderbergh's *Bubble* and how his films, television miniseries, and interactive movie apps re-enact ideas of the video archive. Finally, I will analyze the Screening Room (a streaming platform that enables films to be screened at home on the same day they are released in theaters) and how its use of simultaneous release strategies impacts independent filmmakers and art house exhibition by threatening traditional theatrical windowing.[6]

Simultaneous Release Strategies and Day-and-Date Releasing

With the burgeoning of home video and cable TV in the 1980s, release windows were introduced as a means of maximizing profit across different media (including theatrical release, home video, cable, and broadcast television). As Michael Curtin, Jennifer Holt, and Kevin Sanson note in their introduction to *Distribution Revolution*, "The path from theatrical to digital video disc (DVD), electronic sell-through (EST), and video on demand (VOD) and then on to the networks and library markets has been one of the most significant aspects of navigating the digital distribution revolution."[7] In the twenty-first century, these release windows have started to collapse as the time between windows has shortened from a few months, to a few weeks, to even no time at all. In 1994, the average time between a movie's opening in theaters and its debut on home video was about six months. In 2004, that span fell to four months, with some studios releasing films on DVD even sooner. Since 2014, this window has remained at about ninety days (especially for larger blockbusters like Marvel or Disney films), but it continues to narrow for smaller, indie films, thus limiting these films' box office grosses.

Whereas exhibitors wanted longer windows between theatrical release and other forms of distribution so that they could maximize profits before films were released on other platforms, distributors and filmmakers wanted their films out on as many platforms as possible to more quickly recoup their costs. Audiences, on the other hand, want to see films as soon as possible in the most convenient way; therefore, they are often willing to sacrifice the theatrical experience for the opportunity to see a film sooner at home, especially if the film lacks the special effects and higher production values of the studio blockbusters. In "From the Big Screen to the Small One: How Digitization Is Transforming the Distribution, Exhibition and Consumption of Movies," Alejandro Pardo argues that "the time period of exclusivity is narrowing."[8] As Pardo elaborates, with the continual release of films online by Netflix, Hulu, iTunes, and Amazon, more and more films are omitting their theatrical release altogether and instead are being released solely on demand or on streaming sites. In this context, lower-budget and indie films such as J. C. Chandor's *Margin Call* (2011), Cary Fukunaga's *Beasts of No Nation* (2015), and Noah Baumbach's *The Meyerowitz Stories* (2017) have been released using simultaneous release strategies rather than the traditional theatrical windows.

Pardo reports that "in the 'old distribution world,' theatrical distribution maintained the privilege of exclusivity for several months to guarantee the maximization of revenues before the arrival of other commercial windows (pay-per-view [PPV] and video on demand [VOD], DVD/Blu-ray, free TV broadcasting)."[9] Vladan Nikolic accounts that today, most independent films and even some Hollywood studio films are released simultaneously in theaters and on premium VOD channels.[10] A typical film now earns about half of its revenue from home video and only about 25 percent from theaters. The remainder comes from selling the film to cable and broadcast TV and other sources.[11]

This method of simultaneous release clashes with the usual release strategies of the Hollywood studios, in which the DVD is released about four months after the film's theatrical date and films are released on television once studios and distribution companies have capitalized on their respective markets. In this way, the "day-and-date strategy" challenges current modes of cinematic production, distribution, and exhibition within the context of contemporary digital and independent filmmaking. Thus, John Fithian said of the so-called day-and-date release strategy, "It's the biggest threat to the viability of the cinema industry today."[12] With on-demand viewing on digital and satellite cable, as well as on sites such as Amazon, Netflix, Hulu, and iTunes, films are no longer first viewed primarily in theaters.[13]

Exhibitors and art house theater owners and operators in particular lament the continual narrowing of theatrical windows. For instance, Barry Norman, owner-operator at Eveningstar Cinema in Brunswick, Maine, told *IndieWire*, "Basically, theatrical distribution (both Hollywood blockbusters and art house) are only vehicles to promote VOD/DVD sales and streaming. The blockbusters make back most of their budgets overseas and theatrical release is mandated in order to garner award nominations/wins, which again, serve mostly for DVD sales. Art houses, like mine, actually do the lion's share of the marketing and promotion for their film releases. To have these day-and-date and early VOD releases is just a slap in our face, which they spin as being part of the new paradigm of how people ingest their content."[14] Thus, art house theaters are struggling to manage the marketing and promotion of films that previously would have been the responsibility of the studios. Competing with the audiences for online streaming and video on demand, these theaters also struggle with the increasing quantity of films that are released for shorter and shorter theatrical runs. For example, art house theaters such as the Salt Lake Film Society and the Michigan Theater screen more than 200 film titles a year, often with just a weeklong or two-week run.[15] This means that unlike the studios such as Warner Bros. or Universal, which release and promote only 15 to 25 films a year, independent and art house theaters must promote hundreds of films without the larger marketing budgets of the studios.

Many viewers who do not have access to indie films because they do not live in an urban center with an art house cinema are able to access indie films via streaming services such as Netflix, Hulu, and Amazon, as well as on satellite, cable, VOD, and DVD. Gary Gentile calls this the "creation of a virtual arthouse" at "a time when the theatrical market for smaller films is shrinking."[16] As Joan Hawkins argues in her essay "Dish Towns USA (or Rural Screens) Part One," the "dish towns" across rural America illustrate the lack of possibilities for theatrical screenings of both Hollywood and foreign films.[17] In contemporary media culture, on-demand and streaming services such as Netflix, Amazon, iTunes, and Hulu are replacing satellite dishes and enabling new audiences to have access to indie and foreign films that they would not be able to access theatrically.

This concern over theatrical access has even larger implications when one considers the audiences for independent cinema and art house exhibition. As Gregory Waller has pointed out in *Moviegoing in America: A Sourcebook in the History of Film Exhibition*, much of film exhibition history has been limited to urban experience.[18] But, as noted in the *Economist* in 2009, "American's suburbs are becoming much more diverse places, with more ethnic minorities, more people with degrees and more gays. . . . The potential audience for independent films is thus dispersing beyond the places where independent cinemas concentrated. Not everybody lives near an art-house cinema, but almost everybody has a remote control."[19]

In fact, Netflix continues to maintain its DVD rental service because 34 million Americans still lack broadband internet access.[20] And, as cinemas attempted to make the transition to digital projection systems, art house cinemas in rural communities faced more financial challenges than their urban counterparts.[21] These data on rural audiences are underdiscussed compared with the ongoing concern over net neutrality and online streaming services such as Netflix, Hulu, and Amazon. However, they are also evidence of the demand for independent and international films in locations across the United States and outside of urban centers such as New York and Los Angeles.

Thus, audiences of both Hollywood and independent films are transitioning to on-demand and streaming services as a means of accessing films faster and more conveniently. As Elissa Nelson states in "Windows into the Digital World," "Digital options offer immediacy of access, ease of acquisition, multiple screen/device capabilities, and increased portability on mobile devices."[22] For example, in 2017, reports from the Motion Picture Association of America suggest record highs for viewing of streaming services. Whereas U.S. box office receipts were down 2 percent from the previous year at $11.1 billion, U.S. entertainment spending at home rose to $47.8 billion.[23] Thus, as Chuck Tryon notes in *On-Demand Culture*, "A number of independent film distributors have argued that these on-demand and streaming options have served low-budget films better than theatrical distribution."[24] Films such as the Sundance Film Festival favorite *Mudbound* (Dee Rees, 2017) have been streamed for 20 million hours on Netflix, a number that Netflix insists is drastically higher than theatrical numbers.[25] Thus, there is unlimited potential for indie and art house favorites to surpass box office numbers as streaming services continue to grow.

The next section focuses on the ways in which Steven Soderbergh's use of simultaneous release strategies for his film *Bubble* re-enacts the video archive and creates both online and offline audiences for indie cinema.

(Re-)Enacting the Video Archive: Inside Steven Soderbergh's *Bubble*

When *sex, lies, and videotape* was released in 1989, it heralded a change in the independent film market, making a smash at Cannes and turning the Sundance Film Festival into an overnight sensation that continues to this day. Focusing on video as a means of self-exploration and self-realization, *sex, lies, and videotape* capitalized on the emerging popularity of videotape as a means of representing voyeurism and safe sex. Indeed, the newly burgeoning distribution company Miramax was concerned that the reference to videotape in the film's title would lead audiences to believe that the film was shot on video, thus implying that it was of low quality.[26] Though the accessibility and availability of videotapes have dwindled since the advent of the DVD,[27] now DVDs are also competing with pay-per-view and on-demand viewing, as well as online streaming. This section addresses the impact that these new technologies and new distribution, production, and exhibition practices have on the meaning of independent cinema in a digital age.

To date, Soderbergh has shot a number of films on digital video, including both *Bubble* (2006) and *The Girlfriend Experience* (2009).[28] However, he did not experiment only in the realm of filmic production. These films are the first two films in a series of six shot on digital video and released using a day-and-date strategy by Mark Cuban and Todd Wagner's 2929 production company. Examining the interrelationships between these modes of filmmaking within the independent film industry, this section explores the ways in which Steven Soderbergh's filmic archive re-enacts questions of film and video distribution and re-envisions both indie film production and exhibition.

From his first feature film to two of his most recent films, *Bubble* and *The Girlfriend Experience*, Soderbergh's work has constantly pushed the boundaries between film and video, studio and independent, low budget and high concept. Since 1989, Soderbergh has regularly vacillated between directing larger studio films (the

Ocean's 11 franchise [2001, 2004, 2007] and *Erin Brockovich* [2000]) and smaller, more independent films (such as *Schizopolis* [1996] and *The Limey* [1999]). More recently, Soderbergh has also created multiple television series, including *The Knick* (Cinemax, 2014–2015), *Godless* (Netflix, 2017), and *Mosaic* (HBO, 2017–2018). In 2006, he made a six-picture deal with billionaire entrepreneurs Mark Cuban and Todd Wagner. These films were simultaneously released in theaters, broadcast on HDTV, and made available on DVD.

However, it is worth noting that Wagner and Cuban also created the first all-digital theater empire with Landmark. Financed by HDNet Films and screened in Landmark Theatres (both companies co-owned by media moguls Cuban and Wagner), *Bubble* was part of an experiment, shrinking the theatrical window in the hopes of increasing revenues on all fronts. At the same time, the Wagner/Cuban Companies utilized vertical integration, the integration of production, distribution, and exhibition that was practiced by the "Big Five" studios during the golden age of the Hollywood studio era.[29] As Mark Gallagher argues in *Another Steven Soderbergh Experience*, "Even in the evolving convergence landscape, theatrically released cinema provides the locus for recognition of industrial, economic, and aesthetic formations."[30] In addition to Landmark Theatres, Wagner/Cuban Companies also include the theatrical and home entertainment distribution company Magnolia Pictures, the production company 2929 Productions, and high-definition cable networks HDNet and HDNet Movies.

The day-and-date strategy challenges current modes of cinematic production, distribution, and exhibition within the context of contemporary digital and independent filmmaking. In an interview with *Wired* magazine, Soderbergh states that the day-and-date strategy is also an attempt to combat piracy: "Name any big-title movie that's come out in the last four years. It has been available in all formats on the day of release. It's called piracy. Peter Jackson's *Lord of the Rings*, *Ocean's Eleven*, and *Ocean's Twelve*—I saw them on Canal Street on opening day. Simultaneous release is already here. We're just trying to gain control over it."[31] Thus, the viewing of these films in pirated form, online and on demand, questions the creation of the video and the digital archive. Archiving films on video, DVD, or Blu-ray comes into question when films are also available to download online (often illegally).[32]

As Barbara Klinger points out in her study of piracy and *Titanic* (James Cameron, 1997), in 2005, the Motion Picture Association of America reported that studios lost $6.1 billion in revenue to film piracy.[33] This concern over piracy led the movie industry to further consider narrowing the windows between theatrical release and other forms of distribution. For, as Elissa Nelson argues in "Windows into the Digital World," "In hoping to avoid what happened to the music industry, which suffered at the hands of rampant illegal downloads, the movie business has tried to learn from previous mistakes by giving consumers more attractive options for legal viewing."[34] Thus, the continued utilization of simultaneous release strategies was attractive not only to filmmakers trying to get their films seen by audiences but also to the industry in the face of rampant movie piracy.

However, in January 2006, many theaters refused to screen *Bubble*, not because of its violence or excessive sexual content but over concerns about the success of its theatrical distribution.[35] In fact, filmmaker and director M. Night Shyamalan (*The Sixth Sense* [1999] and *The Happening* [2008]) cautioned theatrical distributors against this practice, saying, "If this thing happens, you know the majority of your theaters are closing. It's going to crush you guys."[36] This method of day-and-date releasing has worked for smaller foreign and independent films such as IFC's *Summer Hours* (Olivier Assayas, 2008) and Soderbergh's *The Girlfriend Experience* (2009).[37] It remains a question as to whether this day-and-date practice will be popularized among the big studios, but, there is buzz that bigger studios like Fox and Warner Bros. may follow suit.[38] In fact, Summit Entertainment's *Twilight* (Catherine Hardwicke, 2008), released simultaneously both on DVD and on demand in March 2009, became the year's top home entertainment title. However, it remains to be seen whether other bigger-budget films like those within the *Star Wars* or Marvel franchises would be as successful under this model.

With the production of these independent films on digital video, as well as their simultaneous releases in theaters, on DVD, and on television, these films also interrogate current film viewing practices. Soderbergh's *Bubble* was available for purchase on DVD in theaters where the film was being viewed. Audiences could purchase a copy of the film in the lobby of the movie theater before or after they viewed the film theatrically rather than waiting to purchase it on DVD months later. Thus, the moment of exhibition was also the moment of the creation of the archive. At the same time, *Bubble* also enabled a new accessibility with regard to independent films.[39] No longer must audiences in towns without art cinemas or independent theaters wait months after a theatrical release in bigger cities like New York or Los Angeles to view an independent film like *Bubble*. Instead, *Bubble* was available for viewing instantly on demand and on DVD. At the same time, however, the day-and-date strategy also raises questions about marketability and profitability.

Soderbergh's *The Girlfriend Experience*, his 2009 film about high-end call girls in Manhattan starring adult film star Sasha Grey, also premiered on demand before its theatrical release. In this context, Katherine Fusco argues, "With its DVD and pay-per-view distribution, *Girlfriend Experience* becomes a film to watch alone and away from theater crowds, a private rather than public viewing experience. . . . The relative brevity of *Bubble* (seventy-three minutes) and *Girlfriend Experience* (seventy-seven minutes) suggests that Soderbergh may be experiencing some of the constraints of working in this format even as it allows him to experiment with production and distribution methods that combat the heavily branded and slow-moving blockbuster."[40] Thus, Fusco points out the ways in which Soderbergh's use of alternative distribution methods such as day-and-date releasing also has implications for both the production and the visual aesthetics of his films.

Following the release of *Side Effects*, his 2013 psychological thriller starring Jude Law and Catherine Zeta-Jones, and after years of rumors surrounding his possible retirement from filmmaking, Soderbergh announced that he would leave Hollywood and start a new career as a painter.[41] He then directed *Behind the Candelabra* (2012), an HBO movie about Liberace starring Michael Douglas and Matt Damon. And, just a few months later, he created his first TV series for Cinemax, an early 1900s medical drama called *The Knick* (2014–2015), starring Clive Owen. In 2017, he made two more films, *Logan Lucky*, a NASCAR heist film distributed by Bleecker Street and Fingerprint Releasing (his own production and distribution company), and *Unsane*, a psychological horror film shot using only iPhones. In 2017 and 2018, he released *Mosaic*, an HBO thriller and miniseries that also included an interactive movie app.

Soderbergh's forays into multiple forms of film distribution and media convergence (via cable television, iPhones, and apps) exemplify a new form of experimentation within the movie industry. But they also draw attention to the myriad ways in which audiences interact with independent film, both on the big screen and on small screens such as televisions, computers, laptops, tablets, and cell phones. As Gallagher notes, Soderbergh's work can be seen as "boundary-pushing examples of screen-media convergence, new production technologies, and exhibition and distribution strategies."[42] In this way, Soderbergh's use of alternative modes of production (via cell phones), distribution (via simultaneous release strategies), and exhibition (via cable television and online apps) also challenges traditional modes of accessing indie cinema.

The next section centers upon the ways in which the Screening Room pushes the boundaries of the relationships between production, distribution, and exhibition of independent cinema by threatening traditional theatrical windowing.

Studios and Same-Day Releasing: The Screening Room as Strategy

Cofounded in 2016 by Sean Parker of Facebook and Napster fame and music executive Prem Akkaraju, the Screening Room is "a streaming platform that aims to make new releases available at home on the same day they hit cinemas, via a set-top box that streams to televisions, similar to Apple TV and Roku."[43] Offering secure antipiracy technology, the Screening Room would charge viewers about $150 for access to the set-top box that transmits the movies and charge $50 per view for a forty-eight-hour rental. Thus, the price of watching a film would be about the same as four movie tickets plus the cost of concessions. According to this plan, exhibitors would also receive $20 for each film purchased. However, this plan would essentially eradicate the need for theatrical windows. Whereas exhibitors such as AMC have expressed interest, exhibitors such as Regal insisted upon an exclusive ninety-day theatrical window in order to screen films in their theaters.[44] While Cinemark refused to reveal its position, its CEO, Mark Zoradi, issued a statement that spelled out his concerns. "The exhibition window has been the most stable window long-term and the theatrical success of a film drives the value proposition for the studios' downstream ancillary markets," he said. "Cinemark believes that any day-and-date propositions must be critically evaluated to avoid the devaluation of the exhibition window and all subsequent revenue streams of our content providers."[45] Concerns over the "devaluation of the exhibition window" also extend to filmmakers, as well as film producers, because the Screening Room makes accessing films online on the same date as they screen in theaters a distinct possibility.

Steven Spielberg, Martin Scorsese, Peter Jackson, Ron Howard, and J. J. Abrams are supporting the plan and have become stakeholders in the company, while James Cameron, Brett Ratner, and Christopher Nolan oppose it. Abrams expressed his support for the Screening Room because of the possibilities it offers for more flexible viewing patterns for his family, telling the *Hollywood Reporter*, "We are in a moment of disruption. I love nothing more than going to the movies. That's the way it has to be. I also know I'm the father of three kids and I haven't been at a theater on opening night [with them] in probably 12 years."[46] Peter Jackson defended his support for the new proposal because of the possibilities of expanding the audience for his films:

> I had concerns about "DirecTV" in 2011, because it was a concept that I believe would have led to the cannibalization of theatrical revenues, to the ultimate detriment of the movie business. Screening Room, however, is very carefully designed to capture an audience that does not currently go to the cinema. . . . This is a critical point of difference with the DirecTV approach—and along with Screening Room's robust anti-piracy strategy, is exactly why Screening Room has my support. Screening Room will expand the audience for a movie—not shift it from cinema to living room. It does not play off studio against theater owner. Instead it respects both, and is structured to support the long-term health of both exhibitors and distributors—resulting in greater sustainability for the wider film industry itself.[47]

Whereas supporters of the Screening Room lauded it for its innovation and sustainability, opponents referenced the devaluing of theatrical exhibition, the fear of piracy, and concerns about revenue sharing, particularly for smaller, independent theaters. Challenging the Screening Room and its possible destruction of the theatrical window, director Brett Ratner explained, "This alternate form of distribution would destroy the exclusive theatrical window which is one of the crucial elements—along with the best possible presentation, the social experience, and the sense of a unique event theatrical creates—that drives the value of the entire distribution chain. There may be certain movies that will lend themselves to this platform, but I am still a firm believer, and as a movie going fan will always support the traditional theatrical experience."[48]

Though the Screening Room also incorporates a plan to share 40 percent of the revenues with exhibitors, exhibitors ultimately did not approve.[49] Even NATO came out against the Screening Room, saying that if there to be new business models, "those models should be developed by distributors and exhibitors in company-to-company discussions, not by a third party."[50] As John Fithian noted, "Exclusive theatrical windows make new movies into events. . . . Success there establishes brand value and bolsters revenue in downstream markets."[51] The Screening Room not only may threaten local economies but also could pose a threat to the entire movie business, especially in relation to global piracy and film exhibition. Without the theatrical window, movies may no longer be "events" and therefore may not be as profitable as "big business."

However, the Screening Room predominantly impacts independently owned and community-driven art house cinemas, since larger theater chains like AMC, Regal, and Landmark would likely receive the lion's share of these shared profits. Single-screen theaters in particular would also be impacted, since they would be able to screen films only for limited periods of time, which would limit their profits. Tim League, one of the most successful independent art house exhibitors and the founder of Alamo Drafthouse, responded to these intricate connections between exhibition and distribution for both the studios and theaters by saying, "As an exhibitor I consider my relationship with the studios a partnership. We're both trying to build large audiences for the movies they finance. I see adoption of this technology and the piracy threat it presents as a grave disservice to that partnership."[52]

Art House Convergence, the nonprofit organization supporting mission-driven, community-based art house theaters across the United States, issued an official statement against the Screening Room on March 15, 2016. Including more than 600 independent exhibitors and allied businesses, the organization overtly indicated that it was not against day-and-date strategies, but in its statement it strongly urged all studios to deny all content to the Screening Room:

> The proposed model is incongruous with the movie exhibition sector by devaluing the in-theater experience and enabling increased piracy. Furthermore, we seriously question the economics of the proposed revenue-sharing model. . . . A model like this will also have a local economic impact by encouraging traditional moviegoers to stay home, reducing in-theater revenue

and making high-quality pirated content readily available. This loss of revenue through box office decline and piracy will result in a loss of jobs, both entry level and long-term, from part time concessions and ticket-takers to full time projectionists and programmers, and will negatively impact local establishments in the restaurant industry and other nearby businesses. How many of today's filmmakers started their careers at their local moviehouse?[53]

Thus, the Screening Room has the potential to negatively impact not only the independent and art house communities but also independent filmmakers themselves. Even film scholar David Bordwell has commented on the dangers of the Screening Room for the movie industry. Calling the Screening Room, "weaponized VOD at $50 a pop," Bordwell purports:

> The studios depend on the theatrical release, but not because it's the biggest source of revenue. (For the top films it can yield a lot, of course, but most films don't recoup their costs in that window.) The theatrical release builds awareness, making it stand out downstream in the ancillaries. Without theatrical release, a film needs a lot of publicity to draw notice. Witness all those films on your Netflix or Hulu menu, all those John Cusack movies you didn't know existed.
>
> Independent films are increasingly relying on day-and-date release between a mild theatrical run and some form of Video on Demand. Other indie titles, along with foreign ones, are going wholly VOD, and the big players—Netflix, Hulu, and Amazon—are vigorously buying titles and backing new projects against the looming day when the studios will license fewer blockbusters to them.[54]

Thus, as Bordwell notes, the Screening Room's threat to the dominance of the theatrical release is also a threat to the studios themselves, as well as to independent filmmakers. Additionally, the Screening Room puts into question the role of publicity in making a film successful (and who is responsible for it: producers, distributors, or exhibitors). Without the publicity provided by the exhibitor, it could be argued that these independent films might never be discovered on streaming sites such as Netflix, Amazon, or Hulu.

The strategies used by the Screening Room also have larger implications for independent films and independent exhibition. As Tom Brueggemann argues, "But their current distribution paradigm is threatened by non-studios with deep pockets like Netflix and Amazon starting to initiate significant projects (both traditional movies and longer-form programming) that have the option of totally bypassing theaters. So the trajectory is moving toward coexistence and finding a model that maintains as much of the status quo as possible while adapting to new paradigms."[55] Unlike larger theater chains like Cinemark and Regal, independent and art house theaters like those represented by Art House Convergence have been some of the only theaters willing to show content that is also screening on-demand.

For example, in 2014, after the major chains refused to show *The Interview* (2014) after Sony was hacked, Art House Convergence drafted a petition with a core group of fellow theater owners to show Sony there was support to release the movie.[56] In addition, when an independent film such as *Love and Friendship* (Whit Stillman, 2016) or *Wonderstruck* (Todd Haynes, 2017) is made available on Amazon just weeks after its theatrical release, these independent and art house theaters are still willing to screen them.[57] Recognizing the advantages of simultaneous release strategies for both distributors and exhibitors, Tim League advocates for day-and-date releasing for specific titles, saying, "When you simply don't have the budget to mount a national campaign twice, once for theatrical and once again for digital/VOD, it helps to compress the windows so that your one press hit is effective in both spaces. An ultraVOD release undoubtedly hurts your theatrical revenue, but if we have confidence that the overall revenue will be greater, we will release it that way. Right now about a third of our titles are day and date or ultraVOD."[58]

Brent Lang and James Rainey of *Variety* note that the appeal of theatrical exhibition is dwindling, especially for larger multiplexes: "Although many theaters have invested heavily in outfitting their locations with comfier chairs, better sound systems and projections, and more diverse snack options, it's not clear that most consumers have the same reverence for hitting the multiplexes that they once did."[59] In an interview at Art House Convergence in 2017, Ira Deutchman (cofounder and managing partner of Emerging Pictures, a New York–based digital exhibition company) maintained that the communal experience is an essential part of theatrical exhibition, noting, "I'm a big believer in the fact that the attraction of going to see a movie in a movie theater as opposed to on a phone, or at home, or even on a big screen at home, has a lot to do with the experience, the audience, the communal experience. No matter what the technology is, the biggest appeal[s] of seeing a movie in a movie theater are all the analog things: which are people, food, drink, conversation. None of that happens if you're sitting at home."[60]

Thus, though the Screening Room endangered theatrical exhibition by threatening traditional windowing, ultimately it failed to come to fruition due to lack of support from both the big chain theaters and the art house and independent theaters. More recently, companies like Warner Bros. and Fox have deliberated over adopting their own models of distribution, "considering charging $30 to stream films after they have played for 30 days."[61] However, in May 2017, Netflix CEO Reed Hastings said the eventual demise of the theatrical release window was "inevitable." He likened "going to the movies to going out to eat," saying, "If you want a communal experience with your friends, you'll go to the theater, just like you'd go to a restaurant even though you know how to cook."[62] This diminishing and possible eradication of theatrical windowing puts into question the interrelationships between producers, distributors, and exhibitors and creates even more challenges for independent filmmakers and the independent and art house cinemas that show their films. In particular, it impacts the box office successes of smaller, indie, and foreign art house fare such as Dee

Rees's *Mudbound* (2017) and Alfonso Cuaron's *Roma* (2018), since their limited theatrical release impacts their possibilities for winning such prestigious awards as the Oscars, Directors Guild of America Awards, and Independent Spirit Awards.

Conclusion

Ira Deutchman recognizes the necessity of acknowledging the history of moviegoing when he considers these changes in distribution, noting, "This is not the first time the movie business has been threatened by an outside force that in theory was going to compete with and take the place of people's time that they were going to spend in a theater. . . . The first time around in my lifetime was back in the fifties and into the early sixties when . . . television first became a mass medium and when Hollywood was having a really hard time figuring out what to do to have audiences come into the theater."[63] Competing with television, multiplexes, and on-line streaming, art house and independent theaters are constantly striving to differentiate themselves in the marketplace.

For instance, in 2010, Alamo Drafthouse (an art house theater chain that now has more than forty locations across the United States) founded Drafthouse Films. Following the earnestly simple motto of "sharing the films we love with the widest audience possible," Drafthouse Films distributes films theatrically, through home video, VOD, and its direct-to-consumer platforms, integrating into the ever-growing Alamo Drafthouse entertainment lifestyle brand.[64] CEO Tim League explains, "Too often in the industry I hear people say, 'Oh, yeah, we bought that, it's a piece of crap, but it'll make money.' But those are words we're never going to utter because what we're trying to do is build up credibility in our brand. We make very few compromises in programming, and we want to do the same on the distribution side."[65]

In fact, other exhibitors and distributors have followed suit. As of 2013, the British Film Institute in London now hosts its own streaming service, the BFI Player.[66] And, in 2015, Lionsgate and Tribeca Shortlist teamed up to create a subscription VOD service.

“The launch of the Tribeca Short List service unites two powerful brands and underscores our commitment to collaborate with blue-chip partners around the world to deliver premium content to online audiences,” said Lionsgate chief executive officer Jon Feltheimer. “The Tribeca name resonates with movie aficionados everywhere, and our service will encompass a highly curated, diverse and prestigious portfolio of quality films.”[67] These alternative streaming services provide even more opportunities to access and watch indie films online. However, they are also a reminder that the opportunities for producers, distributors, and exhibitors to unite and once again be vertically integrated (just as before the Paramount Decree of 1948) seem all the more possible in the era of continuing simultaneous release strategies.

3

DIY Distribution

YouTube, Four Eyed Monsters, *and* Girl Walks into a Bar

In January 2011, the Sundance Institute partnered with YouTube and Acura to release twelve short films from the 2011 Sundance Film Festival.[1] These films were screened in YouTube's Screening Room, a curated wing of YouTube that exhibits foreign and independent films such as *Are You the Favorite Person of Anybody* (2005) from independent directors such as Miguel Arteta (*Star Maps* [1997], *Chuck and Buck* [2000], *Youth in Revolt* [2009], and *Cedar Rapids* [2011]) and Miranda July (*Me and You and Everyone We Know* [2005] and *The Future* [2011]). As a separate channel on YouTube, the YouTube Screening Room was an attempt to redefine YouTube in relation to both professional and quality filmmaking.

YouTube is not usually associated with feature-length films or cinematic aesthetics; rather, it has multiple identities. It is an online space for watching everything from music videos to cat videos, viral videos to political campaign speeches, sports highlights to news clips. Nevertheless, as YouTube continues to develop and grow under the domain of Google and other corporate sponsorship, its investment in quality content has also continued to grow. While YouTube remains the primary space for viewing both music videos and viral videos, it is also working to rebrand itself as a purveyor of high-quality indie cinema online.

Following YouTube's ideal of "broadcasting yourself," more and more independent filmmakers are using this site as a means of self-distributing their films before they get more official distribution deals. Through social networking sites like YouTube, Facebook, and Instagram, filmmakers looking for an alternative means of promoting and distributing their work are building a core audience, often even before their films are released on DVD or in theaters. Perhaps most famously, in 2007, Arin Crumley and Susan Buice promoted their film, *Four Eyed Monsters*, by broadcasting behind-the-scenes footage of the film online before finally releasing the entire film on YouTube. Through word of mouth and viral marketing, the videos garnered more than 1 million hits, and eventually, *Four Eyed Monsters* became the first feature film to be posted on YouTube.

Four Eyed Monsters received a distribution deal on DVD through Withoutabox's Distribution Lab. As stated on the film's website:

> The Distribution Lab is a new system, used by filmmakers, to self distribute independent films. The Lab provides filmmakers with expertise and infrastructure to distribute films using a suite of pioneering distribution techniques such as Demand Ticketing, Social Network Marketing, Active Audience, Fractured Rights, Perpetual Catalog Management, Pay-to-Play Accounting, and more. The Lab will leverage online social networks such as MySpace and Audience—a new proprietary product from Withoutabox to provide a discovery mechanism for an intimate connection to be established with a core audience that will support films in their release. The Distribution Lab will provide filmmakers with flexible and scaleable DVD replication, DVD and merchandise fulfillment, feature film download solutions and the ability for an audience base to request a film to play theatrically in their local area.[2]

This chapter explores the ways in which the availability and accessibility of digital film distribution on YouTube create a space for nontheatrical exhibition and DIY distribution for independent filmmakers. Focusing on the ways in which social networking sites and digital platforms reimagine the role of film directors in producing, distributing, and exhibiting their films, this chapter argues that the presence of these films on YouTube challenges the relationships between producers and consumers. At the same time, the corporate involvement of companies such as Google, Lexus, and American Express in these distribution and exhibition ventures also indicates an ongoing and problematic relationship between independent films and their commercial sponsors. As Jean Burgess and Joshua Green point out in *The YouTube Reader*, "YouTube is disruptive not only because it unsettles the producer-consumer divide, but also because it is the site of dynamic and emergent relations between market and non-market, social and economic activity."[3] Sites like the YouTube Screening Room promote a DIY idea of independent filmmaking, yet they also mask the ways in which the exhibition and distribution of these films are funded through corporate sponsorship. Though the creation of this space for user-generated content on YouTube is often framed around discourses of empowerment and democracy, YouTube is also creating a space for itself as an arbiter of good taste. In this way, YouTube is reframing itself as a media entity that connotes not only popularity but also high aesthetic quality. Focusing on three case studies, *Four Eyed Monsters* (Buice and Crumley, 2007), the YouTube Screening Room, and *Girl Walks into a Bar* (Sebastian Gutierrez, 2011), this chapter will argue that YouTube capitalizes on independent filmmakers and DIY distribution as a means of selling its own aesthetics of quality cinema. Tracing a cultural history of the presence of independent films on YouTube, the chapter posits that from the initial screening of its first feature film (*Four Eyed Monsters*), to the creation of a channel designed exclusively for the exhibition of "quality content" (the YouTube Screening Room), to its continuing foray into feature film distribution with *Girl Walks into a Bar*, YouTube has positioned itself as both an arbiter of "good taste" and a distributor of "quality" independent filmmaking online.

The films considered in this chapter hold a particularly complex and elusive relationship to the film industry, corporate ownership, and mainstream media. While the self-distribution of these films encourages the growth of grassroots movements and DIY film communities, the films' presence on YouTube is a reminder that the films' exhibition and distribution are also dependent on YouTube's and Google's corporate sponsorship. Though YouTube is purportedly seen as a place to "broadcast yourself," a place for creative and personal expression, the corporate sponsorship of Google underlying its usage is often ignored or erased by these discourses of DIY culture, empowerment, and democratic participation. At the same time, YouTube also draws attention to the complex interrelationships between its producers and consumers in an attempt to market both its popularity and the high-art aesthetics of independent films such as *Four Eyed Monsters* and *Girl Walks into a Bar.* In this context, it is important to note both the ways in which YouTube has been understood historically and the means by which it has reframed itself as a purveyor of professional and quality filmmaking online.

YouTube: Reframing Taste in Pursuit of "Quality" Filmmaking and Aesthetics

As Pierre Bourdieu points out in his analysis of bourgeois aesthetics, aesthetics focus on form as opposed to substance or function.[4] These questions of aesthetics and "taste" also hinge on class, cultural capital, and the reinscription of class differences. In the current cultural landscape, cinema itself is often found between the two poles of low and high culture. Whereas "low" culture is associated with the Hollywood blockbuster, "high" culture is associated with the foreign, independent, and world cinema that is available in the YouTube Screening Room. At the same time, however, while the links between high and low cultures often create an artificial binary that conflates low-quality filmmaking with "low-quality" aesthetics (like those found in digital videos and amateur YouTube videos), the presence of professionally made "high-quality" films on YouTube speaks to the need to complicate this divide when it equates professional filmmaking with high culture.

On YouTube, these divisions are also influenced by the construction of independent cinema as a taste culture. In this context, independent cinema is understood in opposition not only to Hollywood, corporatization, and the studio system, but also to the "low" and "popular" cultures of the blockbuster and the megaplex.[5] By reframing itself in opposition to its previous conception as purveyor of amateur and "low-quality" videos, YouTube is working to re-establish itself as an arbiter of "high quality" and professional filmmaking.

Created in 2005 by Chad Hurley, Steve Chen, and Jawed Karim, YouTube was acquired by Google in 2006. Receiving almost 5 billion views a day, YouTube serves as the world's largest online video provider.[6] As of 2018, more than 400 hours of video were uploaded every minute to the site.[7] Originally billed as "Your Digital Video Repository" and designed as a platform for users to share their personal home videos, YouTube has transformed from a mode of video sharing to a mode of video expression. It has become a means of not only sharing video content but also creating shared identity and opportunities for social networking.[8] In its current incarnation, YouTube is a site in which old media (video) collides with new media (online video sharing and social media practices). Creating a new model for archiving, sharing, rating, and (re)circulating digital videos, YouTube is also defined by the interrelationships between the users who generate content, and the viewers and audiences of that content.[9]

As Pelle Snickars and Patrick Vonderau argue in *The YouTube Reader*, YouTube continues to establish a "clip culture"[10] and holds "the broadest repository of moving-image culture to date."[11] In fact, though most of its videos are short (under ten minutes), YouTube also screens feature-length TV shows and films.[12] In 2009, YouTube announced that it had signed deals with Hollywood studios, including Sony, MGM, and others, in order to "showcase thousands of TV episodes and hundreds of movies on its Web site."[13] And, in 2013, YouTube introduced paid premium content. In 2015, YouTube debuted an ad-free subscription service called YouTube Red that was intended to compete with sites such as Netflix and Hulu, but it changed the name to YouTube Premium in 2018 when it incorporated YouTube Music Premium, Google's alternative to Spotify and Apple Music.

These transitions to paid "premium" content are indicative of YouTube's continual pursuit of "quality" content as well as its intention to reframe itself as an arbiter of "good taste." Discourses of quality proliferate on the YouTube site and in the commentary surrounding it. Many YouTube users contribute to this discourse by adding comments and rating the videos on the site itself. Often these discourses redraw the lines between professional and amateur aesthetics, drawing attention to the ways in which notions of elitism, high art, and popular culture circulate on YouTube in this context. These discourses simultaneously redraw and blur the lines between professional and amateur, and between producer and consumer. While YouTube users participate in both the creation of these videos and their critiques, it has become more and more clear that YouTube is attempting to identify itself via these professional aesthetics as it continues to support the high production values and studio-produced content of independent and feature films online.[14]

In hopes of competing with other websites such as Hulu and Netflix (two sites that are already cashing in on paid streaming video services), YouTube is attempting to add more "quality" programming to its repertoire, including feature-length programming by Hollywood studios.[15] In 2011, YouTube created a program called YouTube Next that would "help the video makers with whom YouTube shares ad revenue to produce more professional content by giving them grants and training."[16] This program was an attempt to continue to include more professionally produced original content on the site and underscored YouTube's interest in promoting and purveying "high-quality" videos and professional content for its users. Intriguingly, this focus on quality and professionalism on YouTube also reproduces the distinction between amateur and professional filmmaking and positions YouTube as a space where amateur films may be ghettoized.

Alexandra Juhasz speaks to these complex interrelationships between professionals and amateurs on YouTube in "Learning the Five Lessons of YouTube," stating, "YouTube reifies distinctions between professional (or corporate) culture and that of amateurs (or citizens) even as it celebrates its signature form, the vlog, and the flattening of expertise."[17] On YouTube, these high-quality production values and aesthetics mirror those of independent and art house cinema. Whereas amateur films use "low-end aesthetics," professional videos have the high-quality production values and aesthetics associated with independent cinema.

In fact, YouTube has frequently been critiqued for the low aesthetic quality of its videos, often made on the spot with camera phones, webcams, and digital cameras and posted online unedited. As many of YouTube's critics have noted, videos in the "Most Popular" or "Highest Rated" categories such as "Charlie Bit My Finger"[18] are not necessarily the videos of highest aesthetic quality. These divisions between low- and high-end aesthetics also reflect the divisions between amateur and professional culture. As Kylie Jarrett notes in her essay "Beyond Broadcast Yourself: The Future of YouTube," "The site also encourages users to produce polished content by offering production advice from *Videomaker Magazine* and through the addition of the YouTube Remixer which enables editing, remixing and titling of YouTube content on the site."[19] As Eggo Muller argues, YouTube users are often in conversation online about the quality of the videos even as they are encouraged to rate, share, and add comments on the videos.[20] Thus, discourses of quality are intrinsic to YouTube's creation of a viewing community. In this way, the popular and often amateur videos on YouTube are often constructed in stark opposition to the high art of professionally made feature-length films like *Four Eyed Monsters* or the Sundance shorts in the YouTube Screening Room.

This focus on the producers of YouTube as the creators of its content also highlights what Muller calls the "participation dilemma."[21] On the one hand, YouTube alludes to the possibilities of democratic participation through its ease of use, low budgets, accessibility, and so forth. On the other hand, not all users of YouTube follow the well-established norms of "quality" professional filmmaking and aesthetics. The YouTube mode of exhibition and viewing encourages fan participation and active audiences; however, the aesthetics of YouTube differ depending on its users and audiences.[22] Thus, by supporting independent film distribution and exhibition on its website, YouTube is not only striving to generate more ad revenue but also re-creating itself as a purveyor of "quality" aesthetics and content in an oversaturated media market.

At the same time, however, at the time of this writing, nine of the top ten most popular videos of all time on YouTube are music videos such as Justin Bieber's "Sorry" and Taylor Swift's "Shake It Off." Directed by seasoned music video and Hollywood film directors, these YouTube videos have high production values and aesthetics that rival those of the Hollywood dream factory. Thus, while within the cultural imaginary, YouTube is seen as a video-sharing platform that is both democratic and all-inclusive, the popularity of its videos now leans toward those that are professionally made by the entertainment industry itself. By exhibiting, distributing, and promoting the work of professionals within the industry, YouTube also puts into question its primary status as a space for amateur and nonprofessional filmmakers to share their work. This has severe economic implications for independent filmmakers who are trying to get their work seen on YouTube, since they must compete with the work of celebrities and directors who are already well established within the entertainment industry. In this context, films such as *Four Eyed Monsters* and *Girl Walks into a Bar* also challenge the ways in which YouTube brands itself in relation to notions of both independent cinema and quality filmmaking.

Four Eyed Monsters: DIY Distribution and Social Networking in a New Media Market

Financed with $100,000 in credit cards, Susan Buice and Arin Crumley's semiautobiographical film, *Four Eyed Monsters*, was the first feature-length film (at seventy-two minutes) to be released on YouTube in 2007. An artistic experiment shot on digital video in fourteen months, *Four Eyed Monsters* tells the story of Buice and Crumley's relationship. Buice and Crumley refuse to speak to each other for four months as the film self-reflexively explores the ways in which their alternative means of communication, such as videos, emails, letters, and drawings, impact contemporary understandings of love, romance, and intimacy. In its use of cinematic style and aesthetics, or what Geoff King calls "desktop expressionism" in *Indie 2.0*, the film draws from both documentary and avant-garde cinema.[23] Yet, it is the film's social networking and new media marketing strategies that led to its success as both an independent film and a new form of video self-distribution.[24]

Following its world premiere and critical success at the Slamdance Film Festival in 2005, *Four Eyed Monsters* failed to receive a distribution deal.[25] Rather, its popularity started in 2005, when Buice and Crumley launched their behind-the-scenes video podcasts on their MySpace pages and asked fans to donate money to get their film released in theaters. Capitalizing on the growth of online video streaming and social networking sites, Buice and Crumley launched their new video podcast the day the new video-capable iPod was announced (November 1, 2005).[26] These episodes also screened on the Independent Film Channel and IFC .com. Intended to be DVD extras when the DVD of the film was finally released, the thirteen video podcasts not only chronicle the making of *Four Eyed Monsters* but also serve as a companion to the film. Shot in a similar style and quality as the feature film itself, these shorts also push the boundaries of the interrelationships between professional and amateur filmmaking and between low- and high-art aesthetics. In fact, rather than mimicking the style of video bloggers' "talking heads," the podcasts incorporate behind-the-scenes video footage as well as actual footage from the film itself. Thus, these podcasts also capitalize on ideas of convergence as they investigate the relationships between filmmaking, vlogging, and video extras. In this way, the podcasts are arguably even more notable than the film itself, since they offer up not only a new way of envisioning the video blog but also a new means of cinematic self-promotion.

As Jonathan Gray has argued in *Show Sold Separately*, paratexts like the podcasts for *Four Eyed Monsters* also frame the ways in which industries and audiences see the film itself.[27] Citing the trailers for movies like *The Lord of the Rings* and the spoilers for TV shows like *Lost*, Gray argues that these extratextual materials (or paratexts) are often a means of creating buzz about a film or TV show before it is even seen in theaters. Whereas films like *The Lord of the Rings* trilogy already have a built-in audience because of their high budgets, brand name recognition, and studio backing, *Four Eyed Monsters* capitalized on the popularity and accessibility of its vlog in order to get both a theatrical release and a distributor for the film.

Unlike paratexts such as DVD extras or action figures, one of the advantages of the persistent direct address of the vlog is that it invites feedback from its audiences.[28] Blurring the lines between amateur and professional and between producer and consumer, the vlog also pushes the boundaries between the vlogger and his or her audience. Among the first video podcasts to be made available through the iTunes music store, the *Four Eyed Monsters* podcasts produced a cult following and built the film's audience though online social networking sites such as MySpace and spout.com (a movie rate-and-review site and online fan community). Ease of use and the accessibility of these sites encouraged fan and audience participation. As filmmaker Crumley pointed out, "People were commenting on the videos, then commenting on each other's comments and becoming friends with each other. . . . We wanted to take that social-networking dynamic and bring it into the offline world, so we asked everybody to give us their ZIP codes if they would like to see our film."[29]

Using these social networking tools, Buice and Crumley developed a plan to release the film in the cities (and zip codes) with the most participants and booked themselves into theaters in those cities. Using the internet to generate interest in their film was their strategy, since they didn't have the financial backing to create a larger traditional marketing campaign. Through word of mouth (and through email and MySpace), Buice and Crumley convinced theaters like the IFC Center in New York, the Laemmle Grand 4-Plex in Los Angeles, the Somerville Theater in Boston, and the Gene Siskel Center in Chicago to release the film theatrically in September 2006. With this idea of self-distribution, one requester on MySpace meant one ticket sold in the theaters. Consequently, the theaters themselves did not feel they were taking the risk of losing money by screening the film to an empty theater. Instead, based on the interest and presence of Buice and Crumley's fans on MySpace, the theaters were essentially guaranteed an audience for *Four Eyed Monsters*.

Exposure on iTunes and MySpace, as well as in *IndieWire* and the *New York Times*, increased the film's popularity but also created an online audience for the film. This audience not only influenced new episodes of the video podcast but also impacted the editing of the film itself. Referring to the *Four Eyed Monsters* video podcast series, Buice stated, "It definitely informed our creative process, because we could see how people were responding to an episode and seeing if everyone was getting all the ideas we tried to put in it. And realizing what was working—what wasn't working affected how we would edit the next video and also affected how we would revise the film, which hadn't been released yet."[30] This grassroots approach to distribution also led to more audience and fan participation not only in relation to the social networking sites and film screenings but also in terms of the film's production and postproduction. The filmmakers' capitalization on these new media formats as a means of growing their audience did not end there, however. Crumley and Buice also screened a version of *Four Eyed Monsters* within the video game *Second Life* before landing on YouTube in 2007.[31] Thus, the popularity of *Four Eyed Monsters* was also based on its promotion in multiple markets as not only an indie film but also a vlog and a video game. As an unknown indie film in an era of media convergence, re-envisioning itself via these multiple media platforms led to its success.

Social networking and new media sites continued to grow both profits and audiences for *Four Eyed Monsters*. Through sponsorship from spout.com, the filmmakers made more than $20,000 in referral payments with each new recommendation of *Four Eyed Monsters* by a site visitor.[32] They then started to sell DVDs off their website through Withoutabox.[33] Finally, in 2007, *Four Eyed Monsters* became available on YouTube for free (with YouTube providing ad revenue and spout.com providing sponsorship). To date, the film has received more than 1.4 million views on YouTube.

After the success of *Four Eyed Monsters*, Buice and Crumley remained true to the DIY culture and continued to participate in the DIY filmmaking community. As Burgess and Green note in *YouTube*, the internet is a new "enabling social technology for knowledge."[34] Posting video tutorials on how to make a video podcast and a twenty-nine-minute video about their DIY distribution on YouTube (in the public domain), the filmmakers continued to share their knowledge with online and filmmaking communities as a means of teaching others their DIY distribution strategies.[35] In their presentation at the London International Film Festival in 2007, Buice and Crumley also spoke to the interrelationships between the amateur and the artist as part of their filmmaking process. Chronicling the distribution of *Four Eyed Monsters*, from its initial screening at Slamdance in 2005 to its screening on YouTube in 2007, the filmmakers advocated self-distribution through social networking sites such as MySpace, as well as sponsorship from sites like YouTube and spout.com.

In their video podcasts, these filmmakers promoted use of sites such as YouTube and MySpace as a means of taking film distribution into their own hands. Encouraging audiences to socialize and participate in the promotion of their films by posting comments online and joining social networking sites, these filmmakers also validated their own artistic vision by advocating for self-distribution and self-promotion. For Buice and Crumley, this DIY model provided a space for artistic vision and directorial voice, as well as a space for producing, distributing, and exhibiting their independent film in an increasingly online (and corporate) context.

Within the indie film world, self-distribution and DIY filmmaking have become political and ideological tools that support the antimainstream values associated with independent filmmaking at the margins. Yet these distribution and exhibition models are also dependent on the corporate structures of organizations like YouTube, Google, and even larger theater chains like Regal or AMC. However, like the work of many indie filmmakers, including those of the "Miramax-Sundance era," Buice and Crumley's advocacy of self-distribution does not acknowledge the place of corporate sponsorship within their success.

Four Eyed Monsters's use of social networking as a marketing strategy and its focus on alternative models of independent film distribution suggest the possible future success of subscription models as a next step in the evolution of the film industry. However, as Buice and Crumley point out in their DIY case study presentation, it is a model that may have limited applicability to other independent films and filmmakers, since much of their film's popularity stemmed from the novelty of these alternative marketing schemes and social networking strategies.

When Buice and Crumley were asked how they got the ideas for using the web to self-distribute *Four Eyed Monsters*, they answered that they found their information through Google searches (see Randall Stross's book *Planet Google: One Company's Audacious Plan to Organize Everything We Know*).[36] Thus, though these filmmakers seem to be working outside corporate hierarchies, they are also entrenched within them.[37] In other words, though Buice and Crumley champion the use of YouTube in the distribution of their film, they do not acknowledge the ways in which YouTube controls the continued existence of *Four Eyed Monsters* on its site. To date, *Four Eyed Monsters* is still available for viewing in its entirety for free on YouTube; however, it remains to be seen whether this will be a viable distribution option for future independent filmmakers hoping to get their films produced, distributed, and exhibited in the new media economy.

The YouTube Screening Room: World Cinema, Professional Filmmaking, and Online Distribution

In 2008, YouTube unveiled the Screening Room, a site featuring new releases of high-quality short and feature-length films from around the world. These films included the Academy Award–nominated short *Our Time Is Up* (Rob Pearlstein, 2004), Sundance and Tribeca Film Festival shorts, and the films of Miranda July and Miguel Arteta. Four films were released in the Screening Room every other Friday, and YouTube purported that these films "always appear with the permission and involvement of the filmmakers," so viewers were encouraged to rate and share them and to leave comments.[38] As Michael Learmonth of *Business Insider* points out, "People will be able to communicate directly with filmmakers to share thoughts, exchange opinions with fans, and provide honest feedback using YouTube's features to comment, rate, and share films."[39] In this way, the Screening Room was created not only as an online space for screening and exhibiting these films but also as a social space in which filmmakers and fans could participate in online commentary and networking.

Creating a space for these films (films that were often previously unseen in a theatrical context) to be seen and commented on, YouTube's Screening Room enabled filmmakers and audiences to socially connect in a larger film community that encouraged interaction between producers and consumers. Indeed, this push toward conversation, feedback, and social networking changed how independent films were distributed online as sites like Facebook, Instagram, and YouTube became more and more common places for independent filmmakers to promote and self-distribute their work. As Sara Pollack, film manager for YouTube, stated, "The YouTube Screening Room will serve as a focused destination for people to discover new talent while being entertained and informed through film. . . . We are excited to offer filmmakers around the world a new distribution opportunity and to encourage more conversation within our community around film."[40]

Though now defunct with the introduction of its paid premium content in 2013, the YouTube Screening Room was an attempt to make independent, international, and feature-length films part of YouTube's repertoire. The Screening Room was a place not only to screen and distribute independent films but also to build an audience for these films and to generate revenue (for both YouTube and the filmmakers). In addition to generating revenue through its ad space, the YouTube Screening Room included links to the filmmaker's websites so viewers could buy the films from the filmmakers themselves. A "buy now" button enabled viewers to link to the filmmakers' website to buy DVDs and digital downloads. And YouTube's "High Quality Player," "which offers users the best viewing experience possible," provided more than twice the usual YouTube resolution.[41] However, the presence of these films online while YouTube and Google generated the ad revenue elides the question of who was actually gaining (both economically and culturally) from this enterprise. In fact, YouTube capitalized on these low-budget and independent films (films that were often never screened outside of film festivals and would never be widely distributed theatrically or on DVD) to make a profit.

At the same time, the YouTube Screening Room's primary focus on films that had already screened in film festival circuits and international contexts also points out the ways in which YouTube chose to market films that were already considered both "high culture" and "popular." Like YouTube itself, the Screening Room was designed around name and product recognition. Advertising known cinema brands such as the Sundance Film Festival and the Oscars, the Screening Room exhibited well-known "quality" films rather than more amateur videos such as "Charlie Bit My Finger" or the infamous cat videos usually associated with YouTube. In this context, YouTube was also participating in the cultural economy by cementing its own position as cultural tastemaker.

The launch video for the YouTube Screening Room used celebrities like Moby and indie film stars like Kevin Pollack and Selma

Blair to sell its popularity. As Joshua Gamson has argued in his seminal text on celebrity, *Claims to Fame*, "Celebrities are manufactured as attention-getting bodies, a process complicated but not negated by the fact that celebrities are human beings. Knownness itself is commodified within them."[42] In this way, stars are always already commodified. At the same time, the stars in this video are also indicative of a counterculture (as both Pollack and Blair star in primarily independent films and Moby was part of the punk music and rave scene of the 1990s). The presence of these stars in the video indicates YouTube's association with quality as these well-known celebrities voice their support of this corporate enterprise. Take, for instance, this quote from Moby (included in the press release for the unveiling of the Screening Room): "One of the fantastic things about the digital present is that means of production are so much more egalitarian than in the past." Moby's own MobyGratis program allowed filmmakers to use his music in their films for free. Thus, these celebrities (and their endorsements) stand in for the "independent," the "elite," and the "popular," while at the same time enabling YouTube to elide its own corporate participation in the project by alluding to discourses of empowerment as independent filmmakers were encouraged to self-distribute their work through DIY models.

In the promotional video for the Screening Room, Moby positioned YouTube in relation to discourses of empowerment, saying, "The YouTube Screening Room is about empowering filmmakers and helping them get their work seen. What drives good artists, both filmmakers and musicians, is to create something they love and have other people experience it."[43] But YouTube is not a utopian space that unilaterally empowers its consumers and participants. Some of the commenters on the launch video for the Screening Room pointed out that YouTube was enslaving the artist, paying nothing for the content of these shorts but making millions off the ads.[44]

Additionally, one of the problems with this short-lived DIY distribution format was that the YouTube Screening Room limited its streaming availability to a few weeks. Thus, unlike the YouTube videos that remain on the site from their first posting, the Screening Room posted film with an online expiration date.[45] This limited availability may have drawn users to the site for Sundance and Tribeca festival shorts,[46] but this still left a question as to whether this platform was a viable economic alternative both for independent filmmakers and for YouTube itself.

In this way, Google and YouTube capitalized on small independent filmmakers as a means of making a profit. As Jose van Dijck argues, the interrelationships between the producers of this content (the filmmaker/artist), the consumers/viewers, and YouTube itself have larger cultural and economic implications.[47] Reinscribing the distinctions between popular and high culture, amateur and professional art, and paid and unpaid labor practices, YouTube also must be critiqued for its participation in a capitalist and commercialized media economy. Films like *Girl Walks into a Bar* further cement this relationship between corporate sponsorship and YouTube by re-establishing YouTube as both a purveyor of studio quality feature-length films and an arbiter of luxury and "good taste."

Girl Walks into a Bar: YouTube (and Lexus) as Feature Film Distributor

Billed as "the first major motion picture made exclusively for the internet" and sponsored by the high-end luxury car company Lexus, *Girl Walks into a Bar* (Sebastian Gutierrez, 2011) capitalizes on YouTube's popularity as the first feature film developed and produced exclusively for internet distribution.[48] Available in ten parts as a ten-video playlist during its initial release and currently available for screening in its entirety on YouTube, *Girl Walks into a Bar* premiered both in the YouTube Screening Room and at the SXSW Film Festival in Austin, Texas, on March 11, 2011. Although the film was intended for worldwide distribution on YouTube, it was available to be screened on YouTube only within the United States due to copyright issues.[49]

An independent feature with a Hollywood cast and a budget of less than $1 million, *Girl Walks into a Bar* seems like traditional

Hollywood fare in both style and plot, but it was produced without financial backing from the studios. Starring Josh Hartnett, Danny DeVito, Robert Forster, and Rosario Dawson, the film is also a commentary on the convergence of television, film, and new media cultures in the current global economy. Building off the name recognition of these television and film stars, *Girl Walks into a Bar* promotes both quality filmmaking and cult followings. Capitalizing on DeVito's popularity in *It's Always Sunny in Philadelphia* (FX, 2005–present) and Forster's self-reflexive performance in Quentin Tarantino's *Jackie Brown* (1997), *Girl Walks into a Bar* appeals to savvy media viewers and cult cinema and television audiences.[50]

Joe Leydon of *Variety* called *Girl Walks into a Bar* "the cinematic equivalent of a light but tasty snack."[51] As Nancy Miller writes in her article "Minifesto for a New Age," "Music, television, games, movies, fashion: We now devour our pop culture the same way we enjoy candy and chips—in conveniently packaged bite-size nuggets made to be munched easily with increased frequency and maximum speed. This is snack culture—and boy, is it tasty (not to mention addictive)."[52] Though director Gutierrez hoped viewers would watch the film in its feature-length format, this variety of distribution formats also allowed viewers to watch it in other ways (including a short format more indicative of traditional YouTube viewing practices).[53]

However, even though the film was available for viewing as "snacks," most of the viewings on YouTube have included the film in its entirety. After the film received more than 260,000 views (which translates to ticket sales worth $2.6 million) in the two days following its YouTube release, Gutierrez commented, "This signals a new era in independent film distribution and leaves no doubt that audiences are willing to watch long form content online. . . . I'm so proud of the cast of this movie and fascinated by the direct interaction between them and the actual viewers, who have responded in numbers beyond our expectations."[54] In this way, *Girl Walks into a Bar* is also a reminder of the idea that despite YouTube's propensity for short films, audiences of indie cinema are still willing to view feature-length films online. Though this was Lexus's first foray into filmmaking, it is part of a trend of big corporations tapping into independent film markets.[55]

Questioning theatrical distribution models, *Girl Walks into a Bar* pushes the boundaries of old and new forms of film and media not through its form or aesthetics but through its social media campaigns, marketing strategies, and modes of online distribution. In a press release announcing the film's premiere, director Sebastian Gutierrez stated, "We want to prove that Web distribution is a viable medium for theatrical quality movies which rely on story, characters and dialogue as opposed to special effects."[56] At the time of this writing, the films that are consistently released on YouTube are ones that do not have the wide appeal of Hollywood films like *Avatar* (James Cameron, 2009) or *The Dark Knight* (Christopher Nolan, 2009). Rather, they are films that may not have the special effects or star power of the Hollywood blockbusters.

One month after its release, *Girl Walks into a Bar* had received 550,000 views on YouTube, far exceeding expectations.[57] It is also now available for viewing on YouTube for $1.99. However, the use of sites such as YouTube to exhibit and distribute independent films has larger cultural and economic implications for independent filmmakers hoping to make it in the industry as its continued collaboration with corporate entities such as Google, American Express, and Lexus often limits the kinds of indie stories that can be shared online.

YouTube, DIY Filmmaking, and the Future of Independent Cinema

Four Eyed Monsters and *Girl Walks into a Bar* are not the only films that have participated in this DIY mode of film distribution. Film consultant Peter Broderick and film directors such as Jon Reiss (*Bomb It* [2007]) and Sacha Gervasi (*Anvil: The Story of Anvil* [2008]) have advocated for self-distribution. This is not only because major studios are refusing to distribute independent films, but also because self-distribution enables the filmmakers themselves to control their own work (in terms of both distribution and exhibition). Since the demise of New Line and other independent distribution companies, independent filmmakers have fewer and fewer opportunities for widespread theatrical distribution. Thus, DIY film distribution also enables a possible new model of distribution that encourages multiple forms, rather than sticking only to the major studio model. In other words, it creates what Manohla Dargis calls "a viable, artist-based alternative."[58] This alternative acknowledges the idea that viewers and consumers of films are watching them in different venues. Thus, rather than limiting these venues solely to theatrical experiences, DIY distribution enables viewers to watch these films in multiple exhibition contexts, on their computers, iPods, cell phones, and so forth. In this way, independent cinema's presence is seen not only in theaters or on DVDs but also on Instagram, Facebook, and YouTube.

Whether independent films can be free of studio and corporate intervention is a question that has been asked consistently within academic scholarship about contemporary independent cinema. As noted previously, Chuck Kleinhans has argued that contemporary American independent cinema must be defined in relation to Hollywood itself, not as outside of the corporate machine.[59] Just as the indie cinema of the 1990s was dependent on the corporate ownership of indie distributors like Miramax and Fox Searchlight, in an era of convergence, the relationship between independent cinema and corporate interests is certainly a question that continues to haunt independent cinema and its means of production, distribution, and exhibition, particularly in a new media market in which Google, Lexus, and American Express are sponsoring independent films online.

The presence of independent (and feature) films online also pushes the boundaries of independence itself. No longer framed as working solely in opposition to the studio system, independent filmmakers must also continue to acknowledge the growing corporate interest in this medium of entertainment. In fact, with sponsorship from American Express, the Tribeca films streaming on Tribeca's own Streaming Room may be a reminder that corporate sponsorship is a necessary evil within the independent film industry. As Kylie Jarrett points out, "YouTube's model requires consumers to do most of the immaterial and effective labour of providing the content and creating the communities (market niches) which make the site compelling for users."[60] This has larger implications with regard to who is responsible for the labor behind YouTube's user-generated content. In other words, while users provide the (unpaid) labor, YouTube reaps the economic benefits through its corporate sponsorship and advertising campaigns.[61]

This DIY model of self-distribution is constructed as a means of working against the Hollywood distribution system, but it does not acknowledge the ways in which Google and YouTube work within their own corporate hierarchies. In her essay on YouTube, Alexandra Juhasz discusses the nature of YouTube as a DIY culture. She argues that "YouTube is not *democratic*. Its architecture supports the *popular*. Critical and original expression is easily lost to or censored by its busy users, who not only make YouTube's content, but sift and rate it, all the while generating its business."[62] Though many people can now access the tools for the production and distribution of media on YouTube, the actual viewings are dependent on "popularity." And, as Juhasz argues, those videos that are deemed popular often support the status quo and reinforce hegemonic power.[63]

In an interview with Sasha Costanza-Chock, Henry Jenkins points out the problems of using YouTube and corporate-sponsored sites to distribute artistic work, writing that "these commercial portals present problems of 1) censorship, 2) surveillance, 3) exploitation, and 4) closed technology design."[64] As many critics of YouTube have pointed out, once these films are shown on YouTube, they are subject to YouTube's terms of use. At the same time, YouTube also holds the right to suspend accounts and remove videos based on use violations.[65] Thus, though the YouTube model of self-distribution seems like a viable and democratic alternative, it also has larger political implications in relation to corporate ownership of artistic materials and their availability for both the producers and the consumers of online content.

4

The Fourth Screen

Sundance, Shorts, and Cell Phones

In December 2015, the Independent Film Project's twenty-fifth annual Gotham Independent Film Awards gave away two new awards to Breakthrough Series, Long Form and Short Form. In her introduction to the first of these awards of the evening, Mariska Hargitay (daughter of Jayne Mansfield and best known for her work as Olivia Benson in *Law & Order: Special Victims Unit* [NBC, 1999–present]) remarked, "Just because the screen is a little smaller, doesn't mean that what you're watching isn't a great piece of filmmaking."[1] The nominations for Breakthrough Long Form included *Jane the Virgin* (CW, 2014–2019), *Mr. Robot* (USA, 2015–2019), *Transparent* (Amazon, 2014–2019), *Unbreakable Kimmy Schmidt* (Netflix, 2015–2019), and *Unreal* (Lifetime, 2015–2018).[2] The nominations for Breakthrough Short Form included *Bee and PuppyCat* (Natasha Allegri, Cartoon Hangover, 2013–present), *The Impossibilities* (Anna Kerrigan, seriesofimpossibilities.com, 2015–present), *Qraftish* (Christal, Blackgirldangerous.com, 2015–present), *Shugs and Fats* (Nadia Manzoor and Radhka Vaz, ShugsandFats.TV, 2014–present), and *You're So Talented* (Sam Bailey, Open TV, 2015–present).

Also called "serialized short form narratives" or "indie web series,"[3] these short-form series include everything from an animated series about a woman searching for temporary employment, to the misadventures of two veiled women in Brooklyn, to "an 18-year-old Black queerling, who ponders events and ideas pertaining to race, queerness, gender, feminism, awkwardness, etc., while making crafts."[4] Thus, these independent film awards acknowledge the intertwining of the spaces of independent film with the spaces of television and web-based content. By including television and web series within the concept of independent, this evolution of the Gotham Awards points to the ways in which media convergence is creating a space for short films and web series, both online and on cell phones.

Incorporating an understanding of films made for cell phones that takes into account their status in relation to their production histories, industrial practices, and visual aesthetics, this chapter focuses on web series made for SundanceTV. In *Beyond the Screen: Emerging Cinema and Engaging Audiences*, Sarah Atkinson differentiates between films that are made *on* mobile phones and films that are made *for* mobile phones. For example, films made on mobile phones such as *Cloverfield* (Matt Reeves, 2008), *Rage* (Sally Potter, 2009), *Night Fishing* (Park Chan-wook, 2011), and *Tangerine* (Sean Baker, 2015) became popular even before films were exclusively made *for* mobile phones.[5] However, whereas many critics have focused on films produced *on* cell phones,[6] this chapter will study short films and web series made explicitly *for* mobile phone viewing as a means of further analyzing the intersections between independent films and their means of production, distribution, and exhibition.

To this end, the chapter explores the interrelationships among independent cinema, marketing, and media convergence by analyzing cell phones and their aesthetics through SundanceTV's web series of short films (airing on both the Sundance Channel website and SundanceTV from 2006 to 2015).[7] Independent film organizations like Sundance have created programming specifically for portability and cell phone viewing, ushering in a new era of the digital short. In terms of aesthetics, cinematic form, and filmic style, these digital shorts investigate indie cinema via new modes of visuality, textuality, and aurality.[8] At the same time, they also promote convergence with other media industries, institutions, and technologies. Examining Sundance web series such as *The Art of Seduction* and *Green Porno*, this chapter analyzes how the cell phone redefines the spaces of production, distribution, and exhibition for independent cinema online via the portability of the cell phone.

Taking a three-pronged approach to the ways in which the style of independent filmmaking is transformed on the fourth screen, I will first discuss the ways in which mobile media and cell phone aesthetics are used to create and market alternative forms of indie media. Second, I will discuss the Sundance Channel's transition to SundanceTV and Sundance's first foray into cell phone production, *The Art of Seduction*, as a means of analyzing the multiple ways in which cell phone aesthetics impact understandings of indie programming. Finally, I will focus on Isabella Rossellini's web series for SundanceTV, *Green Porno*, and how it reinvents fourth-screen filmmaking via art cinema and avant-garde aesthetics.

Mobile Media and Cell Phone Aesthetics

In his 2006 book, *Cell Phone Culture*, Gerard Goggin investigates the centrality and growing significance of cell phones in relationship to the growth of "mobile media."[9] Even before the invention of the iPhone, he predicted the interrelationships between the mobile phone and other forms of media such as the camera and video camera. Other authors such as Richard Ling, Larissa Hjorth, Noah Arceneaux, Anandam Kavoori, and J. Katz map out the evolution of the mobile phone as a tool for communication and a technological object, cultural artifact, and distribution platform.[10] In their anthology on the iPhone entitled *Moving Data: The iPhone and the Future of Media*, Pelle Snickars and Patrick Vonderau discuss how the invention of the iPhone and the app, as well as the growth of "mobile studies," "offscreen studies," and "transmedia studies," have impacted motion pictures.[11] In this section, I focus on the ways in which both cinema studies and convergence cultures are intertwined with ideas of cinematic style and aesthetics in a study of short films on cell phones.

In their book *Companion to Mobile Media*, Gerard Goggin and Larrisa Hjorth argue that mobile media can be seen as "a set of practices and cultural artifacts."[12] Noting the relationship between seamlessness and convergence, Francesco Casetti and Sara Sampietro point out the need to account for not only the technological and industrial consequences of convergence but also their social and cultural dimensions. In this context, convergence can be seen as not "a simple combination of various media environments but . . . a continuous mingling of technologies, experience forms, and practices."[13] Harvey May and Greg Hearn call this "the experience economy," "where a broad range of mobile phone users, with or without technical savvy, expendable income and aesthetic ambitions, can harvest from the ever-increasing palette of the digital domain."[14] On SundanceTV, the technologies of film, animation, TV, and the web intermingle to expand upon the stylistic, formal, and narrative elements of independent cinema.

As Goggin has argued, the early twentieth century marks the "second coming of mobile television."[15] Mobile video has been on the rise since the invention of the iPhone in 2007, when video and phone technologies merged. As Juan Miguel Aguado and Inmaculada Martinez point out, the shorter duration and on-demand availability of web video led to a greater compatibility between the aspects of mobile phones and digital video consumption.[16] Goggin notes that mobile video will "increase sixteen-fold between 2012 and 2017."[17] In his book *Post-TV: Piracy, Cord-Cutting, and the Future of Television*, Michael Strangelove notes, "By the end of 2018, there will be over 4.5 billion smartphone subscriptions in the world. The number of mobile-connected devices now exceeds the number of people on earth."[18] He also notes, "Smartphones alone have created a mobile video audience of approximately 240 million people worldwide, including 90 million Americans, using these portable screens."[19] Thus, the mobile video audience is a significant portion of the film viewing audience. Seen as video's next frontier, mobile technologies have also impacted the form and aesthetics of film and video. These aspects of mobile media include their small size and portability, relationship to personal identity (since cell phones and iPods are often considered personal accessories rather than technology), ubiquity, and location sensitivity (mobile media respond to their locations). In this vein, cell phone culture can be defined by (1) portability, (2) ubiquity, (3) personalization, and (4) miniaturization.[20]

The interaction between cell phones and cinema creates new forms of visuality, textuality, aurality, and haptics. At the same time, through personalization, film audiences may find alternative means of viewing such topics as gay pride, activism, environmentalism, music cultures, and so forth. And, the availability of indie films on cell phones creates new audiences for independent cinema online. As chief executive of mobile app company Shopkick Cyriac Roeding argues, "The cellphone is the only interactive medium that you carry with you while you're watching TV *and* while you're shopping in the store. The cellphone is therefore the only interactive medium that can function as a bridge between the TV screen and the store shelf."[21]

In contemporary media culture, the smaller screens of the cell phone and iPod have become ever present and readily available. But the presence of cinematic media on these smaller screens also has implications for how these films are marketed and viewed. Media convergence between cinema, television, and internet technologies has led to a reinvestment in the new "golden age of the digital short"; web videos have embraced the creation of shorter films (one to two minutes) and the use of nonlinear and interactive storytelling formats, simpler story lines, less dialogue, and more colorful art direction.[22] These aesthetic transformations in cinematic style and storytelling are constructed in relation to the smaller size of the cell phone screen.

Michael Strangelove references Gerard Goggin's work in *Global Mobile Media*, stating, "Mobile movies do not recreate earlier use of cell phones or cinemas; rather they foster a new kind of networked culture."[23] In web videos, the camera is often close to the action (close-ups are used instead of wide shots, since broad vistas are hard to discern on the smaller screen).[24] Glen Creeber calls this the "intimate screen," noting "its power to create a particularly close dynamic between image and audience."[25] Movement must also be handled with care, since the frame rate on the web is not up to the twenty-four to twenty-five frames per second of film and television.[26] These films also often incorporate what Max Dawson calls "an aesthetic of efficiency, characterized by streamlined exposition, discontinuous montage and ellipsis, and decontextualized narrative or visual spectacle."[27]

With the advent of cell phone technologies, the content of these web series and short films is also changing. As Vladan Nikolic notes in *Independent Filmmaking and Digital Convergence: Transmedia and Beyond*, "Arguably, the short-film form has now become the dominant format in the world of online streaming video."[28] First, the advent of the web series allows for engagement with taste cultures that exist beyond the fourth screen of the cell phone (such as auteur filmmakers like Guy Maddin and international stars like Isabella Rossellini). Second, the intimate aesthetics of the cell phone also expand upon the aesthetics of independent cinema (engaging with documentary and avant-garde filmmaking practices often associated with the invention of the handheld camera). And, third, the viewing practices of these short films change, since they can be watched in short increments or else binge viewed during the same viewing session.

Intended for viewing within what Nancy Miller calls a "snack culture," these short films are "conveniently packaged bite-size nuggets made to be munched easily with increased frequency and maximum speed."[29] From 2006 to 2015, the creation of these short web series by Sundance was an attempt to address the question of whether the short film might be *the* preferred cinematic form in a culture in which audiences were leaning toward downloading films to their phones and computers instead of seeing them in theaters or on television. At the same time, these films also draw attention to the ways in which cinematic narrative, performance, and direction change when they are designed primarily for the fourth screen. In this vein, the seduction of the cell phone becomes a new means of viewing cinema as well as a new form of cinematic style.

The next section addresses the ways in which indie filmmakers on sites such as SundanceTV use film style and cell phone aesthetics to re-create "indie-ness" on the small screen. The remaining portion of this chapter will focus on two case studies on SundanceTV, *The Art of Seduction* and *Green Porno*, as a means of mapping out the narrative, form, and aesthetics of mobile video.

The Art of Seduction in the Age of the Cell Phone, Sundance Channel, and SundanceTV

As Robert Eberwein notes in "The IFC and Sundance: Channeling Independence," the Sundance Channel launched in 1996 with the film that opened the 1995 Sundance Film Festival, *Before Sunrise* (Richard Linklater, 1995).[30] At that time, the Sundance Channel focused "more toward American independent films that enjoyed little, if any, theatrical distribution," as well as short films, documentaries, and foreign language films.[31] Owned by the cable television network Showtime from 1996 to 2008 and by AMC from 2008 to the present, the Sundance Channel also featured films that focused on issues of ethnic, racial, and sexual diversity, as well as classic films and festival favorites such as *Sweet Sweetback's Baadasssss Song* (Melvin Van Peebles, 1971) and *The Watermelon Woman* (Cheryl Dunye, 1997). As the Sundance Channel evolved, it showed fewer and fewer short films and features, instead focusing on original programming such as *Anatomy of a Scene* (2001–2004), a documentary series focused on the art of filmmaking, and *24 Frame News* (1999–2003), a six-minute news program following the events of the Sundance Film Festival.

The Sundance Channel transitioned to rebranding itself as SundanceTV in 2014 following the success of its original unscripted programming such as *Push Girls* (2012–2013) and fictional series such as *Rectify* (2013–2016) and *Top of the Lake* (2013–present). After this transition, Sundance also hosted the miniseries *The Honourable Woman* (2014) and additional original series such as *The Red Road* (2014–2015) and *Hap and Leonard* (2016–present). At this moment of transition, Sundance TV's senior vice president, Monica Bloom, noted, "We have made great strides in the past few years with our original programming and we see this as the perfect moment to mark that shift with a new name and fresh logo. . . . SundanceTV aims to create television that is as remarkable as the best independent films, and this rebrand embodies that position with confidence."[32] Thus, SundanceTV is utilizing its indie branding to market both its original television series and its web series.

In an effort to acknowledge the mobility of consumers, as well as the diversity of entertainment choices and the new distribution practices of media industries, SundanceTV has attempted to market independent cinema via its web series.[33] As Aymar Christian has noted, "Mobile technologies have been marketed to the public as 'different' from other forms of distribution."[34] He has also stated, "The internet marketplace accommodates independents whose production, storytelling, and distribution strategies push against inequalities and the status quo."[35] SundanceTV markets this notion of mobile video as different by branding their web series as different from/in opposition to the mainstream. At the same time, since these web series are created explicitly for cell phone viewing, this also impacts the content, aesthetics, and modes in which these films are being viewed on the fourth screen.

The Sundance Group already has access to the first screen (cinemas and movie theaters) and the second screen (television).[36] In an era of ever-expanding mobile media and cell phone technologies, Sundance broadened its appeal to both the third screen (computers) and the fourth screen (cell phones and iPods) in its markets. On November 8, 2006, Sundance announced a project collaboration with GSM Association (a global mobile phone company) that would create short films for viewing on mobile phones. Although Sundance was not the first network to create programming specifically for the fourth screen, its press release for *The Art of Seduction* stated, "This pilot project is believed to be the first to commission high caliber independent filmmakers to create original stories specifically for the mobile environment."[37]

As indicated by Sundance Institute president and founder Robert Redford in the press release: "Cell phones are fast becoming the 'fourth screen' medium, after television, cinema and computers. . . . We feel this experiment embodies fully, our quarter-century dedication to exploring new platforms to support wider distribution of independent voices in filmmaking. We are excited about bringing this opportunity to independent filmmakers and most excited to see what they will do with it."[38] The press release goes on to state that Redford commissioned well-established filmmakers and Sundance Film Festival winners and nominees such as Jonathan Dayton and Valerie Faris (*Little Miss Sunshine*, 2006) and Maria Maggenti (*Puccini for Beginners*, 2006) to make short films for mobile phones. In this way, Sundance continued to market its filmmakers through a new medium and tapped into a new market of audiences for that medium.

Coproduced by both Sundance and the National Film Board of Canada in 2006, *The Art of Seduction* is a series of nine short films originally produced for viewing on video cell phones. This was also Sundance's first programming bought specifically for viewing on the web and was released in collaboration with the cell phone carrier Helio. Sundance asked filmmakers such as Guy Maddin, director of *The Saddest Music in the World* (2003) and *My Winnipeg* (2007), and Mark McKinney, director of the Canadian TV Series *Kids in the Hall* (CBC, CBS, HBO, 1989–1995), to create films for the series.

First distributed by the Sundance Channel for two minutes on Monday nights in 2006, *The Art of Seduction* was made available for download on the web at sundancechannel.com. "This is the first time Sundance Channel has acquired programming that will debut on digital platforms," said Christopher Barry, Sundance Channel's vice president for digital media and business Strategy. "Premiering these films on our website and via our mobile partner, Helio, reflects our commitment to seek original content that can be distributed across multiple digital platforms."[39]

Adding films like *The Art of Seduction* to its programming was intended to make Sundance even more accessible, especially for audiences who may no longer watch movies in theaters or on cable television. But, at the same time, the fourth screen also complicates the context in which these films were produced, distributed, and exhibited. In this context, these short films are also reimagining the art of cinematic storytelling in the age of cell phone technologies.

These short films privilege the body in their representations of love, sex, and desire on-screen. Merging cell phone and cinematic technologies, the films also use images of the body in motion to capture relationships between human and animal, beauty and fantasy, and sex and love. Here, the art of seduction is mapped onto not only the bodies on-screen but also the motion of the camera and the kinetic use of the soundtrack. In this vein, seduction becomes a new mode of investigating desire via the intimate screen within a one- to two-minute storytelling medium.

Guy Maddin's film *Nude Caboose* is the first short of *The Art of Seduction* series.[40] Experimenting in the new delivery medium of the cell phone, *Nude Caboose* begins with a close-up of a torso of a nonnormative middle-aged male body. A shirtless man leads a group of lethargic dancers in bodily motions that resemble the motions of a train. As the film cuts back and forth between the male body (the train conductor) and the nude caboose (a nude female body), the music and sounds of a train appear on the soundtrack. The intimate screen aesthetic of the cell phone and the use of nudity made this video marked "Not Safe for Work." Indeed, many of the other films within the series illustrate the idea that the cell phone medium changes the nature of storytelling, requiring shorter narratives and little to no dialogue.

On Fire, one of the other eight films in this series, features a man who dances around a pole that then becomes the pole of a fireman, referencing both the current art of pole dancing and the current fascination with firemen in a post-9/11 world. *Strip Show* redefines the art of seduction through the life of a web cam girl who tries to fulfill her client's every fantasy, from making a smoothie to dressing up like Kenny Rogers and Dolly Parton. *Dirty Dog* is a commentary on current ideas of love and relationships. As a woman throws her boyfriend out of her apartment, he picks up his guitar and serenades her, only to be humped by a dog. In *Electric Chairs*, an elderly couple seduces each other through a choreographed dance involving their wheelchairs. In *SOU*, a word that in Japanese means "noise" and in Chinese means "manic depression," animation and documentary footage are intertwined to create a collage of interculturalism. Though it participates in the traditional "talking heads" style of documentary filmmaking, *Not Pretty, Really*, explores cultural assumptions about beauty and sex. Via the "big heads" of the small forty-by-forty-two-pixel screen, this short redefines the meaning of the close-up. The short film *120 Seconds to Get Elected* features the grainy black-and-white image of an Italian politician who has only 120 seconds to get people to vote for him. As he responds to the nameless and faceless audience, words from his speech such as "happiness," "money," and "jobs" flash on the screen. The animated short *My Obscure Object of Desire* tells the story of an animated heart that turns into a stick person, a dog, and a strawberry. As the genderless stick person smiles, waves, and whistles, it becomes gendered as two giant circles as breasts, long hair, and eyelashes are added to its body.

Uncovering the nature of love, bodies, and desire, these films also explore the art of storytelling for the small screen. In fact, the stories included in these films tend to hinge on the simultaneous presence and absence of the human body as a means of exploring both sex and desire. The films draw attention to the imperfections and flaws of the bodies on-screen, while at the same time both upholding and challenging traditional notions of sex and gender through their use of close-ups, quick-paced editing, and crosscutting. Not all of these films specifically reference sex itself; instead, seduction becomes a new mode of investigating desire within a short-form storytelling medium. These films, when read in tandem as a series, also reimagine the art of storytelling in the age of the cell phone in terms of seriality as well as episodic storytelling.

The popularity of *The Art of Seduction* led to Sundance's promotion of a variety of web series, including the Webby Award–winning series *Green Porno* (2008–2010); *The Captive* (2009), a science fiction thriller web series); *Beginnings* (2011), a documentary web series that explores the early inspirations of artists, musicians, actors, and designers such as Charlotte Gainsbourg, Marjane Satrapi, and Yoko Ono; and *DreamStates* (2011), a collaborative animated video series by the creative agency OptionG. In *DreamStates*, notable artists, musicians, actors, screenwriters, and filmmakers, including Questlove, Will Forte, and Sebastian Junger, recall their dreams. The series included photographic images of the celebrities, as well as both traditional and stop-motion animation sequences to add to its visual appeal.

Animation has also been used in a variety of YouTube video series and podcasts, including John Green's *Crash Course* (2011–present), as well as the MTV series *Braless* from YouTube star Laci Green (2014–present). Thus, Sundance created *The Art of Seduction*, *Green Porno*, and *DreamStates* in an attempt to compete with YouTube's promotion of its own original streaming web series. Attempting to reach an audience already familiar with these star texts, *The Art of Seduction* and *Green Porno* focus on the intersections between intimate video aesthetics, animation, and the avant-garde as a means of reimagining the relationships between the oral, the visual, and the animated.

Already reaching audiences through broadcast television, cable, and satellite, Sundance redefined itself via the fourth screen with *The Art of Seduction* and *Green Porno*, enabling a new means of accessing audiences who are web-savvy. In *Green Porno*, director Isabella Rossellini envisions an alternative form of art cinema and avant-garde aesthetics intended for cell phone viewing audiences.

Green Porno: Art Cinema and Avant-Garde Aesthetics on the Small Screen

A series of eighteen short films conceived, written, codirected by, and starring Isabella Rossellini, *Green Porno* was produced for viewing on both the third and fourth screens. Although the series was originally created for viewing on cell phones and iPods, *Green Porno* first screened at the Sundance Film Festival in Park City, Utah, in January 2008. Since then, the shorts have been available for viewing at the Berlin International Film Festival, the Royal Ontario Museum in Toronto, and the Sundance Channel. Currently, the series is screening online on both the SundanceTV website and YouTube. In its first season, it received 4 million hits and multiple Webby Awards, becoming a viral internet sensation.

Including such creatures as dragonflies, spiders, barnacles, shrimp, and whales, *Green Porno* is a series of one-minute shorts featuring bugs and marine animals communicating, having sex, and reproducing. Selecting the most unusual sexual practices of animals for her shorts, Isabella Rossellini created short stories explaining their bizarre and sometimes scandalous sexualities. Both informative and entertaining, *Green Porno* includes animals present in daily life such as bees and snails, as well as other animals (such as limpets and earthworms) that are hermaphrodites or omnisexual.

In each short, Rossellini opens by saying, “If I were a . . .” fly, snail, starfish, and so on. She describes her body, eyes, length, dominant or unusual features (such as number of legs, or sticky toes), and sexual organs. Then she narrates the peculiar and bizarre ways in which these creatures have sex. The use of avant-garde sets and costumes, using colored paper, cloth, and other simple materials, gives one the impression that even a child could create these creatures, although the films’ explicit sexual content is intended for adult viewing.[41]

Created under the auspices of the environmentally progressive Sundance Channel and designed to be watched in snippets for consumption on YouTube and mobile devices, *Green Porno* represented an intriguing new foray into both independent film and environmental markets.[42] What made these films both unique and odd, though thoroughly entertaining (as evidenced by their 4 million views), was the appearance of Rossellini dressed as a bee, an earthworm, a praying mantis, and several other insects, as well as sea creatures, presenting numerous, varied, and oftentimes hilarious acts of sex as performed in the animal kingdom.

Often, Rossellini played multiple sexes and genders in the films. For instance, in *Bee*, she performed the roles of the queen bee, "daughter" bees, and drones. Dressed as a queen bee, she was fat and laid eggs. She then discussed the various bodily features of the bee, including its antennae, the pads on its feet, its compound eyes, and its stinger. In the costume of a daughter bee, Rossellini showed how bees communicate with each other by dancing among paper flowers. Finally, she performed the mating rituals of the male bee, the drone. Here, she pointed out that drones mate with female bees in flight. After mating, the penis breaks off and gets stuck in the female vagina, "like a cork in a bottle." As Rossellini explained that the drone dies after copulation, she fell to the ground surrounded by blood made of paper. Like *Bee*, each short in the *Green Porno* series is both artistic and scientific, providing an amusing and educational look at the countless ways in which animals mate and reproduce.

Intended for audiences of independent cinema; art cinema; and environmental, educational, and entertainment programming, *Green Porno* capitalized on its quirky and sexy content, Isabella Rossellini's star status, and environmentalism as a means of marketing itself on multiple media platforms. It was Rossellini's body itself that was marketed within these films. Publicity for *Green Porno* featured photos and images of Rossellini posing as a bee, a dragonfly, an earthworm, and a whale; the Sundance Channel website's promos for *Green Porno* highlighted an image of Rossellini embracing a shrimp. It was her body, surrounded by a school of paper anchovies, blinded by the compound eyes of a fly, copulating with a shrimp, that makes both Rossellini and *Green Porno* so eminently watchable and fascinating.[43]

As the founder and president of Sundance and a noted environmentalist and activist since the 1970s, Robert Redford was interested in adding green programming to the Sundance Channel's schedule. In April 2007, Redford launched "The Green," a block of environmental programming intended to encourage "green-themed" television and filmmaking.[44] "The Green" was television's first regularly scheduled programming dedicated to the environment. Included on "The Green" were *Big Ideas for a Small Planet* (a series of programs focusing on environmental innovations); *Eco*

Trip (a series focusing on the environmental impact of everyday products); and a variety of environmental documentaries such as *A Crude Awakening: The Oil Crash* (Basil Gelpke and Ray McCormack, 2006) and *Manufactured Landscapes* (Jennifer Baichwal, 2007). "The Green" also included blogs, discussions, an "Eco-mmunity map" (to search for all things green), links to other educational and environmental sites, and, of course, *Green Porno.* In an attempt to capitalize on consumers' current interest in "going green," *Green Porno* tapped into green markets by promoting a brand image that was both eco-friendly and entertaining.[45] For, as Chris Rojek has argued, "Market organization is actually founded on the perpetual replenishment and development of desire through commodity and brand innovation."[46] Attempting to compete with environmental programming such as *Planet Earth* on the Discovery Channel and independent programming on the Independent Film Channel, Sundance also wanted access to young, green, and tech-savvy consumers.[47] Thus, the marketing for *Green Porno* included cross-network spots (i.e., it was advertised on networks besides the Sundance Channel) and web and even outdoor billboard advertising.[48]

Green Porno's presence, online and on small screens, expands notions of distribution and exhibition. As of this writing, the films are still readily available and easily accessible online through both the SundanceTV website and YouTube. Even the title of the series is rooted in an awareness of how viewers access material on the internet. In an interview with *Wired* magazine, Jody Shapiro, Rossellini's codirector, explained, "What do people mostly go online for, but to look at porn? . . . So we put 'Porno' in, and when people Google it, maybe we'll get lucky and *Green Porno* will come up. We might as well take advantage of the delivery system."[49] By using marketing strategies associated with both new and small-screen media, these films reached larger markets even beyond the green or independent film communities.

Francesco Casetti and Sara Sampietro discuss the ways in which cinema is relocated on the iPhone via both the experiential and the environment, impacting the ways in which viewers experience cinematic technologies, forms, and practices.[50] *Green Porno* began as part of the Sundance Channel's attempt to merge environmental programming with programming specifically designed for internet viewing. As the seasons progressed, the series became more and more educationally and environmentally oriented. With bigger budgets and more time to prepare sets, costumes, and scripts, both season two and season three have more of an educational and scientific approach, incorporating documentary footage and the additional commentary of conservationist and marine biologist Claudio Campagna.[51]

In 2009, in order to promote the selling of the book and DVD (available through HarperCollins), *Green Porno* completed its final season. Interestingly, rather than encouraging the proliferation of more shorts, the release of the book and DVD signaled the end of *Green Porno*. The marketing of the book and "exclusive" DVD (sold together) is an intriguing commentary on the profitability of these fourth-screen technologies. To date, the shorts are still available for free on the SundanceTV website and on YouTube; however, it is likely that purchasing the HarperCollins book and DVD (which sell for twenty-five dollars) will be the only means of viewing these films in the near future.

Nevertheless, the marketing of *Green Porno* continued under another name. On April 20, 2010, Sundance and Rossellini released a new series of shorts, titled *Seduce Me*. And, on May 12, 2013, they released *Mammas*. It is unclear (perhaps deliberately) how these shorts differ from *Green Porno*, since they also focus on the sex lives of animals (such as salmon, bedbugs, and cuttlefish) in the form of short films intended for cell phone viewing. As stated on the Sundance Channel's blog, "Very much the spawn of her multiple Webby Award–winning series, *Green Porno*, *Seduce Me* continues Isabella's explorations of the wild kingdom, only this time concentrating on the courting rituals of nature's quirkiest, from bats to bed bugs."[52] This packaging and marketing of a new series remarketed *Green Porno* by encouraging viewers to "catch up" on all the *Green Porno* episodes as a means of promoting the new series. In 2014 and 2015, Rossellini went on tour performing *Green Porno* live on the theatrical stage, and in 2015, a documentary version of her performance was released by Sundance Productions. This return to the theatrical setting (following the popularity of the three web series, book, and DVD) is also a reminder of the converging media forms of film, television, music, and theater.

Isabella Rossellini has her own opinions about the future of experimental filmmaking online. In an interview with the *Wall Street Journal*, she said, "But the problem of the Internet is that despite its advantages—reaching more people, being more accessible, being free of the traditional time constraints—there's no model to get the money back to the artist, so they can continue to work."[53] Seeing herself as an artist and director (and not just an actress), Rossellini hoped to get work as a director and writer on a feature-length film. However, as of 2018, Sundance is no longer promoting *Green Porno* or its additional web series on SundanceTV. Instead, SundanceTV has transitioned to its own original programming and episodic storytelling such as *Cleverman* (2016–2017) and *Hap and Leonard* (2016–present).

Conclusion

In 2014, Sundance inaugurated its first Episodic Storytelling Lab, "offering writers an opportunity to learn how to develop stories and characters that evolve over multiple episodes in a setting where they can hone their writing skills and gain insight into navigating the changing industry."[54] In 2014, the Independent Filmmakers Project also included web series in their Emerging Visions portion of Independent Film Week. And, as noted previously in this chapter, in 2015, the Gotham Awards acknowledged web series and short-form storytelling in their award for Breakthrough Series.

Adding web series like *The Art of Seduction* and *Green Porno* to its programming makes Sundance even more accessible, especially for audiences who may no longer watch movies in theaters or on cable television. But, the fourth screen also complicates the context in which these films are produced, exhibited, and distributed. The cell phone medium encourages the creation of shorter films (one to two minutes), simpler story lines, and more colorful art direction. With the advent of digital filmmaking, these films are relatively cheap to make. But, the creation of these films raises questions about both their profitability and their sustainability.

Dan Schoenberg, the program manager of the Independent Filmmaker Project, points out, "More and more, we've been seeing creative storytellers moving fluidly across various mediums to tell their stories. The web space is one that's wide open for innovation, and we think that it's going to be daring, forward-thinking storytellers who are going to define and expand its potential. . . . The format democratizes serialized storytelling—it allows anyone the opportunity to develop a series and reach an audience, in whatever form, with whatever business model suits them best."[55] Writing for *IndieWire*, Aaron Dobbs notes that we may be entering a golden age for serialized storytelling via the web.[56] The future of independent cinema on cell phones creates new audiences for independent cinema online, new forms of visual and aural aesthetics, and media convergence with other industries, including film, television, music, and theater. However, it remains to be seen as to whether organizations like Sundance and the Independent Filmmaker Project will be able to profit from the creation, distribution, and marketing of web series made explicitly for cell phones.[57]

Conclusion

The Future of Indie Cinema Online

In July 2018, the new online television platform Rivit TV announced that it would launch Kevin Smith's new pilot, *Hollyweed*, a half-hour sitcom that takes place in a Los Angeles weed dispensary. Labeling itself "audience powered television," the new platform gives viewers the power to greenlight original TV shows by enabling established creators like Smith to screen their works for online audiences and solicit pledges as a means of financing full seasons of their shows.[1] As Marcus Wiley, chief content officer at Rivit TV, states, "This platform allows our industry's top creators like Kevin Smith to focus on passion projects that resonate with their fans without worrying about a committee of executives or advertisers. . . . Our goal is to directly connect creators with their fans, liberate the creative process and invite the audience to greenlight shows from their favorite storytellers."[2]

Like Kickstarter and Indiegogo, this crowdfunding site would greenlight a series based on the success of its fund-raising campaign. After watching a pilot on Rivit TV's website, fans could pay a modest per-episode price (from $1.99 to $5.99) to complete the season. Creators then have forty-five days to convince fans to support their projects. And, as with Kickstarter, if they fail to reach their fund-raising goals, no one is charged. This new model of crowdfunding is becoming more and more popular as sites such as Kickstarter and Indiegogo release trailers and pilots in the hopes of funding full features and series.[3] At the same time, like Netflix and Hulu, online platforms such as Rivit TV also contribute to the accessibility of indie content by making the pilot available to all audiences. Like YouTube, these alternative sites for distribution also encourage grassroots and DIY participation by enabling audiences to choose to fund these projects (rather than basing this funding on the decision making of the executives or the studios).

However, the crowdfunding of established creators such as Kevin Smith or well-known series such as *Veronica Mars* (Rob Thomas, 2014) also has implications for how unknown, less-established indie creators and films will be supported on these crowdfunding sites.[4] Jeff Howe, who coined the term "crowdsourcing," in "The Rise of Crowdsourcing," his 2006 article for *Wired*, notes that this form of crowdsourcing asks a crowd of online laborers to donate money as a means of funding various ideas and products.[5] The dependence on online laborers and funding from fans on these sites also suggests that the future of indie media is enmeshed with the DIY ethos that also supports media production on YouTube and Vimeo.

In this era of media convergence, film and television arms of production and distribution feed into each other by sustaining already well-established industry professionals and limiting the prospects for indie creators who have not yet broken into the Hollywood machine. In fact, as indie cinema online continues to converge with other forms of media such as television, web series, and other internet content, it has also become more and more intertwined with mainstream and Hollywood interests. In this vein, indie cinema online continues to become more immediate, accessible, DIY, and portable as it converges with sites such as Amazon, YouTube, Hulu, and even Disney.

In fact, this DIY form of crowdsourcing content also extends to Amazon and its ongoing focus on original series programming. From its inception in 2010, Amazon Studios encouraged online submissions and crowdsourced feedback. Scriptwriters and series creators submitted proposals for films or series that could include scripts or concept videos. The best scripts and series were then distributed on Amazon Video, and viewers were encouraged to vote on whether or not the show should be picked up for an entire season. In an attempt to compete with original programming on sites such as Netflix and Hulu, Amazon premiered its first original series, *Alpha House* and *Beta*, in 2013. And, in 2015, Jill Soloway's original series based on their trans father's coming-out story, *Transparent*, became the first show produced by Amazon Studios to win a major award and the first show produced by a streaming media service to win a Golden Globe for Best Series.

Amazon Studios' open-door policy not only encourages writers from the Writers Guild of America but also accepts amateur scripts. However, even though amateurs are allowed to apply, most of Amazon's original series are helmed by already established writers, producers, and directors such as Jill Soloway (*Six Feet Under* [HBO, 2002–2005], *Dirty Sexy Money* [ABC, 2007], and *United States of Tara* [Showtime, 2009–2011]) and Amy Sherman-Palladino (*Gilmore Girls* [WB, 2000–2007], *Bunheads* [ABC Family, 2012–2013], and *The Marvelous Mrs. Maisel* [Amazon, 2017–present]). Thus, whereas the company's open-door policy for submissions purportedly enables unknown talent to be supported by Amazon, in fact, it is primarily an opportunity for more well-known content creators to be seen in yet another corporate screening space.

This focus on established talent also extends to Amazon's Original Movies. In 2015, Amazon announced that independent film producer Ted Hope would lead creative development for Amazon Original Movies.[6] Amazon expected to produce about twelve movies per year, with budgets ranging from $5 million to $25 million, augmenting its lineup of original TV series.[7] These films were released on Amazon Prime just four to eight weeks after their theatrical release (compared with up to one year for other windowing).[8]

The first film to be produced by Amazon Studios was Spike Lee's *Chi-Raq* (2015), a modern-day adaptation of Aristophanes's play *Lysistrata*. Coproduced with Lee's company 40 Acres and a Mule Filmworks, it was also distributed theatrically by Roadside Attractions. Later, Amazon also acquired *Love and Friendship* (Whit Stillman, 2016), *Manchester by the Sea* (Kenneth Lonergan, 2016), and *Weiner-Dog* (Todd Solondz, 2016). Acquiring films from these well-known indie directors required very little risk on Amazon's part, since the films had already established a sizable indie viewership and audience at film festivals such as Sundance, Tribeca, Toronto, and Telluride. At the same time, Amazon's narrow window between theatrical and online release (and its intense promotion of these indie films on the Amazon Prime website as "Amazon Originals") also means that most audiences access these films online on Amazon rather than seeing them in theaters in limited release. In 2019, Amazon's multimillion-dollar acquisitions of Nisha Ganatra's *Late Night* and Paul Downs Colaizzo's *Brittany Runs a Marathon* at Sundance are also testing the company's strategy of continuing to theatrically release its films before releasing them on Amazon Prime.

In this way, the indie-ness of online sites such as Netflix and Amazon is becoming more and more in question as these streaming services continue to invest in more mainstream media fare. For example, in 2014, Netflix announced that Adam Sandler would make four movies exclusively for Netflix (of these, *The Ridiculous 6* [Frank Coraci, 2015] and *The Do-over* [Steven Brill, 2016], were released on Netflix to poor reviews). And, in 2015, Netflix partnered with the Weinstein Company on a unique distribution model for the anticipated sequel *Crouching Tiger, Hidden Dragon 2*. The film, which debuted simultaneously on Netflix and in IMAX theaters on August 28, 2015, was the first of several day-and-date titles covered in Netflix's pact to be the sole online distributor of first-run films from the Weinstein Company.[9] However, when asked about why Sandler's film received such popular responses from audiences worldwide, Netflix CEO Ted Sarandos replied, "It's global relevance. People want their work to manifest in the culture and be seen and appreciated, and we can do that like nobody else."[10]

The global relevance of streaming services such as Netflix and Hulu also impacts the accessibility and availability of indie media both in the United States and abroad. As Sarandos points out, "When Netflix has true exclusive rights to a show, it can release it internationally without any major issues. And distributing the show in all 41 global Netflix territories at the same time also has a notable decrease on piracy."[11] In fact, as Andrew Leonard of *Salon* notes, "In 2012, for the first time ever, Americans watched more movies legally delivered via the Internet than on physical formats like Blu-Ray discs or DVDs. The shift signified more than a simple switch in formats; it also marked a major difference in how much information the providers of online programming can gather about our viewing habits. Netflix is at the forefront of this sea change, a pioneer straddling the intersection where Big Data and entertainment media intersect."[12] On June 8, 2016, Netflix released its "binge scale" accounting for which series are watched on Netflix for how long. As noted by Sidneyeve Matrix in "The Netflix Effect," "In the popular press, binge viewing and Netflix are becoming synonymous."[13] Though Netflix does not release viewership data for its programming, this scale analyzed more than 100 serialized TV series between October 2015 and May 2016 based on global viewing across more than 190 countries. The scale reported that shows with complex narratives such as *Mad Men* (AMC, 2007–2015) or *House of Cards* (Netflix, 2013–2018) tend to be savored, whereas genre fare such as *The Walking Dead* (AMC, 2010–present) or *The Fall* (BBC, 2013–2016) are devoured.[14] At the same time, this scale points to the ways in which binging habits are dependent on genre. As Michael Newman argues in *Indie*, genre play is one of the defining characteristics of independent cinema.[15] With the continuation of the streaming wars and the advent of Disney+ in 2019, Netflix no longer hosts its original Marvel superhero series such as *Jessica Jones* (2015–2019), *Daredevil* (2015–2018), and *Iron Fist* (2017–2018), so it is uncertain what will be seen as typical of the Netflix brand in the future, especially globally.

The corporatization of indie media has already been discussed in relation to the advent of Indiewood in the 1990s and the subsequent reign of companies such as Miramax and Lionsgate.[16] Currently, indie cinema online is becoming more and more intertwined with mainstream interests as media conglomerates like Netflix, Amazon, Disney, and Google continue to compete with grassroots and more DIY models of production, distribution, and exhibition.

In particular, with the announcement of the arrival of Disney's own streaming service, Disney+, in November 2019, and WarnerMedia's streaming service to begin in early 2020, along with Disney's merger with Fox and its acquisition of Hulu, the presence of indie cinema online is also in flux. As David Sims of *The Atlantic* wrote in June 2019, "Whether people will be willing to shell out for multiple streaming services remains to be seen, but either way, established platforms such as Netflix will struggle to fill out their offerings as projects such as Disney+ take back their studios' intellectual property."[17] This may lead to more opportunities for indie mediamakers on streaming platforms such as Netflix. Because Netflix has lost its Marvel, Disney, and Warner content, it will be searching for more original content that it can claim sole ownership of. However, it will also be competing with larger media conglomerates like Disney, Amazon, and Google for this content. Thus, it is likely that the future of indie cinema online will continue to be tied to these corporate interests.

Under the domination of Disney's 60 percent share of the company, it is also very likely that Hulu will host less and less indie content. Disney CEO Bob Iger told *Vanity Fair*, "Owning a third of [Hulu] was great—but having control will allow us to greatly accelerate Hulu into that space and become an even greater competitor to those already out there. . . . We'll be able to do that not only by putting more content in Hulu's direction, but by essentially having control to the extent that managing Hulu becomes a little bit more clear, efficient, and effective."[18] In fact, Hulu has already started moving in that direction as it has added live television streaming, an esports package, and premium channels like HBO.

From an examination of the current state of streaming sites such as Netflix, Hulu, and Amazon, it is clear that indie mediamakers still have a multitude of options for producing, distributing, and exhibiting their films. As other online sites such as Facebook and Instagram create their own online programming and more and more streaming services enter the market, however, there is a concern that there are too many streaming service options and that the price of streaming for cordcutters will soon rise to be as high as those for cable and satellite TV. By reclaiming previously alternative online sites for production, distribution, and exhibition such as Netflix and Hulu, companies such as Disney are now taking over formerly indie online spaces. As Yannis Tzioumakis notes, “Media convergence also brought American independent cinema firmly under the fold of the major entertainment conglomerates that also control Hollywood cinema, and in effect helped erase to a great extent notions of the alternative that have been historically associated with many forms of independence in American cinema.”[19]

However, I would argue that indie content may continue to thrive in DIY-oriented and grassroots locations such as YouTube, Vimeo, and SundanceTV. Indie cinema online continues to blur the lines between indie and corporate media through its immediacy, accessibility, and portability. However, as the narrative of independent filmmaking becomes more and more intertwined with television, web series, and other alternative forms of programming, it also becomes more and more entangled with mainstream interests. In an era of media convergence, the future of indie cinema online lies in its ability to navigate the contentious waters of such corporations as YouTube, Amazon, and Netflix and to continue to create alternative spaces and audiences for indie content.

Acknowledgments

This book can be traced back to my love of indie film and art house cinemas. Visiting the Cable Car Cinema in Providence, Rhode Island, for Spike and Mike's Festival of Animation was one of my earliest indie moviegoing experiences, and I joined the Governing Board of the Salt Lake Film Society (the home of our beloved Broadway and Tower Theatres in Salt Lake City, Utah) in 2015. Continually discovering the behind-the-scenes and the flurry of activities that occurs every day at my local art house cinema is a constant reminder of how much I value sharing my cinemagoing experiences with an audience. As this book was being written, those experiences shaped every word in this manuscript, and I am indebted to the many members of Art House Convergence, the Salt Lake Film Society and its filmgoers, the board, the staff, and especially former chair of the board Kevin Hanson and president and CEO Tori A. Baker for continuing to inspire me to think about indie cinema online in new and exciting ways.

I am also thankful for my earliest mentors as I discovered my love of indie film through filmmakers such as John Sayles, Steven Soderbergh, and Jane Campion: Lalitha Gopalan at Georgetown University; Matthew Bernstein at Emory University; and Joan Hawkins, Barbara Klinger, Karma Lochrie, and Phaedra Pezzullo at Indiana University.

I also wish to thank my students and colleagues at Indiana University, Northeastern University, and the University of Utah for never-ending conversations about film and media arts, especially since the coming of the digital age.

I am also grateful for the Faculty Fellowship and the Faculty Research Grant from the University Research Committee at the University of Utah, as well as Research in Progress and Make Time for Research Grants from the College of Fine Arts at the University of Utah that made this book possible.

My acquisitions editor, Nicole Solano, and her assistant Maggie Tibbitt, my production editors Daryl Brower and Gregory Hyman, my copyeditor Susan Ecklund, and my anonymous readers provided thoughtful and helpful comments and advice throughout the process of writing this book.

In addition, I wish to thank everyone who provided feedback on this work at conferences, including Film & History, Flow, History of Moviegoing, Exhibition and Reception Circuits of Cinema, Media Industries, National Communication Association, and Society for Cinema and Media Studies. I also wish to thank the numerous scholars who contributed to this book, from advising me on how to write a book proposal to providing me with new ways of thinking about indie cinema online. Thank you to Yannis Tzioumakis, Cynthia Baron, Chris Holmlund, Geoff King, Gary Needham, Claire Parkinson, Linda Badley, Claire Perkins, Michele Schreiber, Lisa Dombrowski, Justin Wyatt, Alisa Perren, Craig Robertson, Ted Striphas, Aymar Christian, Virginia Crisp, Ira Deutchman, Mark Gallagher, Henry Jenkins, Alexandra Juhasz, Lucas Hilderbrand, Chuck Kleinhans, Emanuel Levy, Ramon Lobato, Amanda Lotz, Sheila Murphy, Michael Newman, E. Deidre Pribram, James Schamus, Chuck Tryon, Gregory Waller, and Patricia Zimmerman.

To my friends and colleagues in Salt Lake City and at the University of Utah for their endless support: Elizabeth Craft, Kevin Hanson, Jane Hatter, James Hughes, Christopher Lee, Ha Na Lee, Paula Lee, Chris Lippard, Colleen McDannell, Andrew P. Nelson, Sara Pickett, Sarah Projansky, Lien Fan Shen, Jennifer Weber, and my research assistant Dana Ware.

To Tonia Edwards, Natasha Ritsma, Cassandra Secrease, and Christy Setzer, for so many conversations about indie film.

To Jasmine Trice, for looking at infinite drafts and joining me in even more infinite conversations.

Ultimately, this book is dedicated to my father, who was always a willing moviegoing companion (even if it was *Y Tu Mamá También* on Father's Day); my mother, who always supported me as a writer and academic and still inspires my future, present, and feminist self (and *She* shall be exalted); and my grandmother Barbara, a fellow cinephile and lover of Nelson Eddy who instilled in me my love of cinema history ("Let Me Call You Sweetheart").

Notes

Introduction

1. Eric Larsen, "Sundance Filmmakers Can Self-Distribute Films Online after Festival," *Mashable*, January 23, 2013, http://mashable.com/2013/01/23/sundance-reelhouse.
2. See Henry Jenkins, *Convergence Culture: Where Old and New Media Collide* (New York: New York University Press, 2006); Tim Dwyer, *Media Convergence* (London: McGraw Hill, 2010); Anne Friedberg, "The End of Cinema: Multi-media and Technological Change," in *Reinventing Film Studies*, ed. Christine Gledhill and Linda Williams (London: Oxford University Press, 2000); Chuck Tryon, *Reinventing Cinema: Movies in the Age of Media Convergence* (New Brunswick, NJ: Rutgers University Press, 2009); Sheila Murphy, *How Television Invented New Media* (New Brunswick, NJ: Rutgers University Press, 2011); Michael Newman and Elana Levine, *Legitimating Television: Media Convergence and Cultural Status* (New York: Routledge, 2011); Elizabeth Evans, *Transmedia Television: Audiences, New Media, Everyday Life* (New York: Routledge, 2013); Henry Jenkins, Sam Ford, and Joshua Green, *Spreadable Media: Creating Value and Meaning in a Networked Culture* (New York: New York University Press, 2013); Amanda Lotz, *The Television Will Be Revolutionized*, 2nd ed. (New York: New York University Press, 2014); Sergio Sparviero, Corinna Peil, and Gabriele Balbi, eds., *Media Convergence and Deconvergence* (Cham, Switzerland: Palgrave Macmillan, 2017); Vladan Nikolic, *Independent Filmmaking and Digital Convergence: Transmedia and Beyond* (New York: Routledge, 2017); Matthew Freeman and William

Proctor, *Global Convergence Cultures: Transmedia Earth* (New York: Routledge, 2018).

3. See Ethan Smith and Lauren A. A. Schuker, "For Indie Films, Video-on-Demand Fills the Revenue Gap," *Wall Street Journal*, January 10, 2011, http://online.wsj.com/article/SB10001424052748704064504576069472667852508.html.
4. See Lee Rainie, "Online Video Audience Surges," Pew Research Center, January 9, 2008, http://pewresearch.org/pubs/682/.
5. Patricia Zimmerman, "Digital Deployment(s)," in *Contemporary American Independent Film*, ed. Chris Holmlund and Justin Wyatt (London: Routledge, 2005), 252.
6. Michael Z. Newman, *Indie: An American Film Culture* (New York: Columbia University Press, 2011); and Yannis Tzioumakis, *American Independent Cinema: An Introduction* (New Brunswick, NJ: Rutgers University Press, 2006).
7. See Tzioumakis, *American Independent Cinema*.
8. The Society for Cinema Studies formally changed its name to Society for Cinema and Media Studies (SCMS) in 2002 as a response to the advent of digital media. For more on the history of this organization and its name, see the Society for Cinema and Media Studies website at http://www.cmstudies.org/?page=org_history.
9. Friedberg, "The End of Cinema," 438–452.
10. For more on these debates, see Toby Miller, "Revising Screen Studies," *Television and New Media* 2 (2001): 91–93; and John Hartley, "Is Screen Studies a Load of Old Cobblers? And If So, Is That Good?," *Cinema Journal* 45, no. 1 (2005): 101–106.
11. See Anna McCarthy, *Ambient Television: Visual Culture and Public Space* (Durham, NC: Duke University Press, 2001); Ina Rae Hark, ed., *Exhibition: The Film Reader* (London: Routledge, 2001); Tryon, *Reinventing Cinema*; and Stephen Groening, *Cinema beyond Territory: Inflight Entertainment and Atmospheres of Globalisation* (London: BFI, 2014), for further discussion of film and television exhibition practices in a nontheatrical context.
12. See Carolyn Marvin, *When Old Technologies Were New* (Oxford: Oxford University Press, 1988); Jeffrey Sconce, "Tulip Theory," in *New Media: Theories of Practices of Digitextuality*, ed. Anna Everett and John T.

Caldwell (New York: Routledge, 2003); Lisa Gitelman, *Always Already New: Media, History and the Data of Culture* (Cambridge, MA: MIT Press, 2008); and Wendy Hui Kyong Chun, Anna Watkins Fisher, and Thomas Keenan, eds., *New Media, Old Media: A History and Theory Reader* (New York: Routledge, 2016), for more discussion of the debates in media studies regarding the relationship between the histories of old and new media.

13. See Gregory Waller, ed., *Moviegoing in America* (Malden, MA: Wiley-Blackwell, 2001); Haidee Wasson, *Museum Movies: The Museum of Modern Art and the Birth of Art Cinema* (Berkeley: University of California Press, 2005); Joshua Greenberg, *From Betamax to Blockbuster: Video Stores and the Invention of Movies on Video* (Cambridge, MA: MIT Press, 2008); Barbara Klinger, *Beyond the Multiplex: Cinema, New Technologies and the Home* (Berkeley: University of California Press, 2006); Charles Acland and Haidee Wasson, *Useful Cinema* (Durham, NC: Duke University Press, 2011); Devin Orgeron, Marsha Orgeron, and Dan Streible, eds., *Learning with the Lights Off* (London: Oxford University Press, 2012).
14. See Manohla Dargis, "Declaration of Indies: Just Sell It Yourself!" *New York Times*, January 14, 2010, http://www.nytimes.com/2010/01/17/movies/17dargis.html.
15. Chris Holmlund and Justin Wyatt, eds., *Contemporary American Independent Film: From the Margins to the Mainstream* (New York: Routledge, 2005).
16. For more on the ways in which *My Big Fat Greek Wedding* pushes the boundaries between indie cinema and Hollywood, see Alisa Perren's "A Big Fat Indie Success Story? Press Discourses Surrounding the Making and Marketing of a 'Hollywood' Movie," *Journal of Film and Video* 56, no. 2 (2004): 18–31.
17. See Holmlund and Wyatt, *Contemporary American Independent Film*; Alisa Perren, *Indie, Inc.* (Austin: University of Texas Press, 2012); Newman, *Indie*; Geoff King, Claire Molloy, and Yannis Tzioumakis, eds., *American Independent Cinema: Indie, Indiewood and Beyond* (New York: Routledge, 2013); and Geoff King, *Indie 2.0: Change and Continuity in Contemporary American Indie Film* (New York: Columbia University Press, 2014).

18. Jim Hillier, ed. "Introduction," in *American Independent Cinema: A Sight and Sound Reader* (London: BFI, 2001), ix.
19. The term "Indiewood" defines the increasingly significant relationship between Hollywood and independent film in the Sundance-Miramax era of independent filmmaking. See Geoff King, *Indiewood, USA* (London: I. B. Tauris, 2009).
20. Chuck Kleinhans, "Independent Features: Hopes and Dreams," in *The New American Cinema*, ed. Jon Lewis (Durham, NC: Duke University Press, 1998), 308.
21. Geoffrey Gilmore, "Long Live Indie Film," *Nation* 272, no. 13 (2001): 17–20.
22. Emanuel Levy, *Cinema of Outsiders: The Rise of American Independent Film* (New York: New York University Press, 1999).
23. Jennifer Holt and Alisa Perren, "Introduction," in *Media Industries: History, Theory, and Method*, ed. Jennifer Holt and Alisa Perren (West Sussex: Wiley-Blackwell, 2009), 1, 5.
24. Perren, *Indie, Inc.*, 8.
25. See Joan Hawkins, "Dark, Disturbing, Intelligent, Provocative and Quirky," in *Contemporary American Independent Film: From the Margins to the Mainstream*, ed. Chris Holmlund and Justin Wyatt (New York: Routledge, 2005), 89–106.
26. Newman, *Indie*, 22.
27. Geoff King, *American Independent Cinema* (Bloomington: Indiana University Press, 2005).
28. E. Deidre Pribram, *Independent Film in the United States, 1980–2001* (New York: Peter Lang, 2002), xi.
29. Pribram, xii.
30. Pribram, xviii.
31. Tzioumakis, *American Independent Cinema*, 11.
32. Rosalind Galt and Kyle Schoonover, *Global Art Cinema: New Theories and Histories* (Oxford: Oxford University Press, 2010); David Andrews, *Theorizing Art Cinemas: Foreign, Cult, Avant-Garde, and Beyond* (Austin: University of Texas Press, 2013); James Tweedie, *The Age of New Waves: Art Cinema and the Staging of Globalization* (Oxford: Oxford University Press, 2013); John White, *European Art Cinema*

(New York: Routledge, 2017); and Geoff King, *Positioning Art Cinema: Film and Cultural Value* (London: I. B. Tauris, 2019).

33. David Bordwell, "The Art Cinema as a Mode of Film Practice," in *Film Theory and Criticism: Introductory Readings*, ed. Marshall Cohen and Leo Baudry (New York: Oxford University Press, 1999), 716–724; and Steve Neale, "Art Cinema as Institution," *Screen* 22, no. 1 (1981): 11–39.
34. Andrews, *Theorizing Art Cinemas*, xi.
35. Andrews, 2.
36. Andrews, 85.
37. King, *Positioning Art Cinema*, 8.
38. King, 73.
39. King, 62.
40. Holmlund and Wyatt, *Contemporary American Independent Film*; Newman, *Indie*; Perren, *Indie, Inc.*; and Yannis Tzioumakis, *American Independent Cinema*.
41. Ramon Lobato, *Netflix Nations: The Geography of Digital Distribution* (New York: New York University Press, 2019).
42. Levy, *Cinema of Outsiders*, 20–51.
43. Yannis Tzioumakis, "American Independent Cinema in the Age of Convergence," *Revue Française d'Études Américaines* 136, no. 2 (2013): 55, https://www.cairn.info/revue-revue-francaise-d-etudes-americaines-2013-2-page-52.htm.
44. Tzioumakis, 56.
45. See Alisa Perren's book *Indie, Inc.* for more discussion on Miramax's relationship to Hollywood in the 1990s.
46. Justin Wyatt, "The Formation of the 'Major Independent': Miramax, New Line and the New Hollywood," in *Contemporary Hollywood Cinema*, ed. Steve Neale and Murray Smith (London: Routledge, 1998), 76.
47. Perren, *Indie, Inc.*, 4.
48. The 1990s ushered in an era of mergers and leveraged buyouts between the major studios and formerly independent production and distribution companies. In 1993, Disney bought Miramax and Time-Warner bought New Line; in 2002, Universal bought Good Machine. This has led to the independent film industry being called Indiewood or dependies rather than indies. For more information on this, see King,

Molloy, and Tzioumakis, *American Independent Cinema*; and Holmlund and Wyatt, *Contemporary American Independent Film*. For more on Hollywood in the new millennium, see Tino Balio, *Hollywood in the New Millennium* (London: BFI, 2013).

49. King, *Indiewood, USA*.
50. James Schamus, "A Rant," in *The End of Cinema as We Know It*, ed. Jon Lewis (New York: New York University Press, 2001), 253–260.
51. Yannis Tzioumakis, *Hollywood's Indies: Classics Divisions, Specialty Labels, and American Independent Cinema* (Edinburgh: Edinburgh University Press, 2012), 4.
52. Tzioumakis, 6.
53. Charles Lyons, "New Machine Comes into Focus," *Variety*, May 13–18, 2002, http://www.variety.com/article/VR1117866761/.
54. Levy, *Cinema of Outsiders*.
55. The five aforementioned films have won Independent Spirit Awards for Best Feature.
56. Gilmore, "Long Live Indie Film," 19.
57. See Levy, *Cinema of Outsiders*; Holmlund and Wyatt, *Contemporary American Independent Film*; Yannis Tzioumakis, *American Independent Cinema*; King, *Indiewood, USA*; Newman, *Indie*; and King, *Indie 2.0*.
58. Cassavetes was a pioneer in independent film production and self-distribution. See Levy, *Cinema of Outsiders*; and Ray Carney, ed., *Cassavetes on Cassavetes* (London: Faber and Faber, 2001). Kevin Smith's direct to DVD and VOD release of *Red State* (2011) on iTunes, Amazon, YouTube, and so on, also underscores the place of DIY exhibition and distribution strategies in today's digital media culture.
59. As many critics have noted, even screening at the Sundance Film Festival is getting more and more difficult as the festival tends to include more and more studio-financed films. The creation of the "anarchic" Slamdance and Slumdance film festivals also attests to this.
60. See the Independent Spirit Awards FAQ page at http://www.spiritawards.com/about/faq/.
61. Anne Thompson, "Sorry, Netflix: The Top DGA Award Won't Consider Day-and-Date Releases," *IndieWire*, June 26, 2019, https://www.indiewire.com/2019/06/dga-day-and-date-theatrical-releases-1202153402/.

62. Newman, *Indie*, 1.
63. Klinger, *Beyond the Multiplex*, 195.
64. Greenberg, *From Betamax to Blockbuster.*
65. Perren, *Indie, Inc.*, 231.
66. Zimmerman, "Digital Deployment(s)," 246.
67. King, *Indie 2.0*, 1.
68. Yannis Tzioumakis, *American Independent Cinema*, 2nd ed. (Edinburgh: Edinburgh University Press, 2017), 219.
69. See McCarthy, *Ambient Television*, for a discussion of the ways in which television viewing practices function outside the home, in sites such as taverns, shopping malls, doctors' offices, and airports.
70. See Jay David Bolter and Richard Grusin, *Remediation: Understanding New Media* (Cambridge, MA: MIT Press, 1999); Lev Manovich, *The Language of New Media* (Cambridge, MA: MIT Press, 2001); Anna Everett and John T. Caldwell, *New Media: Theories of Practices of Digitextuality* (New York: Routledge, 2003); Noah Wardrip-Fruin and Nick Montfort, eds., *The New Media Reader* (Cambridge, MA: MIT Press, 2003); Paul Grainge, ed., *Ephemeral Media* (London: BFI, 2011); David Trend, ed., *Reading Digital Culture* (Oxford: Blackwell, 2001); and David Bell and Barbara M. Kennedy, eds., *The Cybercultures Reader* (New York: Routledge, 2000).
71. Lev Manovich, "New Media: From Borges to HTML," in *The New Media Reader*, ed. Noah Wardrip-Fruin and Nick Montfort (Cambridge, MA: MIT Press, 2003), 17.
72. See Marvin, *When Old Technologies Were New*; Sconce, "Tulip Theory"; Gitelman, *Always Already New*; and Wendy Hui Kyong Chun, Anna Watkins Fisher, and Thomas Keenan, eds., *New Media, Old Media: A History and Theory Reader* for more discussions of the debates in media studies regarding the relationship between old and new media.
73. Tom Ryall, *Alfred Hitchcock and the British Cinema* (Urbana: University of Illinois Press, 1982), 2, quoted in Klinger, *Beyond the Multiplex*, 12.
74. See James Hay and Nick Couldry, "Rethinking Convergence/Culture," *Cultural Studies* 25, no. 4–5 (2011): 473–486.
75. Dwyer, *Media Convergence*, 2.
76. Tzioumakis, *American Independent Cinema*, 2nd ed.
77. Jenkins, *Convergence Culture*.

78. Jenkins, 2. In this context, Jenkins has written about how convergence culture works among the large and global fan bases of *Survivor* (CBS, 2000–present), *American Idol* (Fox, 2002–present), the *Star Wars* franchise, *The Matrix* trilogy, and the *Harry Potter* series.
79. Jenkins, 331.
80. Jenkins, 254.
81. Manuel Castells, "Communication, Power, and Counter-power in the Network Society," *International Journal of Communication* 1 (2007): 253.
82. Manuel Castells, *The Rise of the Network Society* (Cambridge, MA: Wiley-Blackwell, 2007), 72.
83. See Dwyer, *Media Convergence*; Jenkins, *Convergence Culture*; Friedberg, "The End of Cinema"; Murphy, *How Television Invented New Media*; Newman and Levine, *Legitimating Television*; Evans, *Transmedia Television*; Jenkins, Ford, and Green, *Spreadable Media*; Lotz, *The Television Will Be Revolutionized*; Sparviero, Peil, and Balbi, *Media Convergence and Deconvergence*; Nikolic, *Independent Filmmaking and Digital Convergence*; Freeman and Proctor, *Global Convergence Cultures*.
84. Hay and Couldry, "Rethinking Convergence/Culture."
85. Hay and Couldry, "Rethinking Convergence/Culture," 481. Please see also Jean Burgess and Joshua Green, *YouTube* (Cambridge, UK: Polity, 2009).
86. Sarah Kember and Joanna Zylinska, *Life after New Media: Mediation as Vital Process* (Cambridge, MA: MIT Press, 2012), 3.
87. Hay and Couldry, "Rethinking Convergence/Culture."
88. See Newman, *Indie*, 2.
89. See Bolter and Grusin, *Remediation*; Manovich, *The Language of New Media*; and Terry Flew, *An Introduction to New Media* (Oxford: Oxford University Press, 2002).
90. Bolter and Grusin, *Remediation*, 23–24.

1. Indie via Instant Viewing

1. See http://www.oscars.org/sites/oscars/files/91aa_rules.pdf.
2. Zach Sharf, "Netflix Says 20 Million Hours of 'Mudbound' Have Been Streamed, Which Is 'Dramatically Bigger' Than a Theatrical Release," *IndieWire*, June 22, 2018, https://www.indiewire.com/2018/06

/mudbound-netflix-20-million-hours-streaming-reed-hastings -1201977820/.

3. Ramin Setoodeh, "Netflix Pulls Out of Cannes following Rule Change," *Variety*, April 11, 2018, https://variety.com/2018/film/news /netflix-cannes-rule-change-ted-sarandos-interview-exclusive -1202750473/.
4. Nicole Sperling, "Netflix, the Oscars, and the Battle for the Future of Film," *Vanity Fair*, November 20, 2017, https://www.vanityfair.com /hollywood/2017/11/netflix-the-oscars-the-battle-for-the-future-of -film/amp.
5. Barbara Klinger, *Beyond the Multiplex: Cinema, New Technologies, and the Home* (Berkeley: University of California Press, 2006), 2.
6. Klinger, 4.
7. Chris Anderson, *The Long Tail: Why the Future of Business Is Selling Less of More* (New York: Hyperion, 2008).
8. Chuck Tryon, *On-Demand Culture: Digital Delivery and the Future of Movies* (New Brunswick, NJ: Rutgers University Press, 2013), 41.
9. See Michael Newman's discussion of art house institutions in *Indie: An American Film Culture* (New York: Columbia University Press, 2011), as well as his discussion of video in *Video Revolutions: On the History of a Medium* (New York: Columbia University Press, 2014). Both Lucas Hilderbrand, *Inherent Vice: Bootleg Histories of Videotape and Copyright* (Durham, NC: Duke University Press, 2009), and Daniel Herbert, *Videoland: Movie Culture at the American Video Store* (Berkeley: University of California Press, 2014), also provide histories of video culture, videotapes, and movie culture.
10. Wheeler Winston Dixon, *Streaming: Movies, Media, and Instant Access* (Lexington: University Press of Kentucky, 2013).
11. See James Hay and Nick Couldry, "Rethinking Convergence/Culture," *Cultural Studies* 25, no. 4–5 (2011): 473–486.
12. Henry Jenkins, *Convergence Culture: Where Old and New Media Collide* (New York: New York University Press, 2006), 2. In this context, Jenkins has written about how convergence culture works among the large and global fan bases of *Survivor* (CBS, 2000–present), *American Idol* (Fox, 2002–present), the *Star Wars* franchise, *The Matrix* trilogy, and the *Harry Potter* series.

13. Jay David Bolter and Richard Grusin, *Remediation: Understanding New Media* (Cambridge, MA: MIT Press, 1999), 224–225.
14. Hilderbrand, *Inherent Vice*, xvi.
15. Hilderbrand, 10.
16. Herbert, *Videoland*, 19.
17. Anderson, *The Long Tail.*
18. Tryon, *On-Demand Culture*, 3.
19. Tryon, 4.
20. Tryon, 61.
21. Newman, *Indie*, 48.
22. Newman, 61.
23. Newman, 2
24. Internet lists such as "The 25 Worst Movies on Netflix," "19 Netflix Movies So Bad They're Amazing," and "15 of the Worst Movies on Netflix According to Rotten Tomatoes" point to this tendency to search for the worst of the site on review aggregators such as Rotten Tomatoes and Metacritic.
25. Aymar Christian, "Indie TV: Innovation in Series Development," in *Media Independence: Working with Freedom or Working for Free?*, ed. James Bennett and Niki Strange (New York: Routledge, 2015), 162.
26. Adam Sternbergh, "The Age of the Streaming TV Auteur," *Vulture*, September 22, 2014, https://www.vulture.com/2014/09/age-of-the-auteur-on-streaming-tv.html.
27. Herbert, *Videoland*, 45. Also see Kevin Smith's film *Clerks* (1994) for further representation of the relationship between video store clerks and their customers.
28. Cliff Edwards and Sarah Rabil, "Netflix Surges on Streaming-Only Option, DVD Price Increase," *Bloomberg News*, November 22, 2010.
29. Matt Binder, "Netflix Consumes 15 Percent of the World's Internet Traffic, Report Says," *Mashable*, October 4, 2018, https://mashable.com/article/netflix-15-percent-worlds-internet-traffic/#tLf_NtR4EGqI.
30. Paul Bond, "Netflix to Hit 90 Million U.S. Subscribers in 10 Years, Analyst Predicts," *Hollywood Reporter*, June 27, 2018, https://www.hollywoodreporter.com/news/netflix-hit-90-million-us-subscribers-ten-years-analyst-predicts-1123697.

31. See the Netflix company fact page at https://pr.netflix.com/WebClient/loginPageSalesNetWorksAction.do?contentGroupId=10476&contentGroup=Company+Facts.
32. New York Film Academy Ltd., "Get Your Independent Movie on Netflix: What You Need to Know," July 11, 2014, https://www.nyfa.edu/student-resources/get-your-independent-movie-on-netflix/.
33. Michelle L. Martin and Katie O'Connell, "Securing Distribution with Netflix," *The Independent*, January 12, 2011.
34. The conclusion to this book also discusses how Amazon's recent acquisitions address the links between theatrical and digital distribution.
35. Kevin P. McDonald, "Digital Dreams in a Material World: The Rise of Netflix and Its Impact on Changing Distribution and Exhibition Patterns," *Jump Cut: A Review of Contemporary Media*, no. 55 (Fall 2013), http://ejumpcut.org/currentissue/McDonaldNetflix/text.html.
36. Steven Kotler, "Netflix Eager to Grow Indie Pic Eco-System," *Variety*, March 2, 2006, http://variety.com/2006/film/awards/netflix-eager-to-grow-indie-pic-eco-system-1117939103/.
37. Steven Zeitchik, "Netflix Adds Own Pix to the Mix," *Variety*, February 27, 2006. See also Alisa Perren, "Last Indie Standing: The Special Case of Lionsgate in the New Millennium," in *American Independent Cinema: Indie, Indiewood and Beyond*, ed. Geoff King, Claire Molloy, and Yannis Tzioumakis (New York: Routledge, 2013).
38. Times Staff and Wires, "Netflix to Shutter Red Envelope, *Los Angeles Times*, July 22, 2008, http://articles.latimes.com/2008/jul/22/business/fi-briefs22.S5.
39. Anthony Kaufman, "Netflix Folds Red Envelope; Exits Theatrical Acquisition and Production Biz," *IndieWire*, July 23, 2008, http://www.indiewire.com/article/netflix_folds_red_envelope_exits_theatrical_acquisition_and_production_biz.
40. Jon Healey, "Q&A: On a Mission to Change the Economics of Hollywood," *Los Angeles Times*, April 10, 2004.
41. McDonald, "Digital Dreams in a Material World."
42. Chuck Tryon, "TV Got Better: Netflix's Original Programming Strategies and Binge Viewing," *Media Industries* 2, no. 2 (2015): 104–115, http://www.mediaindustriesjournal.org/index.php/mij/article/view/126/201.

43. In fact, noncurrent HBO television series are available for viewing at one of Netflix's competitors, Amazon Prime.
44. Blake Hallinan and Ted Striphas, "Recommended for You: The Netflix Prize and the Production of Algorithmic Culture," *New Media and Society* 18, no. 1 (2016): 117–137.
45. Andrew Leonard, "How Netflix Is Turning Viewers into Puppets," *Salon*, February 1, 2013, http://www.salon.com/2013/02/01/how_netflix_is_turning_viewers_into_puppets/.
46. Beatrice Verhoeven, "Why Fear Streaming Giants? Indie Execs Sing Praises of Amazon, Netflix," *The Wrap*, June 4, 2016, http://www.thewrap.com/broad-green-amazon-studios-netflix-praise-ally-to-indies/.
47. Verhoeven.
48. Kotler, "Netflix Eager to Grow Indie Pic Eco-System."
49. Anne Thompson, "Netflix versus Hollywood: From Oscar Frontrunners to A-List TV Creators, Ted Sarandos Reveals His Master Plan," *IndieWire*, August 24, 2017, https://www.indiewire.com/2017/08/netflix-ted-sarandos-will-smith-adam-sandler-1201866954/2/.
50. Netflix Shareholders File, July 2014, http://files.shareholder.com/downloads/NFLX/3415305831x0x769748/9b21df7f-743c-4f0f-94da-9f13e384a3d2/July2014EarningsLetter_7.21.14_final.pdf.
51. See http://www.youtube.com/watch?v=VvpoUh9gx58&feature=youtu.be. Also cited in Jon Brooks, "For Cinephiles, Netflix Is Less and Less an Option," September 12, 2014, http://ww2.kqed.org/arts/2014/09/12/netflix_streaming_dvds/.
52. Nathan McAlone, "Netflix Now Has Better Programming Than HBO, according to New Survey," *Business Insider*, April 11, 2016, http://www.businessinsider.com/netflix-has-better-programming-than-hbo-2016-4.
53. McAlone.
54. Trefis Team, "Here's How the Exclusive Partnership with Disney Can Impact Netflix," *Forbes*, May 26, 2016, http://www.forbes.com/sites/greatspeculations/2016/05/26/heres-how-the-exclusive-partnership-with-disney-can-impact-netflix/#265aa7b265fe.
55. Netflix Media Center, "Get Ready for Summer on Netflix US," May 23, 2016, https://media.netflix.com/en/company-blog/get-ready-for-summer-on-netflix-us.

56. Alisha Grauso, "Netflix to Begin Exclusive Streaming of Disney, Marvel, Star Wars and Pixar in September," *Forbes*, May 24, 2016, http://www.forbes.com/sites/alishagrauso/2016/05/24/netflix-to-begin-exclusive-streaming-of-disney-marvel-star-wars-and-pixar-in-september/#470f7e26322b.

57. See more on this in the conclusion to this book.

58. Paula Bernstein, "Netflix Reveals Viewership Numbers for *Beasts of No Nation*," *IndieWire*, October 26, 2015, http://www.indiewire.com/2015/10/netflix-reveals-viewership-numbers-for-beasts-of-no-nation-56137/.

59. Bernstein.

60. Bernstein.

61. Press release, "Hulu Grows to over 17 Million Subscribers in 2017," Hulu, January 9, 2018, https://www.hulu.com/press/hulu-grows-to-over-17-million-subscribers-in-2017-emerges-as-powerful-pay-tv-alternative-combining-live-television-with-the-largest-svod-tv-library-in-the-u-s/.

62. See Patricia Zimmerman, "Independent Documentary Producers and American Television Networks," *Screen* 22, no. 4 (1981): 43–53; and Betsy McLane, *A New History of Documentary Film* (New York: Continuum, 2012).

63. Emanuel Levy, *Cinema of Outsiders: The Rise of American Independent Film* (New York: New York University Press, 1999); and Newman, *Indie*.

64. Inside Criterion, "Farewell, Hulu! Hello, Criterion Channel!," *The Criterion Collection*, November 11, 2016, https://www.criterion.com/current/posts/4293-farewell-hulu-hello-criterion-channel.

65. "Morgan Spurlock 'A Day in the Life': Original Series Premieres on Hulu," *Huffington Post*, August 17, 2011, http://www.huffingtonpost.com/2011/08/17/morgan-spurlock-a-day-in-the-life_n_929008.html.

66. According to Andy Forssell, senior vice president of content acquisition and distribution, in *Variety*, "Hulu: Serving Up More Docus and Indie Pix," March 19, 2009, http://weblogs.variety.com/on_the_air/2009/03/hulu-serving-up-more-docus-and-indie-pix.html.

67. Emil Protolinski, "Streaming Services Now Account for Over 70% of Peak Traffic in North America, Netflix Dominates with 37%," *Venturebeat*, December 7, 2015, http://venturebeat.com/2015/12/07/streaming-services

-now-account-for-over-70-of-peak-traffic-in-north-america-netflix -dominates-with-37/.

68. Protolinski.
69. Kaufman, "Netflix Folds Red Envelope."
70. Kaufman.
71. Valentina Valenti, "In VOD We Trust," http://www.documentary.org /magazine/vod-we-trust-navigating-minefield-ever-changing -distribution-platform. Last accessed April 1, 2015.
72. The Film Collaborative, "How I Learned to Stop Worrying and Love VOD," SXSW 2012, http://www.thefilmcollaborative.org/sxsw /American_VOD_SXSW2012.pdf.
73. Jon Reiss, *Think Outside the Box Office: The Ultimate Guide to Film Distribution and Marketing for the Digital Era* (Los Angeles: Hybrid Cinema Publishing, 2010).

2. Simultaneous Release Strategies

1. Paula Bernstein, "Julianne Moore Calls VOD Inferior to the Theatrical Experience," *IndieWire*, April 24, 2015, http://www.indiewire.com/article /julianne-moore-calls-vod-inferior-to-theatrical-experience-20150424.
2. Paula Bernstein, "Is the Day-and-Date Release of 'The Interview' a Success? That Depends," *IndieWire*, December 29, 2014, https://www .indiewire.com/2014/12/is-the-day-and-date-release-of-the-interview-a -success-that-depends-66681.
3. Bernstein, "Julianne Moore Calls VOD Inferior to the Theatrical Experience."
4. Bernstein.
5. See Joan Hawkins, "Dish Towns USA (or Rural Screens), Part One," *FlowTV: A Critical Forum on Media and Culture*, June 29, 2007, https://www.flowjournal.org/2007/06/dish-towns-usa-or-rural-screens -part-one/.
6. This Screening Room should be differentiated from the YouTube Screening Room discussed in the next chapter.
7. Michael Curtin, Jennifer Holt, and Kevin Sanson, "Introduction," in *Distribution Revolution*, ed. Michael Curtin, Jennifer Holt, and Kevin Sanson (Oakland: University of California Press, 2014), 22.

8. Alejandro Pardo, "From the Big Screen to the Small One: How Digitization Is Transforming the Distribution, Exhibition and Consumption of Movies," in *Besides the Screen: Moving Images through Distribution, Promotion and Curation*, ed. Virginia Crisp and Gabriel Menotti Gonring (New York: Palgrave Macmillan, 2015), 31.
9. Pardo, 31.
10. Vladan Nikolic, *Independent Filmmaking and Digital Convergence: Transmedia and Beyond* (New York: Routledge, 2017), 85.
11. Gary Gentile, "'Bubble' Hits Theaters, DVD on Same Day," *USA Today*, January 18, 2006, http://usatoday30.usatoday.com/tech/news/2006-01-18-bubble-theater-threat_x.htm.
12. Gentile.
13. Xeni Jardin, "Thinking Outside the Box Office," *Wired*, December 1, 2005.
14. Eric Kohn, "As Snowpiercer Hits VOD, the Industry's Divided on Distribution's Future," *IndieWire*, July 11, 2014, https://www.indiewire.com/2014/07/as-snowpiercer-hits-vod-the-industrys-divided-on-distributions-future-24403/.
15. Salt Lake Film Society, *Why SLFS Matters 2017 Annual Report*, 2017, https://saltlakefilmsociety.org/about-us/why.
16. Gentile, "'Bubble' Hits Theaters, DVD on Same Day."
17. Hawkins, "Dish Towns USA (or Rural Screens), Part One."
18. Gregory Waller, *Moviegoing in America: A Sourcebook in the History of Film Exhibition* (Malden, MA: Wiley-Blackwell, 2001).
19. *The Economist*, "Saved by the Box," May 23, 2009.
20. Noble McKinley, "Netflix Still Has Millions of DVD Subscribers Because Rural US Broadband Is Terrible," *Quartz Media*, July 19, 2017, https://qz.com/1032779/netflix-still-has-millions-of-dvd-subscribers-because-rural-us-broadband-sucks/.
21. Sarah E. S. Sinwell, "Go Digital or Go Dark: Crowdfunding, Independent Financing and Art House Exhibition on Kickstarter," in *A Companion to American Indie Film*, ed. Geoff King (Malden, MA: Wiley-Blackwell, 2017), 452–468.
22. Elissa Nelson, "Windows into the Digital World: Distributor Strategies and Consumer Choice in a Connected World," in *Connected*

Viewing: Selling, Streaming, and Sharing Media in the Digital Era, ed. Jennifer Holt and Kevin Sanson (New York: Routledge, 2014), 69.

23. Brent Lang, "Global Box Office Hits Record $40.6 Billion in 2017; U.S. Attendance Lowest in 23 Years," *Variety*, April 4, 2018, https://variety.com/2018/digital/news/global-box-office-hits-record-40-6-billion-in-2017-u-s-attendance-lowest-in-23-years-1202742991/.
24. Chuck Tryon, *On-Demand Culture: Digital Delivery and the Future of Movies* (New Brunswick, NJ: Rutgers University Press, 2013), 38.
25. Zach Sharf, "Netflix Says 20 Million Hours of 'Mudbound' Have Been Streamed, Which Is 'Dramatically Bigger' Than a Theatrical Release," *IndieWire*, June 22, 2018, https://www.indiewire.com/2018/06/mudbound-netflix-20-million-hours-streaming-reed-hastings-1201977820/.
26. See Alisa Perren's "Sex, Lies and Marketing: Miramax and the Development of the Quality Indie Blockbuster," *Film Quarterly* 55, no. 2 (Winter 2001–2002): 30–39, for more on this phenomenon.
27. See Charles Acland's "The Last Days of Videotape," *Flow*, November 12, 2009.
28. *The Girlfriend Experience* has also been made into a TV series on Starz (2016–present) and can be watched both on cable and on demand.
29. In 1948, due to the *United States v. Paramount Pictures, Inc.* decision (also known as the Paramount Case, Paramount Decision, or Paramount Decree), the studios were forced to give up their theaters since owning their own theaters and holding distribution rights was considered in violation of antitrust law. In the 1980s, under the Reagan administration, the movie industry was again deregulated.
30. Mark Gallagher, *Another Steven Soderbergh Experience: Authorship and Contemporary Hollywood* (Austin: University of Texas Press, 2013), 13.
31. Jardin, "Thinking Outside the Box Office."
32. See Virginia Crisp, *Film Distribution in the Digital Age: Pirates and Professionals* (New York: Palgrave Macmillan, 2005), for further discussion of film distribution and piracy in the digital age.
33. Barbara Klinger, "Contraband Cinema: Piracy, 'Titanic,' and Central Asia," *Cinema Journal* 49, no. 2 (Winter 2010): 106–124.
34. Nelson, "Windows into the Digital World," 69.
35. Gallagher, *Another Steven Soderbergh Experience*, 13.
36. Ann Homaday, "'Bubble' Vision," *Washington Post*, January 22, 2006.

37. See Landmarktheatres.com.
38. See Diane Garrett, "The Upside of a DVD and VOD Day-and-Date Release," *Variety*, October 17, 2009.
39. See Andrew Sarris, "What's the Deal with Bubble? Soderbergh's Social Experiment Wheezes," *New York Observer*, February 12, 2006.
40. Katherine Fusco, "The Actress Experience: Cruel Knowing and the Death of the Picture Personality in *Black Swan* and *The Girlfriend Experience*," *Camera Obscura* 28, no. 1 (2013): 1–35.
41. Andrew Goldstein, "Steven Soderbergh Confirms Plans to Leave Hollywood and Become a Painter," *Huffington Post*, August 29, 2011, https://www.huffingtonpost.com/artinfo/steven-soderbergh-confirm_b_940528.html.
42. Gallagher, *Another Steven Soderbergh Experience*, 4.
43. Nigel Smith, "Will Sean Parker's Screening Room Hurt or Help the Film Industry?," *The Guardian*, April 8, 2016, https://www.theguardian.com/film/2016/apr/08/sean-parker-screening-room-new-movie-releases-home-viewing-film-industry.
44. Brent Lang, "Studios, Exhibitors Consider Revolutionary Plan for Day-and-Date Movies at Home," *Variety*, March 9, 2016, https://variety.com/2016/film/news/studios-exhibitors-consider-revolutionary-plan-for-day-and-date-movies-at-home-exclusive-1201725168/.
45. Pamela McClintock, "Theater Owner Rejects Proposed $50 Home Movie Service: 'It Feels Like a Half-Baked Plan,'" *Hollywood Reporter*, March 13, 2016, https://www.hollywoodreporter.com/news/theater-owner-rejects-proposed-50-874835.
46. Brent Lang and James Rainey, "Screening Room Proposal Overshadows CinemaCon, Fuels Debate over Release Windows," *Variety*, April 14, 2016, https://variety.com/2016/film/news/cinemacon-analysis-screening-room-1201754079/.
47. McClintock, "Theater Owner Rejects Proposed $50 Home Movie Service."
48. Mike Fleming Jr., "Brett Ratner Joins Growing Filmmaker Chorus against Screening Room Day & Date Home Movie Service," *Deadline Hollywood*, March 17, 2016, https://deadline.com/2016/03/brett-ratner-against-screening-room-day-and-date-home-movie-service-1201722273/.

49. Annlee Ellingson, "New Movies Will Play at Home, Just Not via Screening Room," *LA Biz*, May 31, 2017, https://www.bizjournals.com/losangeles/news/2017/05/31/new-movies-will-not-play-via-screen-room.html.
50. Anita Busch and Anthony D'Alessandro, "NATO on the Screening Room: Any New Model Affecting Exhibs Should Be Handled by Members, 'Not by a Third Party,'" *Deadline Hollywood*, March 16, 2016, https://deadline.com/2016/03/nato-reaction-the-screening-room-1201721117/.
51. Ryan Faughnder, "CinemaCon: Sean Parker's Screening Room a 'Serious Distraction,' Says Theater Group Leader," *Los Angeles Times*, April 12, 2016, http://www.latimes.com/entertainment/envelope/cotown/la-et-ct-cinemacon-2016-screening-room-20160412-story.html.
52. Anthony D'Allessandro, "Art House Theaters Protest the Screening Room in Open Letter," *Deadline Hollywood*, March 15, 2016, https://deadline.com/2016/03/screening-room-art-house-convergence-open-letter-tim-league-1201720859.
53. Art House Convergence, "An Open Letter from Art House Convergence regarding 'Screening Room,'" March 15, 2016, http://www.arthouseconvergence.org/index.php/2016/03/15/an-open-letter-from-art-house-convergence-regarding-screening-room/.
54. David Bordwell, "Weaponized VOD at $50 a Pop," Observations on Film Art Blog, March 15, 2016, http://www.davidbordwell.net/blog/2016/03/15/weaponized-vod-at-50-a-pop/.
55. Tom Brueggemann, "The Screening Room Earns Mixed Reaction, Not Total Rejection," *IndieWire*, March 16, 2016, https://www.indiewire.com/2016/03/the-screening-room-earns-mixed-reaction-not-total-rejection-174822/.
56. D'Allessandro, "Art House Theaters Protest the Screening Room in Open Letter."
57. Whereas Netflix's films such as *The Meyerowitz Stories* (Noah Baumbach, 2017) and *Okja* (Bong Joon-ho, 2017) were exhibited almost exclusively on its streaming sites, Amazon continues to uphold a short theatrical window for its films.
58. Paula Bernstein, "Here's Why 'The Congress' Hit VOD a Month before Its Theatrical Release," *IndieWire*, July 25, 2014, http://www.indiewire

.com/article/heres-why-the-congress-hit-vod-a-month-before-its-theatrical-release-20140725.

59. Lang and Rainey, "Screening Room Proposal Overshadows CinemaCon."
60. Ira Deutchman, interview with Sarah E. S. Sinwell, January 17, 2017.
61. Ellingson, "New Movies Will Play at Home."
62. Ellingson.
63. Ira Deutchman, interview with Sarah E. S. Sinwell.
64. This lifestyle brand of the Alamo Drafthouse Cinemas includes Mondo, the collectible art boutique; Fantastic Fest, the largest international genre film festival in the United States; and the pop culture website Birth.Movies.Death. See the Drafthouse Films website at https://drafthousefilms.com/.
65. Drafthouse Films, https://drafthousefilms.com/.
66. Geoblocking and the BFI's own archive impact the films that can be screened using this service. See Ramon Lobato's study of international digital distribution networks in *Netflix Nations: The Geography of Digital Distribution* (New York: New York University Press, 2019).
67. Kevin Jagernauth, "Lionsgate and Tribeca Enterprises Team Up to Launch Subscription VOD Service in 2015," *IndieWire*, October 20, 2014, http://blogs.indiewire.com/theplaylist/lionsgate-and-tribeca-enterprises-team-to-launch-subscription-vod-service-in-2015-20141020.

3. DIY Distribution

1. See "Sundance Institute, YouTube and Acura to Make 12 Short Films from 2011 Sundance Institute Available for Free on YouTube Screening Room," Sundance Channel press release, January 5, 2011, http://www.sundance.org/press-center/release/sundance-institute-youtube-and-acura-to-make-12-short-films.
2. See "Four Eyed Monsters Announce Self-Distribution through New Without a Box Inc. Initiative," Four Eyed Monsters Blog, http://foureyedmonsters.com/four-eyed-monsters-announce-self-distribution-through-new-withoutabox-inc-initiative/.
3. Jean Burgess and Joshua Green, "The Entrepreneurial Vlogger: Participatory Culture beyond the Professional-Amateur Divide," in *The*

YouTube Reader, ed. Pelle Snickars and Patrick Vonderau (Stockholm: National Library of Sweden, 2009), 90.

4. Pierre Bourdieu, *Distinction: A Social Critique of the Judgment of Taste*, trans. Richard Nice (Cambridge, MA: Harvard University Press, 1987).
5. See Michael Newman, *Indie: An American Film Culture* (New York: Columbia University Press, 2011); Geoff King, *Indie 2.0: Change and Continuity in Contemporary American Indie Film* (New York: Columbia University Press, 2014); Geoff King, *Quality Hollywood: Markers of Distinction in Contemporary Studio Film* (London: I. B. Tauris, 2016); and Geoff King, *Positioning Art Cinema: Film and Cultural Value* (London: I. B. Tauris, 2019). This reference to the multiplex is particularly interesting with regard to the changing nature of independent film distribution and exhibition, both digitally and online through sites like YouTube.
6. Though YouTube's world presence is beyond the scope of this project, the significance of this moniker is also evidence of Google's presence within the global economy. See Kit Smith, "39 Fascinating and Incredible YouTube Statistics," *Brandwatch*, April 12, 2018, https://www.brandwatch.com/blog/39-youtube-stats/.
7. Smith.
8. See Kylie Jarrett, "Beyond Broadcast Yourself: The Future of YouTube," *Media International Australia, Incorporating Culture & Policy* 126 (February 2008): 132–144; and Pelle Snickars and Patrick Vonderau, "Introduction," *The YouTube Reader*, ed. Pelle Snickars and Patrick Vonderau (Stockholm: National Library of Sweden, 2009).
9. See Jean Burgess and Joshua Green, *YouTube* (Malden, MA: Polity, 2009).
10. "Clip culture" is the term Chad Hurley (CEO and founder of YouTube) used to describe the phenomenon of short clips that the creation of YouTube tapped into upon its inception, saying, "There is a complete shift happening in digital media entertainment and users are now in control of what they watch and when they watch it. At YouTube, we are seeing an evolution of entertainment and media distribution—where the audience is now in control more than ever." See Mark Glaser, "Digging Deeper: YouTube CEO Hails 'Birth of a New Clip Culture,'" PBS Media Shift, April 4, 2006, http://www.pbs.org

/mediashift/2006/04/digging-deeperyoutube-ceo-hails-birth-of-a-new-clip-culture094.html.

11. Snickars and Vonderau, "Introduction," *The YouTube Reader*, 11.
12. At its inception, YouTube's ten-minute limit kept bandwidth costs down and made it more difficult for users to post illegal videos online. See Michael Learmonth, "YouTube Shifts Strategy, Tries Long-Form Video," *Business Insider*, June 18, 2008, http://www.businessinsider.com/2008/6/youtube-tries-long-form-video.
13. "YouTube," *New York Times*, Business Day, January 11, 2011, http://topics.nytimes.com/top/news/business/companies/youtube/index.html.
14. Kevin MacDonald's *Life in a Day* (2011) exemplifies this model as a documentary that takes YouTube user videos and creates a feature-length film in that context. Marketed as "made by you" while at the same time capitalizing on the fame and celebrity of Kevin MacDonald and producer Ridley Scott (*Alien* [1979], *Blade Runner* [1982], and *Gladiator* [2000]), *Life in a Day* was envisioned as a global experiment made entirely with user-generated content.
15. See further discussion of *Girl Walks into a Bar* later in this chapter.
16. Claire Cain Miller, "YouTube Acquires a Producer of Videos," *New York Times*, March 7, 2011, http://www.nytimes.com/2011/03/08/technology/08youtube.html.
17. Alexandra Juhasz, "Learning the Five Lessons of YouTube: After Trying to Teach There, I Don't Believe the Hype," *Cinema Journal* 48, no. 2 (Winter 2009): 148.
18. "Charlie Bit My Finger—Again," http://www.youtube.com/watch?v=_OBlgSz8sSM.
19. Jarrett, "Beyond Broadcast Yourself," 133.
20. See Eggo Muller, "Where Quality Matters: Discourses on the Art of Making a YouTube Video," in *The YouTube Reader*, ed. Pelle Snickars and Patrick Vonderau (Stockholm: National Library of Sweden, 2009), 126–139.
21. Muller, 127.
22. See Muller, 126–139.
23. King, *Indie 2.0*.
24. *Four Eyed Monsters* is not the first film to use DIY marketing and self-distribution as a means of promotion. In 1999, *The Blair Witch*

Project (Daniel Myrick and Eduardo Sanchez) used social media and DIY marketing to great effect, as did *Cloverfield* (Matt Reeves) and *Anvil: The Story of Anvil* (Sacha Gervasi) in 2008.

25. Established in 1995, Slamdance is the independent filmmakers' alternative to the hype and Hollywoodization of the Sundance Film Festival. On its website, Slamdance includes finding theatrical distribution for its films as a significant part of its ethos. See "Slamdance: About Us," last modified January 21, 1999, http://www.slamdance.com/site/profile.html.
26. See "Four Eyed Monsters," http://www.neoflix.com/store/FOU37/four-eyed-monsters-dvd-and-music-cd-combo.html.
27. Jonathan Gray, *Show Sold Separately: Promos, Spoilers, and Other Media Paratexts* (New York: New York University Press, 2010).
28. Burgess and Green, "The Entrepreneurial Vlogger," 94.
29. Hugh Hart, "Fans Help Filmmakers Win YouTube Deal," *Wired*, June 25, 2007, http://www.wired.com/entertainment/theweb/news/2007/06/youtubefest.
30. "Discussion about Viewer Habits," posted by Arin Crumley, presented by IFP, video, http://www.youtube.com/watch?v=y6dPPHGtUww.
31. The film was also the first feature film to screen on Second Life. See "Four Eyed Monsters," http://www.neoflix.com/store/FOU37/four-eyed-monsters-dvd-and-music-cd-combo.
32. Hart, "Fans Help Filmmakers Win YouTube Deal."
33. Founded by Davis Straus and Joseph Neulight in 2005, Withoutabox created technology that allowed independent filmmakers to self-distribute their films. Acquired by IMDB (a division of Amazon) in 2008, Withoutabox also enabled online streaming via IMDB and video-on-demand downloads via amazon.com. It closed in 2019. See "Four Eyed Monsters Announce Self-Distribution through New Without a Box Inc. Initiative."
34. Burgess and Green, *YouTube*, 133.
35. See "Four Eyed Monsters DIY Case Study," http://foureyedmonsters.com/four-eyed-monsters-diy-case-study. Independent filmmaking is not new to the DIY scene. As many books and self-help manuals from Robert Rodriguez's *Rebel without a Crew: Or How a 23-Year-Old*

Filmmaker with $7,000 Became a Hollywood Player (New York: Plume, 1996) to Mark Polish, Michael Polish, and Jonathan Sheldon's *The Declaration of Independent Filmmaking: An Insider's Guide to Making Movies Outside Hollywood* (Orlando: Harvest, 2005) attest, one of the central tenets of DIY culture is assisting others in participating in DIY endeavors.

36. Randall Stross, *Planet Google: One Company's Audacious Plan to Organize Everything We Know* (New York: Simon and Schuster, 2008).
37. Even the notion of funding independent films on personal credit cards is evidence of this hierarchy of dependence on corporate greed, as is the sponsorship of Tribeca shorts on YouTube by American Express.
38. However, this also alludes to the idea that YouTube may censor the material and comments on the site based on their political and social implications.
39. Michael Learmonth, "YouTube Unveils 'Screening Room' for Free Indie Movies," *Business Insider*, June 18, 2008, https://www.businessinsider.com/2008/6/youtube-unveils-screening-room-for-free-indie-movies.
40. Learmonth.
41. See YTScreening Room, http://www.youtube.com/user/ytscreeningroom.
42. Joshua Gamson, *Claims to Fame: Celebrity in Contemporary America* (Berkeley: University of California Press, 1994), 104–105.
43. Learmonth. "YouTube Unveils 'Screening Room' for Free Indie Movies."
44. See YouTube Screening Room launch video, http://www.youtube.com/watch?v=j80HN6Hi6bc.
45. The question of how YouTube functions as a cultural archive and who is responsible for its curation is addressed in Robert Gehl's "YouTube as Archive: Who Will Curate This Digital Wunderkammer?" *International Journal of Cultural Studies* 12, no. 1 (January 2009): 43–60.
46. Online streaming of film shorts has become more and more popular as is attested by the presence of Tribeca's short films online on Tribeca's own Streaming Room (http://www.tribecafilm.com/tribecaonline/streaming-room).
47. Jose van Dijck, "Users Like You? Theorizing Agency in User-Generated Content," *Media, Culture and Society* 31, no. 1 (2009): 41.

48. View *Girl Walks into a Bar* at http://www.youtube.com/watch?v =7D4yQPQfFQM.
49. Ben Scuglia, "Girl Walks into a Bar and Gets Free YouTube Distribution," *New Hollywood*, March 10, 2011, http://bravenewhollywood.com /girl-walks-into-a-bar-and-gets-you-tube-distribution/. One of the continuing problems with online film distribution through YouTube is the question of copyright and how it limits what gets shown on YouTube and for how long.
50. As Michael Newman notes in *Indie*, 38, one of the characteristics of contemporary independent cinema is the audience's focus on cinema's self-reflexivity.
51. Joe Leydon, review of *Girl Walks into a Bar*, *Variety*, March 15, 2011, SXSW Reviews, http://www.variety.com/review/VE1117944827/.
52. Nancy Miller, "Minifesto for a New Age," *Wired*, March 1, 2007, http://www.wired.com/wired/archive/15.03/snackminifesto.html.
53. Barbara Klinger has also noted the place of short films online in her discussion of web films in her book *Beyond the Multiplex: Cinema, New Technologies, and the Home* (Berkeley: University of California Press, 2006).
54. Shangri-la Entertainment, "Shangri-la Entertainment Girl Walks into a Bar Attracts More Than 260,000 Viewers," March 14, 2011, PR Newswire, http://finance.yahoo.com/news/ShangriLa-Entertainments -Girl-prnews-3028421673.html?x=0&.v=1.
55. In fact, in July 2011, YouTube released *Life in a Day* (Kevin MacDonald, 2011). Marketed by YouTube and LG as "a historic global experiment to create a user-generated feature film shot in a single day," *Life in a Day* premiered at the Sundance Film Festival in January 2011, simultaneously streamed live on YouTube, and was theatrically released by National Geographic in July 2011.
56. Press release, "Shangri-la Entertainment Announces a Gato Negro Film, 'Girl Walks into a Bar,'" PR Newswire, September 22, 2010, http://www.prnewswire.com/news-releases/shangri-la-entertainment -announces-a-gato-negro-film-girl-walks-into-a-bar-103520559.html.
57. Press release, "Shangri-La Entertainment and Gato Films 'Girl Walks into a Bar' Reaches 550,000 Audience Views on YouTube," PR Newswire, April 25, 2011, http://bx.businessweek.com/lexus/view?url=http%3

A%2F%2Fc.moreover.com%2Fclick%2Fhere.pl%3Fr4550272374%26f%3D9791.

58. Manohla Dargis, "Declaration of Indies: Just Sell It Yourself!" *New York Times*, January 14, 2010, https://www.nytimes.com/2010/01/17/movies/17dargis.html.
59. Chuck Kleinhans, "Independent Features: Hopes and Dreams," in *The New American Cinema*, ed. Jon Lewis (Durham, NC: Duke University Press, 1998), 308.
60. Jarrett, "Beyond Broadcast Yourself," 135.
61. Nevertheless, YouTube does share its ad revenue with artists, but YouTube's criteria for joining the Partners program are vague, and it has offered no concrete revenue numbers.
62. Juhasz, "Learning the Five Lessons of YouTube," 149.
63. Juhasz, 145–150.
64. Henry Jenkins, interview, "DIY Video 2010: Activist Media (Part Three)," Confessions of an Aca-Fan Blog, November 1, 2010, http://henryjenkins.org/2010/11/diy_video_2010_activist_media_2.html.
65. See MIT Free Culture, YouTomb, http://youtomb.mit.edu/.

4. The Fourth Screen

1. "Gotham Independent Film Awards," Livestream, UStream, *Deadline Hollywood*, November 30, 2015, http://deadline.com/2015/11/gotham-awards-2015-live-stream-video-1201647033/.
2. These nominations also point to the significance of Netflix and Amazon in this new digital media landscape (discussed further in chapter 1 and the conclusion to this book).
3. "Gotham Independent Film Awards."
4. Black Girl Dangerous, http://www.blackgirldangerous.org/category/qraftish/. Last accessed January 8, 2020.
5. Sarah Atkinson, *Beyond the Screen: Emerging Cinema and Engaging Audiences* (New York: Bloomsbury, 2014).
6. See Susan Lord and Janine Marcgessault, *Fluid Screens, Expanded Cinema* (Toronto: University of Toronto Press, 2013); Aymar Christian, "Joe Swanberg, Intimacy, and the Digital Aesthetic," *Cinema Journal* 50, no. 4 (Summer 2011): 117–137; Emanuelle Wessels, "'Where Were

You When the Monster Hit?': Media Convergence, Branded Security Citizenship, and the Trans-media Phenomenon of Cloverfield," *Convergence* 17, no. 1 (February 2011): 69–83.

7. In 2014, Sundance was rebranded as SundanceTV as a means of focusing on the production of original series such as *Rectify* (2013–2016), *The Honourable Woman* (2014), and *The Red Road* (2014–2015).
8. Gerard Goggin and Larissa Hjorth, *Mobile Technologies* (New York: Routledge, 2009).
9. Gerard Goggin, *Cell Phone Culture: Mobile Technology in Everyday Life* (London: Routledge, 2006).
10. Richard Ling, *The Mobile Connection* (San Francisco: Morgan Kaufman, 2004); Goggin and Hjorth, *Mobile Technologies*; Noah Arceneaux and Anandam Kavoori, eds., *The Mobile Media Reader* (New York: Peter Lang, 2012); Pelle Snickars and Patrick Vonderau, eds., *Moving Data: The iPhone and the Future of Media* (New York: Columbia University Press, 2012); J. Katz, ed., *Handbook of Mobile Communication* (Cambridge, MA: MIT Press, 2008); Marsha Berry and Max Schleser, *Mobile Media Making in an Age of Smartphones* (New York: Palgrave, 2014); Gerard Goggin and Larissa Hjorth, eds., *Routledge Companion to Mobile Media* (New York: Routledge, 2014).
11. Pelle Snickars and Patrick Vonderau, "Introduction," in *Moving Data: The iPhone and the Future of Media* (New York: Columbia University Press, 2012), 11.
12. Gerard Goggin and Larissa Hjorth, "Introduction: Mobile Media Research: State of the Art," in *Routledge Companion to Mobile Media*, ed. Gerard Goggin and Larissa Hjorth (New York: Routledge, 2014), 2.
13. Francesco Casetti and Sara Sampietro, "With Eyes, with Hands: The Relocation of Cinema into the iPhone," in *Moving Data: The iPhone and the Future of Media.*, ed. Pelle Snickars and Patrick Vonderau (New York: Columbia University Press, 2012), 29.
14. Harvey May and Greg Hearn, "The Mobile Phone as Media," *International Journal of Cultural Studies* 8, no. 2 (2005): 195–211.
15. Gerard Goggin, "The Eccentric Career of Mobile Television," *International Journal of Digital Television* 3 (June 2012): 119.
16. Juan Miguel Aguado and Inmaculada Martinez, "Feeding Digital Omnivores: The Impact of Mobile Media in Digital Entertainment,"

in *Routledge Companion to Mobile Media*, ed. Gerard Goggin and Larissa Hjorth (New York: Routledge, 2014), 185.

17. Gerard Goggin, "Mobile Video: Spreading Stories with Mobile Media," in *Routledge Companion to Mobile Media*, ed. Gerard Goggin and Larissa Hjorth (New York: Routledge, 2014), 146.
18. Michael Strangelove, *Post-TV: Piracy, Cord-Cutting, and the Future of Television* (Toronto: University of Toronto Press, 2015), 133.
19. Strangelove, 134.
20. Goggin and Hjorth, *Mobile Technologies*, 282.
21. Brian Stelter and Bill Carter, "Networks Try a Social Spin at the Upfronts," *New York Times*, May 20, 2012.
22. Barbara Klinger, *Beyond the Multiplex: Cinema, New Technologies and the Home* (Berkeley: University of California Press, 2006).
23. Strangelove, *Post-TV*, 136, Gerard Goggin, *Global Mobile Media* (London: Routledge, 2010), 97.
24. Graham Roberts, "Movie-Making in the New Media Age," in *Web Studies*, ed. David Gauntlett and Ross Horsley (London: Arnold, 2004), 111.
25. Glen Creeber, *Small Screen Aesthetics: From TV to the Internet* (London: BFI, 2013), 121.
26. Roberts, "Movie-Making in the New Media Age," 111.
27. Max Dawson, "Television's Aesthetic of Efficiency: Convergence Television and the Digital Short," in *Television as Digital Media*, ed. James Bennett and Niki Strange (Durham, NC: Duke University Press, 2011), 207.
28. Vladan Nikolic, *Independent Filmmaking and Digital Convergence: Transmedia and Beyond* (New York: Routledge, 2017), 93.
29. Nancy Miller, "Snack Attack," *Wired*, March 1, 2007.
30. Robert Eberwein, "IFC and Sundance: Channeling Independence," in *Contemporary American Independent Film*, ed. Chris Holmlund and Justin Wyatt (New York: Routledge, 2005), 267.
31. L. Beale, "Small Films Find Big Following on Cable Channels," *New York Daily News*, January 24, 1999, 8.
32. Brian Steinberg, "Sundance Channel to Rename Itself SundanceTV," *Variety*, January 27, 2014, https://variety.com/2014/tv/news/sundance-channel-to-rename-itself-sundancetv-1201072666/.

33. Chuck Tryon, "Pushing the (Red) Envelope," in *Moving Data: The iPhone and the Future of Media*, ed. Pelle Snickars and Patrick Vonderau (New York: Columbia University Press, 2012), 126.
34. Aymar Christian, "Not TV, Not the Web," in *The Mobile Media Reader*, ed. Noah Arceneaux and Anandam Kavoori (New York: Peter Lang, 2012), 88.
35. Aymar Christian, "Indie TV: Innovation in Series Development," in *Media Independence: Working with Freedom or Working for Free?*, ed. James Bennett and Niki Strange (New York: Routledge, 2015), 162.
36. The Sundance Group refers to all the businesses that are included within the Sundance corporate umbrella started and run by Robert Redford (SundanceTV, the Sundance Institute, Sundance Catalog, and so forth).
37. GSMA press release, "Robert Redford Announces Sundance Film Festival: Global Short Film Festival Project for Mobile," Sundance .org, November 8, 2006.
38. GSMA press release.
39. "Sundance Channel Acquires U.S. Rights to Ten-Part Short Film Series The Art of Seduction," PR Newswire, October 24 2006. Academic OneFile, http://link.galegroup.com/apps/doc/A153249508 /AONE?u=marriottlibrary&sid=AONE&xid=508b6514.
40. One could imagine that it is listed first because Guy Maddin is the most famous filmmaker included in the series.
41. See https://www.sundancetv.com/shows/green-porno.
42. Sundancechannel.com/greenporno.
43. These narratives of bodily transformation and hardship mirror those of stars such as Robert De Niro and Charlize Theron (who gained weight for their roles in *Raging Bull* [Martin Scorsese, 1980] and *Monster* [Patty Jenkins, 2003], respectively). It should be noted that these stories are also gendered with regard to cultural ideals of beauty and the body.
44. Amanda Griscom Little, "Robert Redford Starts Channeling 'Green,'" April 19, 2007, http://www.msnbc.msn.com/id/18176422/.
45. Stuart Miller, "The Mean Green Marketing Machine," *Multichannel News*, August 12, 2007, http://www.multichannel.com/article/85975 -The_Mean_Green_Marketing_Machine.php.
46. Chris Rojek, 2001, *Celebrity* (London: Reaktion Books, 2001), 189.

47. Sue Adkins, *Cause Related Marketing: Who Cares Wins* (Oxford: Reed Educational and Professional, 1999); and Miller, "The Mean Green Marketing Machine."
48. R. Thomas Umstead, "Sundance Channel Spells 'Green' F-U- N," *Multichannel News*, March 9, 2009, http://www.multichannel.com/article/189625-Sundance_Channel_Spells_Green_F_U_N.php.
49. A. J. Goldmann, "Coming Soon to a Cellphone Near You: Isabella Rossellini Mounting a Housefly," *Wired*, February 12, 2008, http://archive.wired.com/entertainment/theweb/news/2008/02/green_porno.
50. Casetti and Sampietro, "With Eyes, with Hands," 19–32.
51. The inclusion of the expert Claudio Campagna as part of *Green Porno*'s programming also contributes to its environmentalist message, elevating it to conservationist art. Sundance premiered *Green Porno* online on Earth Day, April 21, 2009. Further promoting its green message, the films are linked to environmentalists and environmentalist websites such as Greenmuze and Treehugger.
52. Sundancechannel.com.
53. Michelle Kung, "'Green Porno' Creator Isabella Rossellini on Animal Sex, Crazed Fans and Web Entertainment," *Wall Street Journal*, September 21, 2009, http://blogs.wsj.com/speakeasy/2009/09/21/isabella-rossellini-on-green-porno-crazed-fans-and-web-entertainment/.
54. http://www.sundance.org/programs/episodic-storytelling.
55. Oakley Anderson-Moore, "Will 2014 Be the Year of the Web Series? Sundance and IFP Take On Serialized Content," April 14, 2014, http://nofilmschool.com/2014/04/will-2014-year-web-series-sundance-ifp-take-serialized-content.
56. Aaron Dobbs, "Why Indie Film Institutions Are Turning Their Attention to Web Series," *IndieWire*, April 10, 2014, http://www.indiewire.com/article/television/why-indie-film-institutions-are-turning-their-attention-to-web-series.
57. One also wonders how Sundance will make money on these films if they are available to download for free online. There is an ongoing debate over whether internet users should pay for content. This includes not just *Green Porno* but also news sites such as cnn.com and msnbc.com and online newspapers such as the *New York Times* and the *Washington Post*.

Conclusion

1. Dawn Chmielewski, "TV Platform That Gives Viewers the Power to Greenlight Series Launches with Kevin Smith Stoner Comedy," *Deadline Hollywood*, July 11, 2018, https://deadline.com/2018/07/rivit-tv-viewers-power-greenlight-tv-series-launches-kevin-smith-hollyweed-1202424384/.
2. Joe Otterson, "Kevin Smith Partners with Rivit TV on Comedy Pilot 'Hollyweed,'" *Variety*, July 11, 2018, https://variety.com/2018/tv/news/kevin-smith-hollyweed-rivit-tv-1202869936/.
3. See Sarah E. S. Sinwell, "Go Digital or Go Dark: Crowdfunding, Independent Financing and Art House Exhibition on Kickstarter," in *A Companion to American Indie Film*, ed. Geoff King (Malden, MA: Wiley-Blackwell, 2017).
4. Kickstarter, "The Veronica Mars Movie Project," March 13, 2013, https://www.kickstarter.com/projects/559914737/the-veronica-mars-movie-project.
5. Jeff Howe, "The Rise of Crowdsourcing, *Wired*, June 1, 2006, http://www.wired.com/wired/archive/14.06/crowds_pr.html.
6. Todd Spangler, "Amazon Studios to Produce Movies for Theatrical, Digital Release in 2015," *Variety*, January 19, 2015, http://variety.com/2015/digital/news/amazon-studios-to-produce-movies-for-theatrical-digital-release-in-2015-1201408688/.
7. Todd Spangler, "Amazon's First Movie: Spike Lee Drama 'Chi-raq' to Bow with Theatrical Run," *Variety*, July 15, 2015, http://variety.com/2015/digital/news/spike-lee-chi-raq-amazon-theaters-1201540709/.
8. Spangler, "Amazon Studios to Produce Movies for Theatrical, Digital Release in 2015."
9. Todd Spangler, "Netflix, Weinstein Co. Bust Windows with 'Crouching Tiger' Sequel Day-and-Date Release," *Variety*, September 29, 2014, http://variety.com/2014/digital/news/crouching-tiger-hidden-dragon-sequel-netflix-weinstein-co-1201316645/.
10. Anne Thompson, "Netflix versus Hollywood: From Oscar Frontrunners to A-List TV Creators, Ted Sarandos Reveals His Master Plan,"

IndieWire, August 34, 2017, https://www.indiewire.com/2017/08/netflix-ted-sarandos-will-smith-adam-sandler-1201866954/2/.

11. Liz Shannon Miller, "Netflix and the Future: The Two Things Changing Your Favorite Streaming Platform," *IndieWire*, July 2015, http://www.indiewire.com/2015/07/netflix-and-the-future-the-two-things-changing-your-favorite-streaming-platform-59891/.
12. Andrew Leonard, "How Netflix Is Turning Viewers into Puppets," *Salon*, February 1, 2013, http://www.salon.com/2013/02/01/how_netflix_is_turning_viewers_into_puppets/.
13. Sidneyeve Matrix, "The Netflix Effect: Teens, Binge Watching, and On-Demand Digital Media Trends," *Jeunesse: Young People, Texts, Cultures* 6, no. 1 (2014): 120.
14. Patrick Hopes, "Netflix Unveils Binge Scale with Some Surprising Results," *Deadline*, June 8, 2016, http://deadline.com/2016/06/netflix-binge-scale-data-results-house-of-cards-orange-is-the-new-black-1201769127/.
15. Michael Newman, *Indie: An American Film Culture* (New York: Columbia University Press, 2011).
16. See Alisa Perren, *Indie, Inc.* (Austin: University of Texas Press, 2012), and Perren, "Last Indie Standing: The Special Case of Lionsgate in the New Millennium," in *American Independent Cinema: Indie, Indiewood and Beyond*, ed. Geoff King, Claire Molloy, and Yannis Tzioumakis (New York: Routledge, 2013).
17. David Sims, "Netflix Is a Business, Not a Movement," *The Atlantic*, June 24, 2019, https://www.theatlantic.com/entertainment/archive/2019/06/netflix-business-not-movement/592402/.
18. Nicole Sperling, "Could a Disney-Owned Hulu Bury Netflix for Good?" *Vanity Fair*, December 15, 2017, https://www.vanityfair.com/hollywood/2017/12/disney-owned-hulu-compete-with-netflix-streaming-wars.
19. Yannis Tzioumakis, "American Independent Cinema in the Age of Convergence," *Revue Française d'Études Américaines* 136, no. 2 (2013): 53–54, https://www.cairn.info/revue-revue-francaise-d-etudes-americaines-2013-2-page-52.htm.

Bibliography

Acland, Charles. "The Last Days of Videotape." *Flow*, November 12, 2009. https://www.flowjournal.org/2009/11/the-last-days-of-videotapecharles-r-acland-concordia-university/.

Acland, Charles, and Haidee Wasson. *Useful Cinema*. Durham, NC: Duke University Press, 2011.

Adkins, Sue. *Cause Related Marketing: Who Cares Wins*. Oxford: Reed Educational and Professional, 1999.

Aguado, Juan Miguel, and Inmaculada Martinez. "Feeding Digital Omnivores: The Impact of Mobile Media in Digital Entertainment Media." In *Routledge Companion to Mobile Media*, edited by Gerard Goggin and Larissa Hjorth, 181–194. New York: Routledge, 2014.

Anderson, Chris. *The Long Tail: Why the Future of Business Is Selling Less of More*. New York: Hyperion, 2008.

Anderson-Moore, Oakley. "Will 2014 Be the Year of the Web Series? Sundance and IFP Take On Serialized Content." April 14, 2014. http://nofilmschool.com/2014/04/will-2014-year-web-series-sundance-ifp-take-serialized-content.

Andrews, David. *Theorizing Art Cinemas: Foreign, Cult, Avant-Garde, and Beyond*. Austin: University of Texas Press, 2013.

Arceneaux, Noah, and Anandam Kavoori, eds. *The Mobile Media Reader*. New York: Peter Lang, 2012.

Art House Convergence. "An Open Letter from Art House Convergence regarding 'Screening Room.'" March 15, 2016. http://www.arthouseconvergence.org/index.php/2016/03/15/an-open-letter-from-art-house-convergence-regarding-screening-room/.

Atkinson, Sarah. *Beyond the Screen: Emerging Cinema and Engaging Audiences*. New York: Bloomsbury, 2014.

Balio, Tino. *Hollywood in the New Millennium*. London: BFI, 2013.

Beale, L. "Small Films Find Big Following on Cable Channels." *New York Daily News*, January 24, 1999, 8.

Bell, David, and Barbara M. Kennedy, eds. *The Cybercultures Reader*. New York: Routledge, 2000.

Bernstein, Paula. "Here's Why 'The Congress' Hit VOD a Month before Its Theatrical Release." *IndieWire*, July 25, 2014. http://www.indiewire.com/article/heres-why-the-congress-hit-vod-a-month-before-its-theatrical-release-20140725.

———. "Is the Day-and-Date Release of 'The Interview' a Success? That Depends." *IndieWire*, December 29, 2014. https://www.indiewire.com/2014/12/is-the-day-and-date-release-of-the-interview-a-success-that-depends-66681.

———. "Julianne Moore Calls VOD Inferior to the Theatrical Experience." *IndieWire*, April 24, 2015. http://www.indiewire.com/article/julianne-moore-calls-vod-inferior-to-theatrical-experience-20150424.

———. "Netflix Reveals Viewership Numbers for *Beasts of No Nation*." *IndieWire*, October 26, 2015. http://www.indiewire.com/2015/10/netflix-reveals-viewership-numbers-for-beasts-of-no-nation-56137/.

Berry, Marsha, and Max Schleser. *Mobile Media Making in an Age of Smartphones*. New York: Palgrave, 2014.

Binder, Matt. "Netflix Consumes 15 Percent of the World's Internet Traffic, Report Says." *Mashable*, October 4, 2018. https://mashable.com/article/netflix-15-percent-worlds-internet-traffic/.

Bolter, Jay David, and Richard Grusin. *Remediation: Understanding New Media*. Cambridge, MA: MIT Press, 1999.

Bond, Paul. "Netflix to Hit 90 Million U.S. Subscribers in 10 Years, Analyst Predicts." *Hollywood Reporter*, June 27, 2018. https://www.hollywoodreporter.com/news/netflix-hit-90-million-us-subscribers-ten-years-analyst-predicts-1123697.

Bordwell, David. "The Art Cinema as a Mode of Film Practice." In *Film Theory and Criticism: Introductory Readings*, edited by Marshall Cohen and Leo Baudry, 716–724. New York: Oxford University Press, 1999.

———. "Weaponized VOD at $50 a Pop." Observations on Film Art Blog. March 15, 2016. http://www.davidbordwell.net/blog/2016/03/15/weaponized-vod-at-50-a-pop/.

Bourdieu, Pierre. *Distinction: A Social Critique of the Judgment of Taste.* Translated by Richard Nice. Cambridge, MA: Harvard University Press, 1987.

Brooks, Jon. "For Cinephiles, Netflix Is Less and Less an Option." September 12, 2014. http://ww2.kqed.org/arts/2014/09/12/netflix_streaming_dvds/.

Brueggemann, Tom. "The Screening Room Earns Mixed Reaction, Not Total Rejection." *IndieWire*, March 16, 2016. https://www.indiewire.com/2016/03/the-screening-room-earns-mixed-reaction-not-total-rejection-174822/.

Burgess, Jean, and Joshua Green. "The Entrepreneurial Vlogger: Participatory Culture beyond the Professional-Amateur Divide." In *The YouTube Reader*, edited by Pelle Snickars and Patrick Vonderau, 89–107. Stockholm: National Library of Sweden, 2009.

———. *YouTube.* Cambridge, UK: Polity, 2009.

Busch, Anita, and Anthony D'Alessandro. "NATO on the Screening Room: Any New Model Affecting Exhibs Should Be Handled by Members, 'Not by a Third Party.'" *Deadline Hollywood*, March 16, 2016. https://deadline.com/2016/03/nato-reaction-the-screening-room-1201721117/.

Carney, Ray, ed. *Cassavetes on Cassavetes.* London: Faber and Faber, 2001.

Casetti, Francesco, and Sara Sampietro. "With Eyes, with Hands: The Relocation of Cinema into the iPhone." In *Moving Data: The iPhone and the Future of Media*, edited by Pelle Snickars and Patrick Vonderau, 19–32. New York: Columbia University Press, 2012.

Castells, Manuel. "Communication, Power, and Counter-power in the Network Society." *International Journal of Communication* 1 (2007): 238–266.

———. *The Rise of the Network Society.* Cambridge, MA: Wiley-Blackwell, 2007.

Chmielewski, Dawn. "TV Platform That Gives Viewers the Power to Greenlight Series Launches with Kevin Smith Stoner Comedy." *Deadline Hollywood*, July 11, 2018. https://deadline.com/2018/07/rivit-tv-viewers-power-greenlight-tv-series-launches-kevin-smith-hollyweed-1202424384/.

Christian, Aymar. "Beyond Big Video: The Instability of Independent Networks in a New Media Market." *Continuum: Journal of Media and Cultural Studies* 26, no. 1 (2012): 73–87.

———. "Indie TV: Innovation in Series Development." In *Media Independence: Working with Freedom or Working for Free?*, edited by James Bennett and Niki Strange, 159–181. New York: Routledge, 2015.

———. "Joe Swanberg, Intimacy, and the Digital Aesthetic." *Cinema Journal* 50, no. 4 (Summer 2011): 117–137.

———. "Not TV, Not the Web." In *The Mobile Media Reader.*, edited by Noah Arceneaux and Anandam Kavoori, 87–101. New York: Peter Lang, 2012.

———. *Open TV: Innovation beyond Hollywood and the Rise of Web Television*. New York: New York University Press, 2018.

Chun, Wendy Hui Kyong, Anna Watkins Fisher, and Thomas Keenan, eds. *New Media, Old Media: A History and Theory Reader.* 2nd ed. New York: Routledge, 2016.

Creeber, Glen. *Small Screen Aesthetics: From TV to the Internet*. London: BFI, 2013.

Crisp, Virginia. *Film Distribution in the Digital Age: Pirates and Professionals*. New York: Palgrave Macmillan, 2005.

Curtin, Michael, Jennifer Holt, and Kevin Sanson. "Introduction." In *Distribution Revolution*, edited by Michael Curtin, Jennifer Holt, and Kevin Sanson, 1–20. Oakland: University of California Press, 2014.

D'Allessandro, Anthony. "Art House Theaters Protest the Screening Room in Open Letter." *Deadline Hollywood*, March 15, 2016. https://deadline.com/2016/03/screening-room-art-house-convergence-open-letter-tim-league-1201720859.

Dargis, Manohla. "Declaration of Indies: Just Sell It Yourself!" *New York Times*, January 14, 2010. https://www.nytimes.com/2010/01/17/movies/17dargis.html.

Dawson, Max. "Television's Aesthetic of Efficiency: Convergence Television and the Digital Short." In *Television as Digital Media*, edited by James Bennett and Niki Strange, 204–229. Durham, NC: Duke University Press, 2011.

Deutchman, Ira. Interview with Sarah E. S. Sinwell. January 17, 2017.

Dijck, Jose van. "Users Like You? Theorizing Agency in User-Generated Content." *Media, Culture and Society* 31, no. 1 (2009): 41–58.

Dixon, Wheeler Winston. *Streaming: Movies, Media, and Instant Access.* Lexington: University Press of Kentucky, 2013.

Dobbs, Aaron. "Why Indie Film Institutions Are Turning Their Attention to Web Series." *IndieWire*, April 10, 2014. http://www.indiewire.com/article/television/why-indie-film-institutions-are-turning-their-attention-to-web-series.

Dwyer, Tim. *Media Convergence.* London: McGraw Hill, 2010.

Eberwein, Robert. "IFC and Sundance: Channeling Independence." In *Contemporary American Independent Film*, edited by Chris Holmlund and Justin Wyatt, 265–282. New York: Routledge, 2005.

The Economist. "Saved by the Box." May 23, 2009.

Edwards, Cliff, and Sarah Rabil. "Netflix Surges on Streaming-Only Option, DVD Price Increase." *Bloomberg News*, November 22, 2010.

Ellingson, Annlee. "New Movies Will Play at Home, Just Not via Screening Room." *LA Biz*, May 31, 2017. https://www.bizjournals.com/losangeles/news/2017/05/31/new-movies-will-not-play-via-screen-room.html.

Evans, Elizabeth. *Transmedia Television: Audiences, New Media, Everyday Life.* New York: Routledge, 2013.

Everett, Anna, and John T. Caldwell. *New Media: Theories of Practices of Digitextuality.* New York: Routledge, 2003.

Faughnder, Ryan. "CinemaCon: Sean Parker's Screening Room a 'Serious Distraction,' Says Theater Group Leader." *Los Angeles Times*, April 12, 2016. http://www.latimes.com/entertainment/envelope/cotown/la-et-ct-cinemacon-2016-screening-room-20160412-story.html.

The Film Collaborative. "How I Learned to Stop Worrying and Love VOD." SXSW 2012. http://www.thefilmcollaborative.org/sxsw/American_VOD_SXSW2012.pdf.

Fleming, Mike, Jr. "Brett Ratner Joins Growing Filmmaker Chorus against Screening Room Day & Date Home Movie Service." *Deadline Hollywood*, March 17, 2016. https://deadline.com/2016/03/brett-ratner-against-screening-room-day-and-date-home-movie-service-1201722273/.

Flew, Terry. *An Introduction to New Media.* Oxford: Oxford University Press, 2002.

Forssell, Andy. "Hulu: Serving Up More Docus and Indie Pix." *Variety*, March 19, 2009. http://weblogs.variety.com/on_the_air/2009/03/hulu-serving-up-more-docus-and-indie-pix.html.

"Four Eyed Monsters Announce Self-Distribution through New Without a Box Inc. Initiative." Four Eyed Monsters Blog. http://foureyedmonsters.com/four-eyed-monsters-announce-self-distribution-through-new-withoutabox-inc-initiative/.

Freeman, Matthew, and William Proctor. *Global Convergence Cultures: Transmedia Earth*. New York: Routledge, 2018.

Friedberg, Anne. "The End of Cinema: Multi-media and Technological Change." In *Reinventing Film Studies*, edited by Christine Gledhill and Linda Williams, 438–452. London: Oxford University Press, 2000.

Fusco, Katherine. "The Actress Experience: Cruel Knowing and the Death of the Picture Personality in *Black Swan* and *The Girlfriend Experience*." *Camera Obscura* 28, no. 1 (2013): 1–35.

Gallagher, Mark. *Another Steven Soderbergh Experience: Authorship and Contemporary Hollywood*. Austin: University of Texas Press, 2013.

Galt, Rosalind, and Kyle Schoonover, eds. *Global Art Cinema: New Theories and Histories*. Oxford: Oxford University Press, 2010.

Gamson, Joshua. *Claims to Fame: Celebrity in Contemporary America*. Berkeley: University of California Press, 1994.

Garrahan, Matthew. "YouTube Launches Live Streaming." *Financial Times*, April 8, 2011. https://www.ft.com/content/753e646e-6208-11e0-8ee4-00144feab49a.

Garrett, Diane. "The Upside of a DVD and VOD Day-and-Date Release." *Variety*, October 17, 2009.

Gehl, Robert. "YouTube as Archive: Who Will Curate This Digital Wunderkammer?" *International Journal of Cultural Studies* 12, no. 1 (January 2009): 43–60.

Gentile, Gary. "'Bubble' Hits Theaters, DVD on Same Day." *USA Today*, January 18, 2006. http://usatoday30.usatoday.com/tech/news/2006-01-18-bubble-theater-threat_x.htm.

Gilmore, Geoffrey. "Long Live Indie Film." *Nation* 272, no. 13 (2001): 17–20.

Gitelman, Lisa. *Always Already New: Media, History and the Data of Culture*. Cambridge, MA: MIT Press, 2008.

Glaser, Mark. "Digging Deeper: YouTube CEO Hails 'Birth of a New Clip Culture.'" PBS Media Shift. April 4, 2006. http://www.pbs.org/mediashift/2006/04/digging-deeperyoutube-ceo-hails-birth-of-a-new-clip-culture094.html.

Goggin, Gerard. *Cell Phone Culture: Mobile Technology in Everyday Life.* London: Routledge, 2006.

———. "The Eccentric Career of Mobile Television." *International Journal of Digital Television* 3 (June 2012): 119–140.

———. "Mobile Video: Spreading Stories with Mobile Media." In *Routledge Companion to Mobile Media*, edited by Gerard Goggin and Larissa Hjorth, 146–156. New York: Routledge, 2014.

Goggin, Gerard, and Larissa Hjorth. "Introduction: Mobile Media Research: State of the Art." In *Routledge Companion to Mobile Media*, edited by Gerard Goggin and Larissa Hjorth, 1–8. New York: Routledge, 2014.

———. *Mobile Technologies.* New York: Routledge, 2009.

Goldmann, A. J. "Coming Soon to a Cellphone Near You: Isabella Rossellini Mounting a Housefly." *Wired*, February 12, 2008.

Goldstein, Andrew. "Steven Soderbergh Confirms Plans to Leave Hollywood and Become a Painter." *Huffington Post*, August 29, 2011. https://www.huffingtonpost.com/artinfo/steven-soderbergh-confirm_b_940528.html.

"Gotham Independent Film Awards." Livestream. UStream. *Deadline Hollywood*, November 30, 2015. http://deadline.com/2015/11/gotham-awards-2015-live-stream-video-1201647033/.

Grainge, Paul, ed. *Ephemeral Media.* London: BFI, 2011.

Grauso, Alisha. "Netflix to Begin Exclusive Streaming of Disney, Marvel, Star Wars and Pixar in September." *Forbes*, May 24, 2016. http://www.forbes.com/sites/alishagrauso/2016/05/24/netflix-to-begin-exclusive-streaming-of-disney-marvel-star-wars-and-pixar-in-september/#470f7e26322b.

Gray, Jonathan. *Show Sold Separately: Promos, Spoilers, and Other Media Paratexts.* New York: New York University Press, 2010.

Greenberg, Joshua. *From Betamax to Blockbuster: Video Stores and the Invention of Movies on Video.* Cambridge, MA: MIT Press, 2008.

Groening, Stephen. *Cinema beyond Territory: Inflight Entertainment and Atmospheres of Globalisation.* London: BFI, 2014.

GSMA press release. "Robert Redford Announces Sundance Film Festival: Global Short Film Festival Project for Mobile." Sundance.org. November 8, 2006.

Hallinan, Blake, and Ted Striphas. "Recommended for You: The Netflix Prize and the Production of Algorithmic Culture." *New Media and Society* 18, no. 1 (2016): 117–137.

Hark, Ina Rae, ed. *Exhibition: The Film Reader.* London: Routledge, 2001.

Hart, Hugh. "Fans Help Filmmakers Win YouTube Deal." *Wired*, June 25, 2007. http://www.wired.com/entertainment/theweb/news/2007/06/youtubefest.

Hartley, John. "Is Screen Studies a Load of Old Cobblers? And If So, Is That Good?" *Cinema Journal* 45, no. 1 (2005): 101–106.

Hawkins, Joan. "Dark, Disturbing, Intelligent, Provocative and Quirky." In *Contemporary American Independent Film: From the Margins to the Mainstream*, edited by Chris Holmlund and Justin Wyatt, 89–106. New York: Routledge, 2005.

———. "Dish Towns USA (or Rural Screens), Part One." *FlowTV: A Critical Forum on Media and Culture.* June 29, 2007. https://www.flowjournal.org/2007/06/dish-towns-usa-or-rural-screens-part-one/.

Hay, James, and Nick Couldry. "Rethinking Convergence/Culture." *Cultural Studies* 25, no. 4–5 (2011): 473–486.

Healey, Jon. "Q&A: On a Mission to Change the Economics of Hollywood." *Los Angeles Times*, April 10, 2004.

Herbert, Daniel. *Videoland: Movie Culture at the American Video Store.* Berkeley: University of California Press, 2014.

Hernandez, Eugene. "DIY Distribution: Coming Soon via the Filmmakers . . . 'Four Eyed Monsters' and 'Head Trauma.'" *IndieWire*, August 17, 2006. https://www.indiewire.com/2006/08/diy-distribution-coming-soon-via-the-filmmakers-four-eyed-monsters-and-head-trauma-76252/.

Hilderbrand, Lucas. *Inherent Vice: Bootleg Histories of Videotape and Copyright.* Durham, NC: Duke University Press, 2009.

Hillier, Jim, ed. "Introduction." In *American Independent Cinema: A Sight and Sound Reader*, ix–xvii. London: BFI, 2001.

Holmlund, Chris, and Justin Wyatt, eds. *Contemporary American Independent Film: From the Margins to the Mainstream.* New York: Routledge, 2005.

Holt, Jennifer, and Alisa Perren. "Introduction." In *Media Industries: History, Theory, and Method*, edited by Jennifer Holt and Alisa Perren, 1–16. West Sussex: Wiley-Blackwell, 2009.

Homaday, Ann "'Bubble' Vision." *Washington Post*, January 22, 2006.

Hopes, Patrick. "Netflix Unveils Binge Scale with Some Surprising Results." *Deadline*, June 8, 2016. http://deadline.com/2016/06/netflix-binge-scale-data-results-house-of-cards-orange-is-the-new-black-1201769127/.

Howe, Jeff. "The Rise of Crowdsourcing." *Wired*, June 1, 2006. http://www.wired. com/wired/archive/14.06/crowds_pr.html.

Hughes, Neil. "Netflix Boasts 37% Share of Internet Traffic in North America Compared with 3% for Apple's iTunes." *Apple Insider*, January 20, 2016. http://appleinsider.com/articles/16/01/20/netflix-boasts-37-share-of-internet-traffic-in-north-america-compared-with-3-for-apples-itunes.

Inside Criterion. "Farewell, Hulu! Hello, Criterion Channel!" *The Criterion Collection*, November 11, 2016. https://www.criterion.com/current/posts/4293-farewell-hulu-hello-criterion-channel.

Jagernauth, Kevin. "Lionsgate and Tribeca Enterprises Team Up to Launch Subscription VOD Service in 2015." *IndieWire*, October 20, 2014. http://blogs.indiewire.com/theplaylist/lionsgate-and-tribeca-enterprises-team-to-launch-subscription-vod-service-in-2015-20141020.

Jardin, Xeni. "Thinking Outside the Box Office." *Wired*, December 1, 2005. https://www.wired.com/2005/12/soderbergh/.

Jarrett, Kylie. "Beyond Broadcast Yourself: The Future of YouTube." *Media International Australia, Incorporating Culture & Policy*, no. 126 (February 2008): 132–144.

Jenkins, Henry. *Convergence Culture: Where Old and New Media Collide*. New York: New York University Press, 2006.

———. Interview. "DIY Video 2010: Activist Media (Part Three)." Confessions of an Aca-Fan Blog, November 1, 2010. http://henryjenkins.org/2010/11/diy_video_2010_activist_media_2.html.

Jenkins, Henry, Sam Ford, and Joshua Green. *Spreadable Media: Creating Value and Meaning in a Networked Culture*. New York: New York University Press, 2013.

Juhasz, Alexandra. "Learning the Five Lessons of YouTube: After Trying to Teach There, I Don't Believe the Hype." *Cinema Journal* 48, no. 2 (Winter 2009): 145–150.

Katz, J., ed. *Handbook of Mobile Communication*. Cambridge, MA: MIT Press, 2008.

Kaufman, Anthony. "Netflix Folds Red Envelope; Exits Theatrical Acquisition and Production Biz." *IndieWire*, July 23, 2008. http://www.indiewire.com/article/netflix_folds_red_envelope_exits_theatrical_acquisition_and_production_biz.

Kember, Sarah, and Joanna Zylinska. *Life after New Media: Mediation as Vital Process*. Cambridge, MA: MIT Press, 2012.

Kickstarter. "The Veronica Mars Movie Project." March 13, 2013. https://www.kickstarter.com/projects/559914737/the-veronica-mars-movie-project.

King, Geoff. *American Independent Cinema*. Bloomington: Indiana University Press, 2005.

———. *Indie 2.0: Change and Continuity in Contemporary American Indie Film*. New York: Columbia University Press, 2014.

———. *Indiewood, USA*. London: I. B. Tauris, 2009.

———. *Positioning Art Cinema: Film and Cultural Value*. London: I. B. Tauris, 2019.

———. *Quality Hollywood: Markers of Distinction in Contemporary Studio Film*. London: I. B. Tauris, 2016.

King, Geoff, Claire Molloy, and Yannis Tzioumakis, eds. *American Independent Cinema: Indie, Indiewood and Beyond*. New York: Routledge, 2013.

Kleinhans, Chuck. "Independent Features: Hopes and Dreams." In *The New American Cinema*, edited by Jon Lewis, 307–327. Durham, NC: Duke University Press, 1998.

Klinger, Barbara. *Beyond the Multiplex: Cinema, New Technologies and the Home*. Berkeley: University of California Press, 2006.

———. "Contraband Cinema: Piracy, 'Titanic,' and Central Asia." *Cinema Journal* 49, no. 2 (Winter 2010): 106–124.

Kohn, Eric. "As Snowpiercer Hits VOD, the Industry's Divided on Distribution's Future." *IndieWire*, July 11, 2014. https://www.indiewire.com/2014/07/as-snowpiercer-hits-vod-the-industrys-divided-on-distributions-future-24403/.

Kotler, Steven. "Netflix Eager to Grow Indie Pic Eco-System." *Variety*, March 2, 2006. http://variety.com/2006/film/awards/netflix-eager-to-grow-indie-pic-eco-system-1117939103.

Kung, Michelle. "'Green Porno' Creator Isabella Rossellini on Animal Sex, Crazed Fans and Web Entertainment." *Wall Street Journal*, September 21, 2009. http://blogs.wsj.com/speakeasy/2009/09/21/isabella-rossellini-on-green-porno-crazed-fans-and-web-entertainment/.

Lang, Brent. "Global Box Office Hits Record $40.6 Billion in 2017; U.S. Attendance Lowest in 23 Years." *Variety*, April 4, 2018. https://variety.com/2018/digital/news/global-box-office-hits-record-40-6-billion-in-2017-u-s-attendance-lowest-in-23-years-1202742991/.

———. "Studios, Exhibitors Consider Revolutionary Plan for Day-and-Date Movies at Home." *Variety*, March 9, 2016. https://variety.com/2016/film/news/studios-exhibitors-consider-revolutionary-plan-for-day-and-date-movies-at-home-exclusive-1201725168/.

Lang, Brent, and James Rainey. "Screening Room Proposal Overshadows CinemaCon, Fuels Debate over Release Windows." *Variety*, April 14, 2016. https://variety.com/2016/film/news/cinemacon-analysis-screening-room-1201754079/.

Larsen, Eric. "Sundance Filmmakers Can Self-Distribute Films Online after Festival." *Mashable*, January 23, 2013. http://mashable.com/2013/01/23/sundance-reelhouse.

Learmonth, Michael. "YouTube Shifts Strategy, Tries Long-Form Video." *Business Insider*, June 18, 2008. http://www.businessinsider.com/2008/6/youtube-tries-long-form-video.

———. "YouTube Unveils 'Screening Room' for Free Indie Movies." *Business Insider*, June 18, 2008. https://www.businessinsider.com/2008/6/youtube-unveils-screening-room-for-free-indie-movies.

Leonard, Andrew. "How Netflix Is Turning Viewers into Puppets." *Salon*, February 1, 2013. http://www.salon.com/2013/02/01/how_netflix_is_turning_viewers_into_puppets/.

Levy, Emanuel. *Cinema of Outsiders: The Rise of American Independent Film*. New York: New York University Press, 1999.

Leydon, Joe. Review of *Girl Walks into a Bar. Variety*, March 15, 2011. SXSW Reviews. http://www.variety.com/review/VE1117944827/.

Ling, Richard. *The Mobile Connection*. San Francisco: Morgan Kaufman, 2004.

Little, Amanda Griscom, "Robert Redford Starts Channeling 'Green.'" April 19, 2007. http://www.msnbc.msn.com/id/18176422/.

Lobato, Ramon. *Netflix Nations: The Geography of Digital Distribution.* New York: New York University Press, 2019.

Lord, Susan, and Janine Marcgessault. *Fluid Screens, Expanded Cinema.* Toronto: University of Toronto Press, 2013.

Lotz, Amanda. *The Television Will Be Revolutionized.* 2nd ed. New York: New York University Press, 2014.

Lyons, Charles. "New Machine Comes into Focus." *Variety*, May 13–18, 2002. http://www.variety.com/article/VR1117866761/.

Manovich, Lev. *The Language of New Media.* Cambridge, MA: MIT Press, 2001.

———. "New Media: From Borges to HTML." In *The New Media Reader*, edited by Noah Wardrip-Fruin and Nick Montfort, 13–25. Cambridge, MA: MIT Press, 2003.

Martin, Michelle L., and Katie O'Connell. "Securing Distribution with Netflix." *The Independent*, January 12, 2011.

Marvin, Carolyn. *When Old Technologies Were New.* Oxford: Oxford University Press, 1988.

Matrix, Sidneyeve. "The Netflix Effect: Teens, Binge Watching, and On-Demand Digital Media Trends." *Jeunesse: Young People, Texts, Cultures* 6, no. 1 (2014): 119–138.

May, Harvey, and Greg Hearn. "The Mobile Phone as Media." *International Journal of Cultural Studies* 8, no. 2 (2005): 195–211.

McAlone, Nathan. "Netflix Now Has Better Programming Than HBO, according to New Survey." *Business Insider*, April 11, 2016. http://www.businessinsider.com/netflix-has-better-programming-than-hbo-2016-4.

McCarthy, Anna. *Ambient Television: Visual Culture and Public Space.* Durham, NC: Duke University Press, 2001.

McClintock, Pamela. "Theater Owner Rejects Proposed $50 Home Movie Service: 'It Feels Like a Half-Baked Plan.'" *Hollywood Reporter*, March 13, 2016. https://www.hollywoodreporter.com/news/theater-owner-rejects-proposed-50-874835.

McDonald, Kevin P. "Digital Dreams in a Material World: The Rise of Netflix and Its Impact on Changing Distribution and Exhibition Patterns." *Jump Cut: A Review of Contemporary Media*, no. 55 (Fall 2013). http://ejumpcut.org/currentissue/McDonaldNetflix/text.html.

McLane, Betsy. *A New History of Documentary Film*. New York: Continuum, 2012.

Miller, Claire Cain. "YouTube Acquires a Producer of Videos." *New York Times*, March 7, 2011. http://www.nytimes.com/2011/03/08/technology/08youtube.html.

Miller, Liz Shannon. "Netflix and the Future: The Two Things Changing Your Favorite Streaming Platform." *IndieWire*, July 2015. http://www.indiewire.com/2015/07/netflix-and-the-future-the-two-things-changing-your-favorite-streaming-platform-59891/.

Miller, Nancy. "Minifesto for a New Age." *Wired*, March 1, 2007. http://www.wired.com/wired/archive/15.03/snackminifesto.html.

———. "Snack Attack." *Wired*, March 1, 2007. https://www.wired.com/2007/03/snackattack/.

Miller, Stuart. "The Mean Green Marketing Machine." *Multichannel News*, August 12, 2007. http://www.multichannel.com/article/85975-The_Mean_ Green_Marketing_Machine.php.

Miller, Toby. "Revising Screen Studies." *Television and New Media* 2 (2001): 91–93.

"Morgan Spurlock 'A Day in the Life': Original Series Premieres on Hulu." *Huffington Post*. August 17, 2011. http://www.huffingtonpost.com/2011/08/17/morgan-spurlock-a-day-in-the-life_n_929008.html.

Muller, Eggo. "Where Quality Matters: Discourses on the Art of Making a YouTube Video." In *The YouTube Reader*, edited by Pelle Snickars and Patrick Vonderau, 126–139. Stockholm: National Library of Sweden, 2009.

Murphy, Sheila. *How Television Invented New Media*. New Brunswick, NJ: Rutgers University Press, 2011.

Neale, Steve. "Art Cinema as Institution." *Screen* 22, no. 1 (1981): 11–39.

Nelson, Elissa. "Windows into the Digital World: Distributor Strategies and Consumer Choice in a Connected World." In *Connected Viewing: Selling, Streaming, and Sharing Media in the Digital Era*, edited by Jennifer Holt and Kevin Sanson, 62–78. New York: Routledge, 2014.

Netflix Media Center. "Get Ready for Summer on Netflix US." May 23, 2016. https://media.netflix.com/en/company-blog/get-ready-for-summer-on-netflix-us.

Netflix Shareholders File. July 2014. http://files.shareholder.com/downloads/NFLX/3415305831x0x769748/9b21df7f-743c-4f0f-94da-9f13e384a3d2/July2014EarningsLetter_7.21.14_final.pdf.

Newman, Michael. *Indie: An American Film Culture*. New York: Columbia University Press, 2011.

———. *Video Revolutions: On the History of a Medium*. New York: Columbia University Press, 2014.

Newman, Michael, and Elana Levine. *Legitimating Television: Media Convergence and Cultural Status*. New York: Routledge, 2011.

New York Film Academy Ltd. "Get Your Independent Movie on Netflix: What You Need to Know." July 11, 2014. https://www.nyfa.edu/student-resources/get-your-independent-movie-on-netflix/.

Nikolic, Vladan. *Independent Filmmaking and Digital Convergence: Transmedia and Beyond*. New York: Routledge, 2017.

Noble, McKinley. "Netflix Still Has Millions of DVD Subscribers Because Rural US Broadband Is Terrible." *Quartz Media*, July 19, 2017. https://qz.com/1032779/netflix-still-has-millions-of-dvd-subscribers-because-rural-us-broadband-sucks/.

"O'Doyle Rules! Adam Sandler Heads to Netflix." Press release. October 2, 2014.

Orgeron, Devin, Marsha Orgeron, and Dan Streible, eds. *Learning with the Lights Off*. London: Oxford University Press, 2012.

Otterson, Joe. "Kevin Smith Partners with Rivit TV on Comedy Pilot 'Hollyweed.'" *Variety*, July 11, 2018. https://variety.com/2018/tv/news/kevin-smith-hollyweed-rivit-tv-1202869936/.

Pardo, Alejandro. "From the Big Screen to the Small One: How Digitization Is Transforming the Distribution, Exhibition and Consumption of Movies." In *Besides the Screen: Moving Images through Distribution, Promotion and Curation*, edited by Virginia Crisp and Gabriel Menotti Gonring, 23–45. New York: Palgrave Macmillan, 2015.

Parr, Ben. "YouTube Surpasses Two Billion Video Views Daily." *Mashable*, May 17, 2010. http://mashable.com/2010/05/17/youtube-2-billion-views/.

Perren, Alisa. "A Big Fat Indie Success Story? Press Discourses Surrounding the Making and Marketing of a 'Hollywood' Movie." *Journal of Film and Video* 56, no. 2 (2004): 18–31.

———. *Indie, Inc.* Austin: University of Texas Press, 2012.

———. “Last Indie Standing: The Special Case of Lionsgate in the New Millennium.” In *American Independent Cinema: Indie, Indiewood and Beyond*, edited by Geoff King, Claire Molloy, and Yannis Tzioumakis, 108–120. New York: Routledge, 2013.

———. “Sex, Lies and Marketing: Miramax and the Development of the Quality Indie Blockbuster.” *Film Quarterly* 55, no. 2 (Winter 2001–2002): 30–39.

Popper, Ben. “Netflix Whizzes Past 75 Million Subscribers Thanks to Record International Growth.” January 19, 2016. *The Verge*. http://www.theverge.com/2016/1/19/10790282/netflix-q4-2015-earnings.

Pribram, E. Deidre. *Independent Film in the United States, 1980–2001*. New York: Peter Lang, 2002.

Protolinski, Emil. “Streaming Services Now Account for Over 70% of Peak Traffic in North America, Netflix Dominates with 37%.” *Venturebeat*, December 7, 2015. http://venturebeat.com/2015/12/07/streaming-services-now-account-for-over-70-of-peak-traffic-in-north-america-netflix-dominates-with-37/.

Rainie, Lee. “Online Video Audience Surges.” Pew Research Center. January 9, 2008. http://pewresearch.org/pubs/682/.

Reiss, Jon. *Think Outside the Box Office: The Ultimate Guide to Film Distribution and Marketing for the Digital Era*. Los Angeles: Hybrid Cinema Publishing, 2010.

Richmond, Will. “CES Takeaway #3: Mobility Is Video’s Next Frontier.” *Video Nuze*. January 12, 2011.

Roberts, Graham. “Movie-Making in the New Media Age.” In *Web. Studies*, edited by David Gauntlett and Ross Horsley, 103–113. London: Arnold, 2004.

Rojek, Chris. *Celebrity*. London: Reaktion Books, 2001.

Salt Lake Film Society. *Why SLFS Matters 2017 Annual Report*. 2017. https://saltlakefilmsociety.org/about-us/why.

Sarris, Andrew. “What’s the Deal with Bubble? Soderbergh’s Social Experiment Wheezes.” *New York Observer*, February 12, 2006.

Schamus, James. “A Rant.” In *The End of Cinema as We Know It*, edited by Jon Lewis, 253–260. New York: New York University Press, 2001.

Sconce, Jeffrey. "Tulip Theory." In *New Media: Theories of Practices of Digitextuality*, edited by Anna Everett and John T. Caldwell, 179–196. New York: Routledge, 2003.

Setoodeh, Ramin. "Netflix Pulls Out of Cannes following Rule Change." *Variety*, April 11, 2018. https://variety.com/2018/film/news/netflix-cannes-rule-change-ted-sarandos-interview-exclusive-1202750473/.

Shangri-la Entertainment. "Shangri-la Entertainment Girl Walks into a Bar Attracts More Than 260,000 Viewers." March 14, 2011. PR Newswire. http://finance.yahoo.com/news/ShangriLa-Entertainments-Girl-prnews-3028421673.html?x=0&.v=1.

Sharf, Zach. "Netflix Says 20 Million Hours of 'Mudbound' Have Been Streamed, Which Is 'Dramatically Bigger' Than a Theatrical Release." *IndieWire*, June 22, 2018. https://www.indiewire.com/2018/06/mudbound-netflix-20-million-hours-streaming-reed-hastings-1201977820/.

Sims, David. "Netflix Is a Business, Not a Movement." *The Atlantic*, June 24, 2019. https://www.theatlantic.com/entertainment/archive/2019/06/netflix-business-not-movement/592402/.

Sinwell, Sarah E. S. "Go Digital or Go Dark: Crowdfunding, Independent Financing and Art House Exhibition on Kickstarter." In *A Companion to American Indie Film*, edited by Geoff King, 452–468. Malden, MA: Wiley-Blackwell, 2017.

Smith, Ethan, and Lauren A. A. Schuker. "For Indie Films, Video-on-Demand Fills the Revenue Gap." *Wall Street Journal*, January 10, 2011. http://online.wsj.com/article/SB10001424052748704064504576069472667852508.html.

Smith, Nigel. "Will Sean Parker's Screening Room Hurt or Help the Film Industry?" *The Guardian*, April 8, 2016. https://www.theguardian.com/film/2016/apr/08/sean-parker-screening-room-new-movie-releases-home-viewing-film-industry.

Snickars, Pelle, and Patrick Vonderau. "Introduction." In *Moving Data: The iPhone and the Future of Media*, edited by Pelle Snickars and Patrick Vonderau, 1–18. New York: Columbia University Press, 2012.

———. "Introduction." In *The YouTube Reader*, edited by Pelle Snickars and Patrick Vonderau, 9–21. Stockholm: National Library of Sweden, 2009.

Spangler, Todd. "Amazon's First Movie: Spike Lee Drama 'Chi-raq' to Bow with Theatrical Run." *Variety*, July 15, 2015. http://variety

.com/2015/digital/news/spike-lee-chi-raq-amazon-theaters-1201540709/.

———. "Amazon Studios to Produce Movies for Theatrical, Digital Release in 2015." *Variety*, January 19, 2015. http://variety.com/2015/digital/news/amazon-studios-to-produce-movies-for-theatrical-digital-release-in-2015-1201408688/.

———. "Netflix, Weinstein Co. Bust Windows with 'Crouching Tiger' Sequel Day-and-Date Release." *Variety*, September 29, 2014. http://variety.com/2014/digital/news/crouching-tiger-hidden-dragon-sequel-netflix-weinstein-co-1201316645/.

Sparviero, Sergio, Corinna Peil, and Gabriele Balbi, eds. *Media Convergence and Deconvergence*. Cham, Switzerland: Palgrave Macmillan, 2017.

Sperling, Nicole. "Netflix, the Oscars, and the Battle for the Future of Film." *Vanity Fair*, November 20, 2017. https://www.vanityfair.com/hollywood/2017/11/netflix-the-oscars-the-battle-for-the-future-of-film/amp.

Steinberg, Brian. "Sundance Channel to Rename Itself SundanceTV." *Variety*, January 27, 2014. https://variety.com/2014/tv/news/sundance-channel-to-rename-itself-sundancetv-1201072666/.

Stelter, Brian, and Bill Carter. "Networks Try a Social Spin at the Upfronts." *New York Times*, May 20, 2012.

Sternbergh, Adam. "The Age of the Streaming TV Auteur." *Vulture*, September 22, 2014. https://www.vulture.com/2014/09/age-of-the-auteur-on-streaming-tv.html.

Strangelove, Michael. *Post-TV: Piracy, Cord-Cutting, and the Future of Television*. Toronto: University of Toronto Press, 2015.

Stross, Randall. *Planet Google: One Company's Audacious Plan to Organize Everything We Know*. New York: Simon and Schuster, 2008.

"Sundance Channel Acquires U.S. Rights to Ten-Part Short Film Series The Art of Seduction." PR Newswire. October 24, 2006. Academic OneFile. http://link.galegroup.com/apps/doc/A153249508/AONE?u=marriottlibrary&sid=AONE&xid=508b6514.

"Sundance Institute, YouTube and Acura to Make 12 Short Films from 2011 Sundance Institute Available for Free on YouTube Screening Room." Sundance Channel press release. January 5, 2011. http://www.sundance.org/press-center/release/sundance.

Thompson, Anne. "Netflix versus Hollywood: From Oscar Frontrunners to A-List TV Creators, Ted Sarandos Reveals His Master Plan." *IndieWire*, August 24, 2017. https://www.indiewire.com/2017/08/netflix-ted-sarandos-will-smith-adam-sandler-1201866954/2/.

———. "Sorry, Netflix: The Top DGA Award Won't Consider Day-and-Date Releases." *IndieWire*, June 26, 2019. https://www.indiewire.com/2019/06/dga-day-and-date-theatrical-releases-1202153402/.

Times Staff and Wires. "Netflix to Shutter Red Envelope." *Los Angeles Times*, July 22, 2008. http://articles.latimes.com/2008/jul/22/business/fi-briefs22.S5.

Trefis Team. "Here's How the Exclusive Partnership with Disney Can Impact Netflix." *Forbes*, May 26, 2016. http://www.forbes.com/sites/greatspeculations/2016/05/26/heres-how-the-exclusive-partnership-with-disney-can-impact-netflix/#265aa7b265fe.

Trend, David, ed. *Reading Digital Culture*. Oxford: Blackwell, 2001.

Tryon, Chuck. *On-Demand Culture: Digital Delivery and the Future of Movies*. New Brunswick, NJ: Rutgers University Press, 2013.

———. "Pushing the (Red) Envelope." In *Moving Data: The iPhone and the Future of Media*, edited by Pelle Snickars and Patrick Vonderau, 124–139. New York: Columbia University Press, 2012.

———. *Reinventing Cinema: Movies in the Age of Media Convergence*. New Brunswick, NJ: Rutgers University Press, 2009.

———. "TV Got Better: Netflix's Original Programming Strategies and Binge Viewing." *Media Industries* 2, no. 2 (2015): 104–115. http://www.mediaindustriesjournal.org/index.php/mij/article/view/126/201.

Tweedie, James. *The Age of New Waves: Art Cinema and the Staging of Globalization*. Oxford: Oxford University Press, 2013.

Tzioumakis, Yannis. *American Independent Cinema: An Introduction*. New Brunswick, NJ: Rutgers University Press, 2006.

———. *American Independent Cinema*. 2nd ed. Edinburgh: Edinburgh University Press, 2017.

———. "American Independent Cinema in the Age of Convergence" *Revue Française d'Études Américaines* 136, no. 2 (2013): 52–66. https://www.cairn.info/revue-revue-francaise-d-etudes-americaines-2013-2-page-52.htm,

———. *Hollywood's Indies: Classics Divisions, Specialty Labels and American Independent Cinema*. Edinburgh: Edinburgh University Press, 2012.

Umstead, R. Thomas. "Sundance Channel Spells 'Green' F-U- N." *Multichannel News*, March 9, 2009. http://www.multichannel.com/ article/189625-Sundance_Channel_Spells_Green_F_U_N.php.

Valenti, Valentina. "In VOD We Trust." http://www.documentary.org/magazine/vod-we-trust-navigating-minefield-ever-changing-distribution-platform. Last accessed April 1, 2015.

Verhoeven, Beatrice. "Why Fear Streaming Giants? Indie Execs Sing Praises of Amazon, Netflix." *The Wrap*, June 4, 2016. http://www.thewrap.com/broad-green-amazon-studios-netflix-praise-ally-to-indies/.

Waller, Gregory. *Moviegoing in America: A Sourcebook in the History of Film Exhibition*. Malden, MA: Wiley-Blackwell, 2001.

Wardrip-Fruin, Noah, and Nick Montfort, eds. *The New Media Reader*. Cambridge, MA: MIT Press, 2003.

Wasson, Haidee. *Museum Movies: The Museum of Modern Art and the Birth of Art Cinema*. Berkeley: University of California Press, 2005.

Wessels, Emanuelle. "'Where Were You When the Monster Hit?': Media Convergence, Branded Security Citizenship, and the Transmedia Phenomenon of Cloverfield." *Convergence* 17, no. 1 (February 2011): 69–83.

White, John. *European Art Cinema*. New York: Routledge, 2017.

Wyatt, Justin. "The Formation of the 'Major Independent': Miramax, New Line and the New Hollywood." In *Contemporary Hollywood Cinema*, edited by Steve Neale and Murray Smith, 74–90. London: Routledge, 1998.

"YouTube." *New York Times*, Business Day, January 11, 2011. http://topics.nytimes.com/top/news/business/companies/youtube/index.html.

Zeitchik, Steven. "Netflix Adds Own Pix to the Mix." *Variety*, February 27, 2006.

Zimmerman, Patricia. "Digital Deployment(s)." In *Contemporary American Independent Film*, edited by Chris Holmlund and Justin Wyatt, 245–264. London: Routledge, 2005.

———. "Independent Documentary Producers and American Television Networks." *Screen* 22, no. 4 (1981): 43–53.

Mediagraphy

Almost Kings (Philip G. Flores, 2010)
Alpha House (Amazon, 2013)
American: The Bill Hicks Story (Matt Harlock and Paul Thomas, 2009)
American Idol (Fox, 2002–present)
Anatomy of a Scene (Sundance, 2001–2004)
Anvil: The Story of Anvil (Sacha Gervasi, 2008)
Arrested Development (Netflix, 2013–present)
The Art of Seduction (Sundance, 2006)
Avatar (James Cameron, 2009)
Beasts of No Nation (Cary Fukunaga, 2015)
Bee and PuppyCat (Natasha Allegri, Cartoon Hangover, 2013–present)
Before Sunrise (Richard Linklater, 1995)
Beginnings (Sundance, 2011)
Behind the Candelabra (HBO, 2012)
Beta (Amazon, 2013)
Big Ideas for a Small Planet (Sundance, 2007)
Black Swan (Darren Aronofsky, 2010)
The Blair Witch Project (Daniel Myrick and Eduardo Sanchez, 1999)
Bomb It (Jon Reiss, 2007)
Born into Brothels (Ross Kauffman and Zana Briski, 2004)
Brahman Naman (Qaushiq Mukherjee, 2016)
Braless (MTV, 2014–present)
Breaking Bad (AMC, 2008–2013)

Brittany Runs a Marathon (Paul Downs Colaizzo, 2019)
Bubble (Steven Soderbergh, 2005)
Bunheads (ABC Family, 2012–2013)
Captain Fantastic (Matt Ross, 2016)
The Captive (Sundance, 2009)
Charlie's Angels: Full Throttle (Joseph McGinty Nichol, 2003)
Chi-Raq (Spike Lee, 2015)
Clerks (Kevin Smith, 1994)
Cleverman (Sundance, 2016–2017)
Cloverfield (Matt Reeves, 2008)
Comic-Con Episode IV: A Fan's Hope (Morgan Spurlock, 2011)
Crash Course (John Green, 2011–present)
Crawford (David Modigliani, 2008)
Crouching Tiger, Hidden Dragon (Ang Lee, 2000)
The Crown (Netflix, 2016–present)
A Crude Awakening: The Oil Crash (Basil Gelpke and Ray McCormack, 2006)
The Crying Game (Neil Jordan, 1992)
The Daily Show (Comedy Central, 1996–present)
Daredevil (Netflix, 2015–2018)
The Dark Knight (Christopher Nolan, 2009)
A Day in the Life (Hulu, 2011)
Dexter (Showtime, 2006–2013)
Dirty Sexy Money (ABC, 2007)
The Do-over (Steven Brill, 2016)
DreamStates (Sundance, 2011)
East Los High (Hulu, 2013–2017)
Eco Trip (Sundance, 2007)
Embedded Live (Tim Robbins, 2005)
Eraserhead (David Lynch, 1977)
Erin Brockovich (Steven Soderbergh, 2000)
Faces (John Cassavetes, 1968)
The Fall (BBC, 2013–2016)
Family Guy (Fox, 1998–present)
F for Fake (Orson Welles, 1973)
Finding Dory (Andrew Stanton, 2016)

The Flaw (David Singleton, 2011)
Four Eyed Monsters (Buice and Crumley, 2007)
4 Months, 3 Weeks and 2 Days (Cristian Mungiu, 2007)
The Fundamentals of Caring (Rob Burnett, 2016)
Gangs of New York (Martin Scorsese, 2002)
Get Out (Jordan Peele, 2017)
Gilmore Girls (WB, 2000–2007)
The Girlfriend Experience (Steven Soderbergh, 2009)
Girl Walks into a Bar (Sebastian Gutierrez, 2011)
Godless (Netflix, 2017)
Green Porno (Sundance, 2008–2010)
Grey Gardens (Albert and David Maysles, 1975)
The Handmaid's Tale (Hulu, 2017–present)
Hap and Leonard (Sundance, 2016–present)
The Happening (M. Night Shyamalan, 2008)
Happiness (Todd Solondz, 1998)
Hemlock Grove (Netflix, 2013–2015)
The Honourable Woman (Sundance, 2014)
Hoop Dreams (Steve James, 1994)
House of Cards (Netflix, 2013–2018)
The Hulk (Ang Lee, 2003)
The Impossibilities (Anna Kerrigan, seriesofimpossibilities.com, 2015–present)
The Interview (Evan Goldberg and Seth Rogen, 2015)
Iron Fist (Netflix, 2017–2018)
It's Always Sunny in Philadelphia (FX, 2005–present)
Jackie Brown (Quentin Tarantino, 1997)
Jane the Virgin (CW, 2014–2019)
Jessica Jones (Netflix, 2015–2019)
The Jungle Book (Jon Favreau, 2016)
Juno (Jason Reitman, 2007)
Kids in the Hall (CBC, CBS, HBO, 1989–1995)
The Knick (Cinemax, 2014–2015)
Late Night (Nisha Ganatra, 2019)
Law & Order: Special Victims Unit (NBC, 1999–present)
Life in a Day (Kevin Macdonald, 2011)

Lilyhammer (Netflix, 2012–2014)
The Limey (Steven Soderbergh, 1999)
Little Miss Sunshine (Jonathan Dayton and Valerie Faris, 2006)
Logan Lucky (Steven Soderbergh, 2017)
Lord of the Rings (Peter Jackson, 2001)
Love and Friendship (Whit Stillman, 2016)
Mad Men (AMC, 2007–2015)
Manchester by the Sea (Kenneth Lonergan, 2016)
Manufactured Landscapes (Jennifer Baichwal, 2007)
Margin Call (C. Chandor, 2011)
The Marvelous Mrs. Maisel (Amazon, 2017–present)
The Matrix (Lana and Lilly Wachowski, 1999)
Melancholia (Lars von Trier, 2011)
The Meyerowitz Stories (Noah Baumbach, 2017)
Monster (Patty Jenkins, 2003)
Mosaic (HBO, 2017–2018)
The Most Dangerous Man in America (Judith Ehrlich and Rick Goldsmith, 2009)
Mr. Robot (USA, 2015–2019)
Mudbound (Dee Rees, 2017)
My Big Fat Greek Wedding (Joel Zwick, 2002)
My Winnipeg (Guy Maddin, 2007)
Newlyweds (Edward Burns, 2011)
Night Fishing (Park Chan-wook, 2011)
No Direction Home (Martin Scorsese, 2005)
No End in Sight (Charles Ferguson, 2007)
Ocean's 11 (Steven Soderbergh, 2001)
Ocean's 12 (Steven Soderbergh, 2004)
Ocean's 13 (Steven Soderbergh, 2007)
Okja (Bong Joon-ho, 2017)
Orange Is the New Black (Netflix, 2013–2019)
Our Time Is Up (Rob Pearlstein, 2004)
The Passion of the Christ (Mel Gibson, 2004)
Puccini for Beginners (Maria Maggenti, 2006)
The Puffy Chair (Duplass Brothers, 2005)
Pulp Fiction (Quentin Tarantino, 1994)

Push Girls (Sundance, 2012–2013)
Qraftish (Christal, Blackgirldangerous.com, 2015–present)
Rage (Sally Potter, 2009)
Raging Bull (Martin Scorsese, 1980)
Rectify (Sundance, 2013–2016)
The Red Road (Sundance, 2014–2015)
Red State (Kevin Smith, 2011)
The Ridiculous 6 (Frank Coraci, 2015)
Roma (Alfonso Cuaron, 2018)
The Saddest Music in the World (Guy Maddin, 2003)
Schizopolis (Steven Soderbergh, 1996)
Seduce Me (Sundance, 2010)
Sense8 (Netflix, 2015–2018)
sex, lies, and videotape (Steven Soderbergh, 1989)
Shadows (John Cassavetes, 1959)
Sherrybaby (Laurie Collyer, 2006)
Shugs and Fats (Nadia Manzoor and Radhka Vaz, ShugsandFats.TV, 2014–present)
Side Effects (Steven Soderbergh, 2013)
Six Feet Under (HBO, 2002–2005)
The Sixth Sense (M. Night Shyamalan, 1999)
Snowpiercer (Bong Joon-ho, 2013)
Spoilers with Kevin Smith (Hulu, 2011)
Sports Night (ABC, 1998–2000)
Spotlight (Tom McCarthy, 2015)
Still Alice (Richard Glatzer and Wash Westmoreland, 2014)
Stranger Than Paradise (Jim Jarmusch, 1984)
Stranger Things (Netflix, 2016–present)
Summer Hours (Olivier Assayas, 2008)
Supersize Me (Morgan Spurlock, 2004)
Survivor (CBS, 2000–present)
Sweet and Lowdown (Woody Allen, 1999)
Sweet Sweetback's Baadasssss Song (Melvin Van Peebles, 1971)
Tangerine (Sean Baker, 2015)
Take the Money and Run (Woody Allen, 1969)
This Film Is Not Yet Rated (Kirby Dick, 2006)

This Filthy World (Jeff Garlin, 2006)
The Times of Harvey Milk (Rob Epstein, 1984)
Titanic (James Cameron, 1997)
Top of the Lake (Sundance, 2013–present)
Transparent (Amazon, 2014–2019)
24 Frame News (Sundance, 1999–2003)
Twilight (Catherine Hardwicke, 2008)
Two Days in Paris (Julie Delpy, 2007)
Unbreakable Kimmy Schmidt (Netflix, 2015–2019)
United States of Tara (Showtime, 2009–2011)
Unreal (Lifetime, 2015–2018)
Unsane (Steven Soderbergh, 2017)
Up to Speed (Hulu, 2011)
Veronica Mars (Rob Thomas, 2014)
The Walking Dead (AMC, 2010–present)
The Watermelon Woman (Cheryl Dunye, 1997)
Weiner-Dog (Todd Solondz, 2016)
Whale Rider (Niki Caro, 2002)
A Woman under the Influence (John Cassavetes, 1974)
Wonderstruck (Todd Haynes, 2017)
You're So Talented (Sam Bailey, Open TV, 2015–present)
Zootopia (Byron Howard, Rich Moore, Jared Bush, 2015)

Index

ABC network, 39, 41
Abrams, J. J., 57
Academy Awards, 25, 45, 78
accessibility, 16, 22, 23, 111; appearance of infinite access to indie cinema, 28–31; social networking sites and, 74; streaming services and, 108; Sundance Channel and, 95–96, 103; YouTube and, 72
Acme Video (Providence), 1
advertising revenue, 43, 70, 72, 76, 79, 141n61
aesthetics, 18, 24, 65; avant-garde, 89, 98–103; of cell phones and mobile media, 88, 89–93; "high" and "low" culture, 68–69, 81; professional versus amateur, 70, 71, 81; VCRs and, 28–29; YouTube aesthetics of quality cinema, 23, 68–72
Age of New Waves, The (Tweedie, 2013), 9
Aguado, Juan Miguel, 90
airports/airplanes, exhibition in, 5, 123n69
Akkaraju, Prem, 56
Alamo Drafthouse, 59, 63
algorithms, 30, 31, 34, 35
Allegri, Natasha, 87
Allen, Woody, 37
Almost Kings (Flores, 2010), 33
Alpha House (Amazon series, 2013), 107
Amazon, 2, 5, 27, 34, 110, 122n58; Amazon Prime, 38, 107, 108, 128n43; Amazon Studios, 106; Amazon Video, 42, 106; Fox Searchlight compared to, 31; future of independent cinema and, 111; IMDb (Internet Movie Database), 138n33; on-demand viewing and, 49; Original Movies, 107, 108; publicity and, 61; rural audiences and, 50; share of internet traffic, 42; theatrical releases omitted by, 48; theatrical windows and, 134n57
AMC (American Movie Classics), 32, 34, 35, 41, 93
AMC theater chain, 38, 57, 59
American Express, as corporate sponsor, 67, 83, 84, 139n37
American Idol (Fox series, 2002–present), 19, 124n78, 125n12
American Independent Cinema (King), 8
American Independent Cinema: An Introduction (Tzioumakis, 2006), 3
American: The Bill Hicks Story (Harlock and Thomas, 2009), 43
American Zoetrope, 14
Anatomy of a Scene (SundanceTV series, 2001–2004), 93
Anderson, Chris, 27, 29
Andrews, David, 9, 10
animation, 90, 97, 98
anime, 41
Another Steven Soderbergh Experience (Gallagher), 53

Anvil: The Story of Anvil (Gervasi, 2008), 83
Apple TV, 57
apps, online, 47, 56
Arceneaux, Noah, 89
Are You the Favorite Person of Anybody (Arteta, 2005), 65
Aronofsky, Darren, 13
Arrested Development (Netflix, 2013, 2018), 32, 34, 35
art cinema, 9, 40, 89; decline of art cinemas, 16; as "subcultural aggregate," 10
"Art Cinema as a Mode of Film Practice, The" (Bordwell, 1979), 9
"Art Cinema as Institution" (Neale, 1981), 9
Arteta, Miguel, 65
art house cinema, 2, 8, 36; Alamo Drafthouse theater chain, 63; urban theaters, 27
Art House Convergence, 59, 61, 62
Art of Seduction, The, 24, 89, 94–98, 103
Assayas, Olivier, 54
Association of Independent Video and Filmmakers, 11
Atkinson, Sarah, 88
audiences, 16, 32, 42, 74; accessibility and, 22, 103; age of online audiences, 3; art house, 33; competition for, 49–50; creation of new audiences, 5; DIY distribution and, 75; image and, 92; immediacy and, 22; mainstream, 6; migratory behavior of, 28; mobile media, 90; mobility of video access and, 27; multiple media devices and, 23; Netflix, 35–36; nontheatrical, 22, 26; self-reflexivity of cinema and, 82, 140n50; simultaneous release strategies and, 46, 48; social media and, 66; YouTube and, 72, 78, 79
aurality, 24, 88
auteurs, 10, 41, 92
avant-garde film, 8, 9, 73
Avatar (Cameron, 2009), 83
Avon Cinema (Providence), 1

Baichwal, Jennifer, 101
Bailey, Sam, 87
Baker, Sean, 88
Barry, Christopher, 95
Baumbach, Noah, 48, 134n57
BBC (British Broadcasting Corporation), 34
Beasts of No Nation (Fukunaga, 2015), 36, 38, 48
Bee and PuppyCat (Allegri, Cartoon Hangover, 2013–present), 87
Before Sunrise (Linklater, 1995), 93
Beginnings (SundanceTV series, 2011), 97–98
Behind the Candelabra (Soderbergh, 2012), 56
Berlin International Film Festival, 99
Bernard, Tom, 45–46
Beta (Amazon series, 2013), 107
"Beyond Broadcast Yourself: The Future of YouTube" (Jarrett), 71
Beyond the Multiplex (Klinger), 15–16, 18, 26
Beyond the Screen: Emerging Cinema and Engaging Audiences (Atkinson), 88
BFI Player, 63, 135n66
Big Ideas for a Small Planet (Sundance series), 100
Biography Channel, 41
Black Swan (Aronofsky, 2010), 13
Blair, Selma, 79–80
Blair Witch Project, The (Myrick and Sanchez, 1999), 137–138n24
Bleecker Street Media, 36, 56
blockbusters, 13, 29, 34, 48, 55; licensing of, 60; "low" culture associated with, 68; star power of, 83
Blockbuster video stores, 31
Bloom, Monica, 94
Blu-ray, 49, 54, 109
Bolter, Jay David, 22, 28
Bomb It (Reiss, 2007), 83

Bong Joon-ho, 23, 25, 46, 134n57
Bordwell, David, 9, 60
Born into Brothels (Kauffman and Briski, 2004), 33
Bourdieu, Pierre, 68
Bowles, Eamonn, 43
box office revenue, 2, 7, 45, 48, 51, 62
Brahman Naman (Mukherjee, 2016), 34
Braless (Green, MTV series, 2014–present), 98
branding, 28, 32; desire and, 101; indie branding, 40; of YouTube, 65, 72
Bravo network, 41
Breaking Bad (AMC series, 2008–2013), 35
Breakthrough Series, 87, 103
Brill, Steven, 108
Briski, Zana, 33
British Film Institute (BFI), 63, 135n66
Brittany Runs a Marathon (Colaizzo, 2019), 108
Broderick, Peter, 83
Brueggemann, Tom, 61
B-Side, 44
Bubble (Soderberg, 2005), 22, 46, 47, 51, 52–56
Buice, Susan, 66, 73, 75–77
Bunheads (ABC Family, 2012–2013), 107
Burgess, Jean, 20, 21, 76
Burnett, Rob, 34
Burns, Edward, 46
Bush, George W., 41
Bush, Jared, 38

Cable Car Cinema (Providence), 1
cable television, 4, 11, 16, 22, 39, 103; audience abandonment of, 96; high price of, 110–111; release windows and, 47
Cameron, James, 45, 54, 57, 83
Campagna, Claudio, 102, 145n51
Campbell, Billy, 33
Cannes Film Festival, 25, 34, 52
Captain Fantastic (Ross, 2016), 36
Captive, The (SundanceTV series, 2009), 97
Caputo, Dave, 42
Caro, Niki, 34
Casetti, Francesco, 90, 101
Cassavetes, John, 13, 15, 40, 122n58
Castells, Manuel, 20
cat videos, 79
Cedar Rapids (Arteta, 2011), 65
Cell Phone Culture (Goggin), 89
cell phones, 2, 3, 5, 17, 56; aesthetics of, 88, 89–93, 103–104; *The Art of Seduction* series produced for viewing on, 95; cinema experienced on, 27; DIY distribution and, 84; as fourth screen, 94; intertwined with other media forms, 20; media convergence and, 104; portability and, 23, 89; web series and, 88
censorship, 85, 139n38
CGI (computer-generated imagery), 22
Chandor, J. C., 48
Chaplin, Charlie, 14
"Charlie Bit My Finger" (amateur video on YouTube), 71, 79
Charlie's Angels: Full Throttle (Nichol, 2003), 34
Chen, Steve, 69
Chi-Raq (Lee, 2015), 107
Christal, 87
Christian, Aymar, 30, 94
Chuck and Buck (Arteta, 2000), 65
Cinelan, 44
cinema (film): between "high" and "low" culture, 68; cell phones and, 24; convergence with television, 30; as film objects, 4; as first screen, 94; immediacy and, 22; media convergence and, 27; platform mobility and, 29; as theatrical and nontheatrical medium, 26
Cinemark theater chain, 38, 57, 61
cinema studies, 89, 118n8
Cinemat (Bloomington, Ind., video store), 1
Cinemax, 56
Cinetic, 44

Claims to Fame (Gamson), 80
class differences, 68
Clerks (Smith, 1994), 126n27
Cleverman (SundanceTV series, 2016–2017), 103
"clip culture," 69, 136n10
Cloverfield (Reeves, 2008), 88
Colaizzo, Paul Downs, 108
Columbia Pictures, 12
Colyer, Laurie, 34
Comic-Con Episode IV: A Fan's Hope (2011), 40
Companion to Mobile Media (Goggin and Hjorth), 90
computers, 3, 5, 17, 56; cinema experienced on, 27; DIY distribution and, 84; intertwined with other media forms, 20; as third screen, 94
Contemporary American Independent Film (Holmlund and Wyatt, 2005), 6
convergence cultures, 4, 5, 6; cinematic style/aesthetics and, 89; convergence culture studies, 18; definition of independent cinema and, 11, 14; discourses of, 18; hybridity and, 21; meaning of cinema and, 27; podcasts and, 74; revisiting/rethinking of, 17–21; self-distribution and, 23; transformation in meaning of indie cinema and, 16. *See also* media convergence
Convergence Culture: Where Old and New Media Collide (Jenkins), 18–19
Copland, Liesl, 42–43
Coppola, Francis Ford, 14
copyright, 81, 140n49
Coraci, Frank, 108
corporate sponsorship, 23, 65, 67, 68; DIY culture and, 77, 139n37; self-distribution and, 77
Costanza-Chock, Sasha, 85
Couldry, Nick, 20, 21
Crash Course (Green, 2011–present), 98
Crawford (Modigliani, 2008), 41, 44
Criterion Channel, 1, 27, 40–41
Crouching Tiger, Hidden Dragon 2 (Yuen, 2016), 108
crowdfunding, 105
Crude Awakening, A: The Oil Crash (Gelpke and McCormack, 2006), 101
Crumley, Arin, 66, 73, 74, 75–77
Crunchyroll, 41
Crying Game, The (Jordan, 1992), 12
Cuaron, Alfonso, 63
Cuban, Mark, 52, 53
Cultural Studies (journal), 20
Curtin, Michael, 47
cybercultures, 17

Daily Show, The (Comedy Central, 1996–present), 39
Damon, Matt, 56
Daredevil (Netflix series, 2015–2018), 109
Dargis, Manohla, 84
Dark Knight, The (Nolan, 2009), 83
Dawson, Max, 92
Dawson, Rosario, 82
day-and-date releases, 2, 23, 45, 47, 59; effect on profit and ticket sales, 46; simultaneous releases compared with, 47–51
Day in the Life, A (Spurlock, 2011), 41
Dayton, Jonathan, 6, 13, 95
debut window, home entertainment, 38
Delpy, Julie, 31
De Niro, Robert, 144n43
Deutchman, Ira, 62, 63
DeVito, Danny, 82
Dexter (TV series), 35
Dick, Kirby, 33
"Digital Deployment(s)" (Zimmerman), 16
digital media technologies, 4, 14, 17, 18, 23, 118n8
Dijck, Jose van, 81
Directors Guild of America, 15, 63
DirecTV, 58
Dirty Dog (short film), 96–97

Dirty Sexy Money (ABC series, 2007), 107
Discovery Channel, 39
"Dish Towns USA (or Rural Screens) Part One" (Hawkins), 50
Disney, 13, 26, 48, 106, 121n48; Disney+, 109, 110; "Disney Decade," 12; Hulu acquired by, 110; Netflix and, 38
distribution, 2, 5, 10, 16, 32, 58; alternative practices/spaces for, 7, 24; broadband internet as channel for, 16; of cinema, 26–27; corporate ownership and, 18; digital, 14, 16, 20, 33, 47; independent cinema defined in relation to, 3; industrial affiliation of distributors, 7; mobile technologies and, 94; Netflix and, 33–34; nontheatrical, 17; online, 20, 78–81, 83; simultaneous release strategies and, 56; studio/big-business model of, 14; vertical integration and, 53; VOD (video on demand), 43; windowing strategy and, 26. *See also* DIY (do it yourself) distribution; self-distribution
Distribution Lab, 66
Distribution Revolution (Curtin, Holt, and Sanson, eds.), 47–48
Dixon, Wheeler Winston, 27
DIY (do it yourself) distribution, 15, 16, 20, 106, 109, 122n58, 137–138n24; as alternative to theatrical release, 46; assistance to others in DIY culture, 138–139n35; changing cultural meaning of, 21; convergence cultures and, 22; distribution and, 23; *Four Eyed Monsters* and, 73–78; future of independent cinema and, 83–85; YouTube and, 67, 80. *See also* self-distribution
Dobbs, Aaron, 104
doctors' offices, exhibition in, 5, 123n69
documentaries, 5, 28, 73; on Hulu, 39–40, 41; on Netflix, 30, 34; "talking heads" style, 97; VOD distribution strategies for, 43; YouTube and, 137n14
Do-over, The (Brill, 2016), 108
DreamStates (OptionG, 2011), 98
Dunye, Cheryl, 93
Duplass Brothers, 33
DVDs (digital video discs), 1, 2, 16, 32, 44, 84; day-and-date release strategies and, 23; decline of videotape and, 52; DVD culture, 41; exclusive rights to, 33; extras included with, 73; lack of access to broadband internet and, 51; Netflix distribution by mail, 34; outperformed by video streaming, 42, 109; rare and out-of-print, 37; release windows and, 47, 48; simultaneous release strategies and, 5, 22, 49, 55; unlimited delivery of, 31; YouTube movies and, 66
Dwyer, Tim, 18

East Los High (Hulu series, 2013–2017), 3
Ebert, Roger, 7
Eberwein, Robert, 93
Eco Trip (Sundance series), 100–101
Ehrlich, Judith, 40
Electric Chairs (short film), 97
electronic sell-through (EST), 47
electronics stores, 16
Ellsberg, Daniel, 40
Embedded Live (Robbins, 2005), 33
emergent media, 17, 18
Emerging Pictures, 62
Emmy Awards, 35
"End of Cinema, The" (Friedberg, 2000), 4
Epstein, Rob, 41
Eraserhead (Lynch, 1977), 33, 40
Erin Brokovich (Soderbergh, 2000), 53
European Art Cinema (White, 2017), 9
Eveningstar Cinema (Brunswick, Maine), 49

exhibition, 2, 84; alternative practices/spaces for, 7, 24; of cinema, 26–27; corporate ownership and, 18; digital, 14; DIY strategies, 15, 77, 110, 122n58; independent cinema defined in relation to, 3; mainstream first-run, 29; nontheatrical, 5, 16, 17, 67; studio/big-business model of, 14; theatrical window and, 45; as urban experience, 50; vertical integration and, 53; via cable television and apps, 56
exhibition, theatrical, 43, 45, 58; communal experience of, 62; high cost of, 42; limits of, 25
Expressionism, German, 9

Facebook, 66, 78, 84, 110
Faces (Cassavetes, 1968), 13
Fairbanks, Douglas, 14
Fall, The (BBC series, 2013–2016), 109
Family Guy (Fox series, 1998–present), 39
Faris, Valerie, 6, 13, 95
Favreau, Jon, 38
Feltheimer, Jon, 64
Ferguson, Charles, 31
F for Fake (Welles, 1973), 40
film. *See* cinema
Film Collaborative, 43
film critics, 7, 8, 10
film festivals, 10, 11, 15, 33, 108
Film Independent, 33, 36
FilmStruck, 40–41
film studies, 4
financing, 7, 10, 11, 15, 32
Finding Dory (Stanton, 2016), 38
Fingerprint Releasing, 56
Fithian, John, 46, 49, 58–59
Flaw, The (Singleton, 2011), 40
Flores, Philip G., 33
Forster, Robert, 82
Forte, Will, 98
Four Eyed Monsters (Buice and Crumley, 2007), 23, 66–68, 71, 72, 73–78, 83, 137n24
4 Months, 3 Weeks and 2 Days (Mungiu, 2007), 34
fourth screen, 94, 96, 98, 102
Fox network, 39, 41
Fox Searchlight, 31, 84
Fox studio, 26, 54, 62
Friedberg, Anne, 4
From Betamax to Blockbuster (Greenberg), 16
"From the Big Screen to the Small One" (Pardo), 48
Frost, Alex, 33
Fukunaga, Cary, 36, 48
Fundamentals of Caring, The (Burnett, 2016), 34
Fusco, Katherine, 55
Future, The (July, 2011), 65

Gainsbourg, Charlotte, 98
Gallagher, Mark, 53, 56
Galt, Rosalind, 9
Gamson, Joshua, 80
Ganatra, Nisha, 108
Gangs of New York (Scorsese, 2002), 6
Garlin, Jeff, 33
Gelpke, Basil, 101
Gene Siskel Center (Chicago), 75
Gentile, Gary, 50
Gervasi, Sacha, 83
Get Out (Peele, 2017), 14
Gibson, Mel, 14
Gilmore, Geoffrey, 7
Gilmore Girls (WB series, 2000–2007), 107
Girlfriend Experience, The (Soderbergh, 2009), 52, 54, 55, 72
Girlfriend Experience, The (Starz series, 2016–present), 132n28
Girl Walks into a Bar (Gutierrez, 2011), 67, 68, 81–83
Glatzer, Richard, 45
Global Art Cinema (Galt and Schoonover, 2010), 9
Global Mobile Media (Goggin), 91
Godless (Netflix series, 2017), 53

Goggin, Gerard, 89, 90, 91
Goldberg, Evan, 45
Golden Globe Awards, 34, 107
Goldsmith, Rick, 40
Good Machine, 121n48
Google, 5, 15, 23, 65, 68, 83, 110; capitalizing on independent cinema, 81; DIY distribution and, 85; YouTube acquired by, 69; YouTube Music Premium and, 70
Gotham Independent Film Awards, 87, 88, 103
grassroots media, 21, 22, 23, 68, 106, 111. *See also* DIY (do it yourself) distribution
Gray, Jonathan, 74
Green, John, 98
Green, Joshua, 20, 21, 76
Green, Laci, 98
"Green, The" (environmental series), 100–101
Greenberg, Joshua, 16
Green Porno (SundanceTV series, 2008–2010), 24, 89, 93, 97, 98–103, 145n51
Grey, Sasha, 55
Grey Gardens (Maysles brothers, 1975), 40
Griffith, D. W., 14
Grusin, Richard, 22, 28
GSM Association, 94
Gutierrez, Sebastian, 67, 81, 82

Hallinan, Blake, 35–36
Handmaid's Tale, The (Hulu series, 2017–present), 39
Hap and Leonard (SundanceTV series, 2016–present), 93, 103
Happening, The (Shyamalan, 2008), 54
Happiness (Solondz, 1998), 8
haptics, 24
Hardwicke, Catherine, 54
Hargitay, Mariska, 87
Harlock, Matt, 43
Harry Potter series, 19, 124n78, 125n12
Hartnett, Josh, 82
Hastings, Reed, 31–32, 34, 62
Hawkins, Joan, 50
Hay, James, 20, 21
Haynes, Todd, 61
HBO (Home Box Office), 31, 32, 34, 35, 39, 110; Amazon Prime and, 128n43; surpassed by Netflix in programming quality, 37–38
HDNet Films, 53
HDTV, 53
Hemlock Grove (Netflix series, 2013–2015), 32, 34
Herbert, Daniel, 29, 31
Hilderbrand, Lucas, 28–29
Hillier, Jim, 6
History Channel, 39
Hjorth, Larissa, 89
Hollyweed (Smith, 2018), 105
Hollywood, 2, 9, 14, 69; blockbusters, 34, 49, 68, 83; classics divisions, 13; corporate media embodied by, 19; distribution system of, 85; entertainment conglomerates and, 11–12; golden age "Big Five" studios, 53; indie cinema (re)defined in relation to, 6–9, 84; media convergence and, 111; simultaneous release strategies and, 22; specialty labels, 13; staggered releases and, 47; television as competition for, 63; transition to on-demand and streaming services, 51; YouTube and, 69, 70, 72
Holmlund, Chris, 6, 10
Holt, Jennifer, 7, 47
Honourable Woman, The (SundanceTV miniseries, 2014), 93, 142n7
Hoop Dreams (James, 1994), 40
Hope, Ted, 107
House of Cards (Netflix series, 2013–2018), 32, 34, 35, 38, 109
Howard, Byron, 38
Howard, Ron, 57
Howe, Jeff, 106
"How I Learned to Stop Worrying and Love VOD" (Film Collaborative), 43

Hulk, The (Lee, 2003), 34
Hulu, 2, 5, 25, 34, 106; appeal to younger viewers, 3; appearance of unlimited programming access, 27; branding of, 39–41; Disney's acquisition of, 110; Hulu Plus, 40; immediacy and, 22, 26; media convergence and, 28; on-demand viewing and, 49; as one of most prolific streaming sites, 27; publicity and, 61; rural audiences and, 50; share of internet traffic, 42; taste culture of, 30; theatrical releases omitted by, 48; theatrical windows on, 26; YouTube Red/Premium as competitor to, 70
Hurley, Chad, 69, 136n10

"IFC and Sundance, The: Channeling Independence" (Eberwein), 93
IFC Center (New York), 75
Iger, Bob, 110
IMDb (Internet Movie Database), 138n33
immediacy, 22, 26, 28, 29, 51, 111
Impossibilities, The (Kerrigan, seriesofimpossibilities.com, 2015–present), 87
independent cinema, 2, 3; brief history (1989–1999), 11–14; defined and redefined, 6–9, 18; as distinctly American film culture, 11; genre play as defining characteristic, 109; "high culture" construction of, 30; historical evolution in online spaces, 5; as "Hollywood art films," 10; mainstream media culture and, 20; "major independents," 12; online access to (1999–present), 21–24; visibility and popularity of, 22, 26
Independent Feature Project, 11
Independent Film Channel (IFC), 36, 54, 73, 101
Independent Filmmakers Project, 103, 104
Independent Filmmaking and Digital Convergence: Transmedia and Beyond (Nikolic), 92
Independent Film Project, 87
Independent Spirit Awards, 11, 13, 15, 36, 63
Indie (Newman), 8
Indie, Inc (Perren), 7, 12
Indie 2.0 (King), 16–17, 73
Indie: An American Film Culture (Newman, 2011), 3, 29–30
IndieFlix, 27
Indiegogo, 105
"Indie TV: Innovation in Series Development" (Christian), 30
indie web series, 87–88
IndieWire (daily news website), 36, 44, 49, 104
IndieWire Picks: Inspired by the 2013 Oscar Doc Nominees, 40
"Indiewood," 13, 109, 120n19
Inherent Vice: Bootleg Histories of Videotape and Copyright (Hilderbrand), 28–29
Instagram, 66, 78, 84, 110
international cinema, 9
International Documentary Association, 43
internet, 16, 76, 103; broadband, 16, 17; debate over free content on, 145n57; lack of access to, 51; Netflix share of traffic on, 32; net neutrality, 51; physical formats exceeded by movies viewed through, 109
Interview, The (Goldberg and Rogen, 2014), 45
iPhones, film shot using, 56, 89, 90, 101
iPods, 5, 16, 73, 91, 98; DIY distribution and, 84; as fourth screen, 94
Iron Fist (Netflix series, 2017–2018), 109
It's Always Sunny in Philadelphia (FX series, 2005–present), 82
iTunes, 2, 42, 43, 122n58; DIY distribution and, 75; revenue sales, 43; on-demand viewing and, 49; rural audiences and, 50; theatrical releases omitted by, 48; video podcasts and, 74

Jackie Brown (Tarantino, 1997), 82
Jackson, Peter, 53, 57–58
James, Steve, 40
Jane the Virgin (CW series, 2014–2019), 87
Jarmusch, Jim, 13
Jarrett, Kylie, 71, 85
Jenkins, Henry, 20, 21, 124n78, 125n12; on art and corporate sponsorship, 85; definition of media convergence, 18–19, 28
Jenkins, Patty, 144n43
Jessica Jones (Netflix series, 2015–2019), 109
Jordan, Neil, 12
Juhasz, Alexandra, 71, 85
July, Miranda, 65
Junger, Sebastian, 98
Jungle Book, The (Favreau, 2016), 38
Juno (Reitman, 2007), 8, 13

Kanopy, 27
Karim, Jawed, 69
Karpen, Andrew, 36
Katz, J., 89
Kauffman, Ross, 33
Kavoori, Anandam, 89
Kerrigan, Anna, 87
Kickstarter, 105
Kids in the Hall (CBC, CBS, HBO series, 1989–1995), 95
King, Geoff, 6, 8, 9, 10; on "desktop expressionism," 73; on digital video and broadband internet, 16–17
Kino Lorber, 40
Kleinhans, Chuck, 7, 84
Klinger, Barbara, 15–18, 26, 54
Knick, The (Cinemax series, 2014–2015), 53, 56

Laemmle Grand 4-Plex (Los Angeles), 75
Landmark Theatres, 53, 59
Lang, Brent, 62
laptops, 16, 27, 56
Late Night (Ganatra, 2019), 108
Law, Jude, 55
Law & Order: Special Victims Unit (NBC series, 1999–present), 87
League, Tim, 59, 61, 63
Learmonth, Michael, 78
"Learning the Five Lessons of YouTube" (Juhasz), 71
Lee, Ang, 34
Lee, Spike, 107
leveraged buyouts, 13, 121n48
Lexus, as corporate sponsor, 23, 67, 81, 82–83, 84
Leydon, Joe, 82
licensing, 30, 37, 43
Life in a Day (MacDonald, 2011), 137n14, 140n55
Lilyhammer (Netflix series, 2012–2014), 32, 34
Limey, The (Soderbergh, 1999), 53
Ling, Richard, 89
Linklater, Richard, 41, 93
Lionsgate, 34, 63, 64, 109
Little Miss Sunshine (Dayton and Faris, 2006), 6, 13, 95
Logan Lucky (Soderbergh, 2017), 56
London International Film Festival, 76
Lonergan, Kenneth, 107
Long Tail, The: Why the Future of Business Is Selling Less of More (Anderson), 27
Lord of the Rings series (Jackson, 2001–2003), 53, 74
Los Angeles Film Festival, 15, 33
Lost (ABC series, 2004–2010), 74
Love and Friendship (Stillman, 2016), 61, 107
Lucas, George, 14
Lucasfilm, 38
Lynch, David, 33, 40
Lyons, Charles, 13

MacDonald, Kevin, 137n14
Maddin, Guy, 92, 95, 96, 144n40

Mad Men (AMC series, 2007–2015), 35, 109
Maggenti, Maria, 95
Magnolia Pictures, 43, 53
Mammas (SundanceTV series, 2013), 102
Manchester by the Sea (Lonergan, 2016), 107
Manovich, Lev, 17
Manufactured Landscapes (Baichwal, 2007), 101
Manzoor, Nadia, 87
Margin Call (Chandor, 2011), 48
marketing, 3, 23, 83; ancillary markets, 11; budgets, 50; media convergence and, 88
Martinez, Inmaculada, 90
Marvel franchise, 38, 48, 55, 109, 110
Marvelous Mrs. Maisel, The (Amazon, 2017–present), 107
Matrix, Sidneyeve, 109
Matrix trilogy (Wachowski and Wachowski, 1999–2003), 19, 124n78, 125n12
Matsushita, 12
Maysles, Albert and David, 40
MCA Universal, 12
McCarthy, Tom, 14
McCormack, Ray, 101
McKinney, Mark, 95
McLane, Betsy, 39
Me and You and Everyone We Know (July, 2005), 65
media, mainstream, 20, 68, 108
media conglomerates, 31, 109, 110
media convergence, 2, 8, 9, 11, 56; cell phones and, 104; circulation of cinema and, 17, 26; definition of, 18–19, 28; dependence on technology, finances, and content, 31; future of independent cinema and, 111; "golden age of the digital short" and, 91; *Green Porno* series and, 103; indie cinema (re)defined in era of, 14; meaning of cinema and, 27; as rhetorical construct, 18; short films/web series and, 88; streaming services and, 28–31. *See also* convergence cultures
Media Convergence (Dwyer), 18
media studies, 4, 5
medium specificity, 29
megaplex, 69
Melancholia (Trier, 2011), 46
mergers, 13, 121n48
Metacritic, 126n24
Meyerowitz Stories, The (Baumbach, 2017), 48, 134n57
MGM studio, 69
Miller, Nancy, 82, 92
"Minifesto for a New Age" (Miller), 82
mini-majors, 13
Miramax, 6, 7, 11, 13, 109; bought by Disney, 121n48; corporate ownership of, 84; indie branding and, 40; Netflix compared to, 30–31; rise and fall of, 11; specialty divisions for indie films, 12
Mr. Robot (USA series, 2015–2019), 87
mobile media, 89–93, 94
mobile phones, 88
Moby, 79, 80
Modigliani, David, 41
Moore, Julianne, 45
Moore, Rich, 38
Mosaic (HBO series, 2017–2018), 53, 56
Most Dangerous Man in America, The (Ehrlich and Goldsmith, 2009), 40
Motion Picture Association of America, 51, 54
Movie Gallery, 31
Moviegoing in America: A Sourcebook in the History of Film Exhibition (Waller), 50
Moving Data: The iPhone and the Future of Media (Snickars and Vonderau), 89
Mudbound (Rees, 2017), 25–26, 51, 63
Mukherjee, Qaushiq, 34
Muller, Eggo, 71, 72
multiplexes, 16, 62, 136n5
Mungiu, Cristian, 34
museums, indie cinema in, 10

music, 24, 104
music videos, 65, 72
My Big Fat Greek Wedding (Zwick, 2002), 6
My Obscure Object of Desire (short film), 97
Myrick, Daniel, 138n24
MySpace, 66, 73–76
My Winnipeg (Maddin, 2007), 95

narrative cinema, classical, 9
National Association of Theatre Owners (NATO), 26, 46, 58
National Film Board of Canada, 95
NBC network, 39, 41
Neale, Steve, 9
Nelson, Elissa, 51, 54
Neorealism, Italian, 9
Netflix, 1, 5, 11; appeal to younger viewers, 3; appearance of unlimited programming access, 27; binge viewing associated with, 109; immediacy and, 22, 26, 28; indie content distributed on demand, 31–38; investment in mainstream media, 108; licensing fees, 43; limited theatrical releases and, 25–26; media convergence and, 28–31; Netflix feature films, 25; on-demand viewing and, 49; as one of most prolific streaming sites, 27; persistence of DVD rental service, 51; publicity and, 61; rural audiences and, 50; share of internet traffic, 42; taste culture of, 30; theatrical releases omitted by, 48; theatrical windows on, 26; YouTube Red/Premium as competitor to, 70
"Netflix Effect, The" (Matrix), 109
Neulight, Joseph, 138n33
New Directors/New Films festival, 15
New Hollywood, 10
New Line, 11, 12, 13, 84, 121n48
Newlyweds (Burns, 2011), 46
Newman, Michael, 3, 6, 10, 29–30, 109, 140n50
new media, 17, 18, 26; immediacy as defining characteristic, 22; new media studies, 21; old media interaction with, 19, 69; YouTube and, 69, 76
New Wave, French, 9
New York Film Academy, 32
New York Film Festival, 15
niche content, 41, 85
Nichol, Joseph McGinty, 34
Night Fishing (Park, 2011), 88
Nikolic, Vladan, 49, 92
NoBudge, 27
No Direction Home (Scorsese, 2005), 40
No End in Sight (Ferguson, 2007), 31
Nolan, Christopher, 45, 57, 83
Norman, Barry, 49
Not Pretty, Really (short film), 97
Nude Caboose (Maddin, 2006), 96

Ocean's 11 franchise (Soderbergh, 2001, 2004, 2007), 53
offscreen studies, 89
Okja (Bong, 2017), 25–26, 134n57
On-Demand Culture: Digital Delivery and the Future of Movies (Tryon), 27, 29, 51
on-demand services, 2, 27; audiences' desire for access and, 29; cost of, 3; Netflix model, 31–38; simultaneous release strategies and, 22, 47; speed and convenience of access through, 51. *See also* VOD (video on demand)
120 Seconds to Get Elected (short film), 97
On Fire (short film), 96
Ono, Yoko, 98
Orange Is the New Black (Netflix series, 2013–2019), 32, 34
Oscars, 25, 40, 45, 63
Our Time Is Up (Pearlstein, 2004), 78
Owen, Clive, 56

Palme d'Or, 34
Paramount Decree [*United States v. Paramount Pictures, Inc.*] (1948), 54, 64

paratexts, 74
Pardo, Alejandro, 48–49
Park Chan-wook, 88
Parker, Sean, 56
participatory culture, 19
Passion of the Christ, The (Gibson, 2004), 14
pay-per-view (PPV), 48, 52
Pearlstein, Rob, 78
Peele, Jordan, 14
Perren, Alisa, 6, 7, 10, 12
Pickford, Mary, 14
piracy, 53–54, 58, 59, 60, 109
Pixar, 38
Planet Google: One Company's Audacious Plan to Organize Everything We Know (Stross), 77
platform mobility, 29
podcasts, 73–74, 76
Pollack, Kevin, 79, 80
Pollack, Sara, 78–79
portability, 16, 22, 23, 24, 89, 111; of cell phone culture, 91; of mobile media, 90
Positioning Art Cinema (King, 2019), 9, 10
Post-TV: Piracy, Cord-Cutting, and the Future of Television (Strangelove), 90
Potter, Sally, 88
Pribram, E. Deidre, 8
producer–consumer divide, 19
production, 3, 32; DIY model of, 15, 77, 109; studio/big-business model of, 14; vertical integration and, 53; via cell phones, 56
production values, 3, 14
product tie-ins, 3
publicity, 60–61
Puccini for Beginners (Maggenti, 2006), 95
Puffy Chair, The (Duplass Brothers, 2005), 33
Pulp Fiction (Tarantino, 1994), 8, 12
Push Girls (SundanceTV series, 2012–2013), 93
Qraftish (Christal, Blackgirldangerous .com, 2015–present), 87
Questlove, 98

Rage (Potter, 2009), 88
Raging Bull (Scorsese, 1980), 144n43
Rainey, James, 62
Randolph, Marc, 31
Ratner, Brett, 57, 58
Ravid, Orly, 43
reception discourses, 8
Rectify (SundanceTV series, 2013–2016), 93, 142n7
Redbox, 16
Red Envelope Entertainment, 31, 33, 34, 43
Redford, Robert, 95, 100, 144n36
Red Road, The (SundanceTV series, 2014–2015), 93, 142n7
Red State (Smith, 2011), 15, 22, 46, 47, 122n58
Reelhouse, 2
Rees, Dee, 25, 62–63
Reeves, Matt, 88
Regal theater chain, 38, 57, 59, 61
Reiss, Jon, 43–44, 83
Reitman, Jason, 8, 13
release strategies. *See* day-and-date releases; simultaneous releases; theatrical releases
Remediation (Bolter and Grusin), 22
remote control, 4
representational discourses, 8
revenue sharing, 58
Ridiculous 6, The (Coraci, 2015), 108
"Rise of Crowdsourcing, The" (Howe, 2006), 106
Rivit TV, 27, 105–106
Robbins, Tim, 33
Roeding, Cyriac, 91
Rogen, Seth, 45
Rojek, Chris, 101
Roku, 57
Roma (Cuaron, 2018), 63
Ross, Matt, 36

Rossellini, Isabella, 89, 92, 98–103
Rotten Tomatoes, 126n24
Royal Ontario Museum (Toronto), 99

Saddest Music in the World, The (Maddin, 2003), 95
Salt Lake Film Society, 1
Sampietro, Sara, 90, 101
Sanchez, Eduardo, 138n24
Sandler, Adam, 108
Sandvine, 42
Sanson, Kevin, 47
Sarandos, Ted, 36, 37, 38, 42, 108–109
satellite television, 22, 39, 49, 111
Satrapi, Marjane, 98
Schamus, James, 13
Schizopolis (Soderbergh, 1996), 40, 53
Schoenberg, Dan, 104
Schoonover, Kyle, 9
Scorsese, Martin, 6, 40, 57, 144n43
Scott, Ridley, 137n14
Screening Room (streaming platform), 47, 56–63, 130n6
Screening Room, YouTube, 64, 71, 130n6; DIY idea and, 23, 67; "high" culture associated with, 68; professional filmmaking and online distribution, 77–81. *See also* YouTube
screen studies, 4
Second Life video game, 75, 138n31
Seduce Me (SundanceTV series, 2010), 24, 102
self-distribution, 17, 23, 73, 83; DIY film communities and, 68; social media and, 75, 76–77. *See also* DIY (do it yourself) distribution
semi-indies, 13
Sense8 (Netflix series, 2015–2018), 32
seriality, 97
serialized short form narratives, 87–88
sex, lies, and videotape (Soderbergh, 1989), 11, 13, 52
Shadows (Cassavetes, 1959), 15
"Shake It Off" (Swift music video), 72
Shapiro, Jody, 101
Sherman-Palladino, Amy, 107
Sherrybaby (Colyer, 2006), 34
shopping malls, 123n69
short films, digital, 16, 23, 82, 89–93
Show Sold Separately (Gray), 74
Showtime channel, 93
Shudder, 40
Shugs and Fats (Manzoor and Vaz, ShugsandFats.TV, 2014–present), 87
Shyamalan, M. Night, 54
Side Effects (Soderbergh, 2013), 55
Sims, David, 110
simultaneous releases, 2, 5, 45–47, 51, 64; day-and-date releases compared with, 47–51; Hollywood compared to indie cinema, 22; Netflix and, 38; for Soderbergh's *Bubble*, 52–56
Singleton, David, 40
Six Feet Under (HBO series, 2002–2005), 107
Sixth Sense, The (Shyamalan, 1999), 54
Slamdance Film Festival, 11, 73, 76, 122n59, 138n25
Slumdance Film Festival, 122n59
smartphones, 90
Smith, Kevin, 22, 105, 106, 122n58, 126n27; DIY model and, 15; "movie revue" series, 41; simultaneous release strategies and, 46, 47
SnagFilms, 27, 40, 44
Snickars, Pelle, 69, 89
Snowpiercer (Bong, 2013), 23, 46
social media/social networking, 36, 41, 66, 69; DIY distribution and, 73–78; online distribution and, 78
Society for Cinema and Media Studies (SCMS), 4, 118n8
Soderbergh, Steven, 11, 13, 22, 40; boundaries pushed by, 52–53, 56; simultaneous release strategies and, 46, 47, 51
Solondz, Todd, 8, 107
Soloway, Jill, 107
Somerville Theater (Boston), 75
Sony, 12, 69

Sony Pictures Classics, 45
"Sorry" (Bieber music video), 72
SOU (short film), 97
specialty divisions, 11, 12, 13, 31
Spielberg, Steven, 57
Spoilers with Kevin Smith (Smith, 2012–present), 41
Spotlight (McCarthy, 2015), 13–14
spout.com website, 74, 76
Spurlock, Morgan, 40, 41
Stanton, Andrew, 38
Star Maps (Arteta, 2005), 65
Star Wars franchise, 19, 124n78, 125n12
Starz, 35, 38, 132n28
Sternbergh, Adam, 30–31
Still Alice (Glatzer and Westmoreland, 2014), 45
Stillman, Whit, 61, 107
storytelling, episodic, 97, 103
Strangelove, Michael, 90, 91
Stranger Than Paradise (Jarmusch, 1984), 13
Stranger Things (Netflix series, 2016–present), 3
Straus, Davis, 138n33
Streaming: Movies, Media, and Instant Access (Dixon), 27
streaming services, 1, 3, 25, 40–41; advent of, 5; algorithms of, 30, 34, 35; "dish towns" and, 50; growth of, 44; immediacy and, 22, 29; on-demand culture and, 27; proliferation of, 110–111; rise of, 16; theatrical windows on, 26. *See also* Hulu; Netflix
Striphas, Ted, 35–36
Strip Show (short film), 96
Stross, Randall, 77
studios, independent, 2
studio system, 12, 69, 84
subscription fees, 3
Summer Hours (Assayas, 2008), 54
Summit Entertainment, 54
Sundance Channel, 93, 95, 102
Sundance Film Festival, 2, 11, 15, 25, 31, 108, 140n55; creation of, 11; *Four Eyed Monsters* premiere at, 73; Hollywoodization of, 138n25; Netflix and, 33; news program following events of, 93; shorts at, 81, 98; studio-financed films at, 122n59; theatrical releases and, 46
Sundance Group, 94, 144n36
Sundance Institute, 2, 64, 95, 144n36
"Sundance-Miramax era," 3, 77, 120n19; specialty divisions and, 31; theatrical model of, 15
SundanceTV website, 5, 23–24, 88, 89, 93, 142n7; cell phone culture and, 93–98; future of independent cinema and, 111; *Green Porno* series on, 99, 102, 103
Supersize Me (Spurlock, 2004), 40
Survivor, (CBS series, 2000–present), 19, 124n78, 125n12
Swasey, Steve, 32–33
Sweet and Lowdown (Allen, 1999), 37
Sweet Sweetback's Baadasssss Song (Van Peebles, 1971), 37, 93
SXSW (South by Southwest) Film Festival, 43, 81

tablets, 2, 3, 16, 17, 56; cinema experienced on, 27; intertwined with other media forms, 20
Take the Money and Run (Allen, 1969), 37
Tangerine (Baker, 2015), 88
Tarantino, Quentin, 8, 12, 82
taste culture, 30, 40, 69
taverns, exhibition in, 123n69
television, 2, 3, 5, 19, 111; accessibility and, 22; cell phones and, 24; convergence with film, 30; day-and-date release strategies and, 23; "end of cinema" and, 4; Hulu and, 39–40; intertwined with other media forms, 20; mobile media and, 91; Netflix original series, 32, 34–35, 37–38;

original series, 16; platform mobility and, 29; rise as competitor to Hollywood, 63; as second screen, 94; simultaneous release strategies and, 5, 55. *See also* cable television; satellite television
Telluride Film Festival, 15, 46, 108
textuality, 24, 88
theaters, movie, 2, 3, 5, 45; art house, 27, 46, 49; audience abandonment of, 96; day-and-date release strategies and, 23; as first screen, 94; increase in number of, 11; limited theatrical releases, 25; as marketing platforms for awards, 26; simultaneous release strategies and, 5, 22; single-screen, 59; theater chains, 38, 59, 61, 63, 77; theatrical revenue, 43
theatrical releases, 33, 41, 46, 60; documentaries, 5; elided, 2; financing of, 23; indie branding and, 40; less availability of indie cinema through, 22, 42, 47; limited, 25–26, 63; as primary standard for success/failure of films, 15; simultaneous release strategies and, 22; as vehicles for VOD/DVD sales and streaming, 49
Theorizing Art Cinemas (Andrews, 2013), 9, 10
Theron, Charlize, 144n43
Think Outside the Box (Reiss), 43
third screen, 94, 98
This Film Is Not Yet Rated (Dick, 2006), 33
This Filthy World (Garlin, 2006), 33
Thomas, Paul, 43
Thomas, Rob, 106
3D, 22
ticket prices, 3
Times of Harvey Milk, The (Epstein, 1984), 41
Time-Warner, 12, 13, 121n48
Titanic (Cameron, 1997), 54
Top of the Lake (SundanceTV series, 2013–present), 93
Toronto Film Festival, 15, 33, 46, 108
Tower Theatre Archive (Salt Lake City video store), 1
trade publications, 8
transmedia, 17, 89
Transparent (Amazon series, 2014–2019), 87, 107
Travel Channel, 41
Tribeca Film Festival, 7, 11, 15, 78, 81, 108, 139n37
Tribeca Shortlist, 63–64
Tribeca Streaming Room, 84
Tryon, Chuck, 27, 29, 35
Tugg, 27
Turner Broadcasting Company, 12
Turner Classic Movies, 41
"TV Got Better" (Tryon), 35
Tweedie, James, 9
24 Frame News (SundanceTV, 1999–2003), 93
Twilight (Hardwicke, 2008), 54
Two Days in Paris (Delpy, 2007), 31
Tzioumakis, Yannis, 3, 8, 10, 13, 18; on "de-institutionalising" of American indie cinema, 17; on effects of media convergence, 111; on reconglomeration, 12

Unbreakable Kimmy Schmidt (Netflix series, 2015–2019), 87
United Artists, 14
United States of Tara (Showtime series, 2009–2010), 107
Universal, 13, 50, 121n48
Unreal (Lifetime series, 2015–2018), 87
Unsane (Soderbergh, 2017), 56
Up to Speed (Linklater, 2012–present), 41

Van Peebles, Melvin, 37, 93
Variety (trade magazine), 13, 62, 82
Vaz, Radhka, 87
VCRs (video cassette recorders), 4, 28–29
Veronica Mars (Thomas, 2014), 106
vertical integration, 53, 64

VHS (Video Home System), 1, 16
video, digital, 14, 16, 52, 68
video, home, 11, 15, 16, 63, 69; revenues from, 49; simultaneous release strategies and, 47; windowing and, 26, 48
video, mobile, 90, 94
video archive, 51, 52–56
Videodrome (Atlanta video store), 1
video games, 75, 76
Videoland: Movie Culture at the American Video Store (Herbert), 29, 31
Videomaker Magazine, 71
video stores, 1, 16, 27; degree of access to movie culture and, 29; relationship of store clerks and customers, 31, 126n27
Video Vault (Alexandria, VA, video store), 1
viewing practices, 16, 17, 23, 123n69
Vimeo, 106, 111
viral videos, 65
virtual reality, 22
visuality, 24, 88
visual style, 9
vlogging, 74, 76
VOD (video on demand), 2, 43, 46, 47, 49, 63; revenues from, 3; Screening Room and, 60; ultraVOD, 61. *See also* on-demand services
Vonderau, Patrick, 69, 89

Wachowski, Lana and Lilly, 19
Wagner, Todd, 52, 53
Wagner/Cuban Companies, 53
Walking Dead, The (AMC series, 2010–present), 35, 109
Waller, Gregory, 50
Warner Bros., 50, 54, 62
Warner-Media, 110
Watermelon Woman, The (Dunye, 1997), 93
Waters, John, 33
Web 2.0, 19
Webby Award, 97, 99, 102
web series, 2, 104, 106, 111; cell phone technologies and, 92; Gotham Awards and, 88; return of theatrical setting and, 103; on SundanceTV, 5, 23, 24, 88, 89, 92, 94, 97–98
Weiner-Dog (Solondz, 2016), 107
Weinstein Company, 108
Welles, Orson, 40
Westmoreland, Wash, 45
Whale Rider (Caro, 2002), 34
White, John, 9
Wiley, Marcus, 105
windowing, theatrical, 26, 45, 47, 56; Amazon and, 134n57; collapse of release windows, 48; eventual demise of, 62; movies as "events" and, 59
"Windows into the Digital World" (Nelson), 51, 54
Withoutabox, 66, 76, 138n33
Woman under the Influence, A (Cassavetes, 1974), 15, 40
Wonderstruck (Haynes, 2017), 61
Writers Guild of America, 107
Wyatt, Justin, 6, 10, 12

You're So Talented (Bailey, Open TV, 2015–present), 87
Youth in Revolt (Arteta, 2009), 65
YouTube, 1, 2, 11, 84, 106, 122n58, 136n5; ad revenue, 85, 140n55; animation in videos on, 98; censorship on, 85, 139n38; "clip culture" and, 69, 136n10; copyright issues and, 81, 140n49; DIY distribution on, 23, 65–68; feature-length films released on, 73, 79, 81–83; free content from, 3; future of independent cinema and, 83–85, 111; indie films screened on, 5, 15; initial ten-minute limit, 69, 137n12; as largest online video provider, 69, 136n6; multiple identities of, 65; "quality" filmmaking and aesthetics, 68–72; share of internet traffic, 42; Sundance Film Festival and, 64; taste culture of, 67, 69; YouTube

Next, 70; YouTube Red/Premium, 70. *See also* Screening Room, YouTube
YouTube (Burgess and Green), 20, 76
YouTube Reader, The (Snickars and Vonderau), 69
Zeta-Jones, Catherine, 55
Zimmerman, Patricia, 3, 16, 39
Zootopia (Howard, Moore, and Bush, 2015), 38
Zoradi, Mark, 57
Zwick, Joel, 6

About the Author

SARAH E. S. SINWELL is an assistant professor in the Department of Film and Media Arts at the University of Utah. She has published essays on Kickstarter, *Green Porno*, and *Mysterious Skin* in *A Companion to American Indie Film* (2017), *Women's Studies Quarterly* (2010), and *Asexualities: Feminist and Queer Perspectives* (2014).